Southeast Asian Sources

Exploratory Essays in Critical Reconstruction

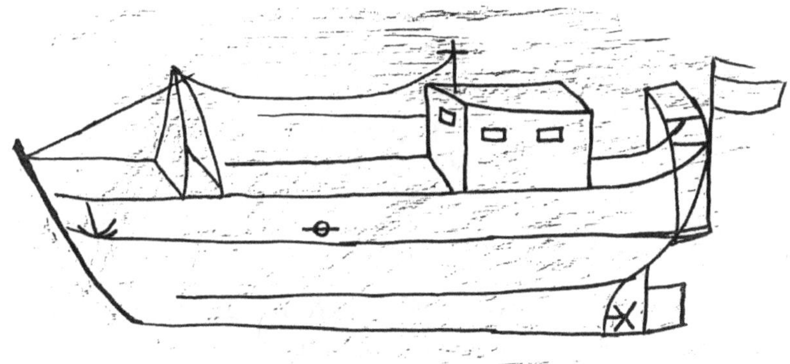

By Hugh M. Lewis

1994

ISBN
9798415576036

Archaeological Anthropology
Indie Anthropology
Poor Hugh's E-Press
Lewis Micro-Publishing

Contents

For Humankind
Past, present and yet to be

That all people will make it to the end
Of that long, uphill, rocky and windy road

Foreword: 1992 to 2022

This text was originally composed and finished thirty years ago preparatory to doctoral fieldwork in the Southeast Asian region. Scholarship has since moved on and there are undoubtedly many more recent and important texts to include in an updated study of Southeast Asia.

To some undeterminable extent this lapse before its publication in a hard-print text retains some degree of scholarly and historical value in its own right, even if scholarship has moved on.

Revolutions of knowledge as a result of widespread on-line publications, also represented by this text, would not have been possible twenty or even ten years previously, and as a result of new DNA analytical profiling techniques now being more widely used around the world, and is leading to the development of extensive globally available data-bases.

These developments perhaps well spell a second information revolution in making available for comparative analysis and study and for holistic construction of taxonomies and comparative human descent structures that in detail and range were previously unavailable and largely undreamt of.

It is not known to what degree these new knowledge foundations and means of inquiry and research have impacted an areal and regional studies approach such as Southeast Asian Studies.

Undoubtedly these new forms and frameworks of knowledge and systematic inquiry will complement and find further contextualizing the broader normative foundations of this kind of inter-regional scholarly knowledge.

We know for instance that new historical linguistic constructions of the region have discarded some of the older reconstructions found within this text, but this does not change the overall emphasis or requirements of a genuine ethno-cultural, ethno-linguistic and ethno-historical approach to these regional studies, particularly in a region with a relatively shallow history, a deeper proto-history, and a very deep prehistory, rendered quite sketchy by the common condition of poor preservation of organic material evidence.

Having finished this and a few other texts during those couple of years preparatory to fieldwork, I went ahead and conducted fieldwork in 1993-1995 upon the Overseas Chinese of Georgetown, Pulau Penang, in Malaysia. It was only unfortunate in hindsight that much of this work didn't get carried forward and become the foundation of longer-term studies of change in the region.

Preface: On the Construction of the Concept of "Southeast Asia"

Its parts do not know a complete elephant

The term "Southeast Asia" has only recently become stabilized as a conventional term for a region on the world map.[1]

The variations of the name Southeast Asia (South East Asia, South-East Asia, Southeastern Asia etc.) have occurred with differential frequencies in the literature, and have in part reflected varying political relations with the region adopted by the naming country. "Thus in East and West alike the word 'Asia' is really an equivoque. It has no fixed meaning—no clear-cut denotation—but it is extraordinarily rich in emotional connotations. Though these make it the despair of the logician, they enhance its value for the poet, the artist—and the politician." (J. Steadman, The Myth of Asia, 1969: 35.)[2]

---

[1] "By 'making up' the region out of nations, Americans tended to politicize the idea of 'Southeast Asia' as a whole…American researchers who studied nonpolitical subjects tended to do so sub-nationally. The result was a now-conventional division of academic labor between 'macropolitical science' and 'microanthropology.'" (Donald Emmerson, "'Southeast Asia': What's in a Name?" JSEAS, Vol. 19, pg. 13.)

[2] "…No less interesting is the first element, 'Southeast,' it implies additional peripheries: south of China, east of India…not only 'Southeast Asia' but, by the same logic of adjacency, Malte-Brun's 'Indochina,' Logan's 'Indonesia,' and Purcell's less successful 'Indosinesia.' Variations in the rendering of 'Southeast'—it has been spelled a dozen ways in English alone—have even reflected political

Southeast Asian Sources

The term "Southeast Asia" leads to a reification and projection of a spurious sense of homogeneity, unity and boundedness onto the region it delimits on the globe. It is a region that is actually as culturally diverse and complicated as it has been historically entangled and unbounded. As the crossroads of the orient, it has long been a meeting place, and a region of cultural intermingling between many different kinds of people.

One will find anywhere one travels in Southeast Asia a profusion of different religions, ethnic identities, and cultural orientations within the same marketplace, within the same city limits, even under the same roof. Southeast Asia, from a regional perspective, becomes a veritable mosaic of human difference and variation.

It is predictable that alternative hyphenated forms should have given way to a single compound. Such a stabilization of an entire region also represents the ossification of a modern area of imagination. Southeast Asia as a place has become more clearly and conventionally bounded than it was before.

We know now to exclude Australia, Melanesia, Taiwan, Southern and Southeastern China, Northeastern India, Nepal, and Sri Lanka, if only for reasons of political culture, though all of these areas may have had some more or less distant or direct relationship to the region.

It would have made little sense to have called the area East-South Asia, as this would have conflicted with our geographical sense of the cardinal directions of the compass—a sense of direction which lends solidity, and hence credibility, to our region of imagination that we have so labeled.

---

differences between Western governments." (Donald K. Emmerson, "'Southeast Asia': What's in a Name?" JSEAS, Vol. 19: 3-4)

The inter-regionality and fuzziness of Southeast Asia is reflected in the cross-disciplinary character of its study. If we want to get beyond a simplistic, textbook tour of tropical Southeast Asian exotica, then we must entertain the problem of diversity and the inherent complexity of such diversity.

No single point of view is by itself sufficient or comprehensive enough to provide an adequate theoretical basis for understanding the complex historical processes and patterns of Southeast Asian civilization.

The diversity in which such a cross-disciplinary approach to Southeast Asian studies is rooted entails that any final or complete picture must be in the last analysis of a synthetic character. Perfect agreement between all different points will never be found, and any emergent, general picture must compromise some of the detail.

Like the history of its name, Southeast Asian studies begins and ends with the understanding of the place it stands for in our own mind's eye, as a representation we bring to a mystified region.

My objectives in writing this collection of exploratory essays were threefold.

First, it is an attempt to bring to the foreground a number of alternative hypotheses regarding the origin, history, dynamics and patterns of Southeast Asian Civilization. Its aim is one of demonstrating the regional distinctiveness and sui generis continuity of character that makes Southeast Asia more than a mere bastardization of South and East Asia.

Second, I wish to critique within the same set of essays certain attitudes, approaches and conventions that underlie or are implicit in many of our theoretical preconceptions about Southeast Asia, as well as in our approaches to the study of human history.

Southeast Asian Sources

Third, I wish to make my critiques constructive by offering what I believe to be serious and viable alternatives to those aspects of our anthropological and areal studies that I seek to deconstruct. These alternatives are framed as theoretical and procedural examples based upon the evidence derived from research in Southeast Asian studies, in support of the major hypothesis that I offer for consideration in critique of what we know and do not know about Southeast Asia.

Any comprehension of Southeast Asia must eventually be poly-thematic and eclectic in attempting to incorporate many diverse views from very different disciplines. This exploratory essay attempts to weave together in a critical manner several different hypothetical themes to create a tapestry of Southeast Asia as a cultural region.

Generally, it is the question of how we go about representing and modeling past life-ways, viewpoints, languages, and worlds. It is a matter of what we select for such representation and what we choose to ignore, and how these reconstructions are in part prejudiced by our own preconceptions about the past and models rooted in the present.

These themes are offered as alternative hypothesis for critical consideration of their merit in shedding constructive light upon the patterns common to Southeast Asian peoples and their cultures.

The essays I offer in this collection are exploratory not just for their content, but also because they together compose a statement of the place and contribution that cultural anthropology might make in constructive criticism of other studies, especially linguistics, biology and archaeology.

Furthermore, they represent a form of poly-thematic elaboration that is in style, organization, and tonality, unique to the forums of anthropological and Southeast Asian studies, and that contradict in many deliberate ways the canons of good scholarly writing.

Centrally, they treat the general problem that I refer to as reconstruction. They concern the question of how we go about representing and modeling past life-ways, viewpoints, languages, and worlds; of what we select for such representation; what we choose to ignore; and how these reconstructions may be at least in part prejudiced by our own representations.

Because we have little else to work with when we are trying to establish a direct connection to the past, we are left with the challenge of rendering our reconstructions as close to the ground, and as systematically unbiased and value-free as possible— objective in the most scientific of senses.

We must pass our models again and again through the wringer of criticism and debate, and ultimately they must withstand the same litmus test—the test of time—that has judged all previous work as well before or after the fact of publication.

An ethnocultural approach, similar to ethno-historical research, is offered as an alternative research paradigm for framing hypotheses in regard to the cultural orientations of people. It shares with ethno-history the central project of comprehensively embracing all extant documentary sources and the points of view represented by such sources, as well as the problem of integrating these sources into a single credible picture.

I have long identified myself as a cultural anthropologist interested in Southeast Asian studies. From my initial introduction to the area its mystique and mystification has only fascinated me to further inquiry. If I can convey even a little of this fascination and mystery to the reader, I will have more than repaid my growing debt to the field of Southeast Asian studies.

Southeast Asian Sources

It has been a mixed blessing that ultimately was not in my stars to fulfill, to focus primarily in one region like specializing in Southeast Asian studies, rather than to become distracted by the crosscutting demands of life, of making a living, raising a family, or learning new areas of intellectual engagement and stimulation.

Looking back though, it appears that many scholars of the curious and fascinating region of Southeast Asian studies have also moved on with lives leading in other directions.

I have no regrets in this regard but am only grateful to have had what time I could to devote to these studies, and now, the time, means and grateful opportunity to finally push some of these works through to some finished form of publication and greater public availability and awareness.

Introduction: Critical Reconstruction of the Southeast Asian "Context"

Southeast Asia stands out as an internally coherent cultural region. As a coherent region, it is characterized by two main features—(1.), great age, and (2.) great diversity. Of course, these two aspects have always in Southeast Asia been deeply intertwined.

Southeast Asia remains one of the most heterogeneous, long settled, and most culturally, ethnically, racially, linguistically and historically complicated regions in the World—evidence in its own right of its great cultural age.

Geographically, it has been divided between insular, or island Southeast Asia, including Malaysia, Borneo, Singapore, Brunei, and the vast arc of island archipelagos including Indonesia and the Philippines, and peninsular, or Mainland Southeast Asia, including Thailand, Burma, Kampuchea, Laos and Vietnam.

This distinction between insular and peninsular Southeast Asia reflects another important contrast in the region between the maritime orientation of the many miles of shoreline, and the mountain orientation of the highlands, large spiny chains that separate the Great Rivers flowing python-like through the valleys, lowland piedmonts, and large alluvial deltas.

Strong culture historical reasons are sometimes given for including Sri Lanka, the Andamans, the Nicobars, Assam, Yunnan, Hainan, Formosa and even New Guinea and Madagascar, although these political entities are conventionally peripheral to the region circumscribed by the designation of Southeast Asia.

<u>Southeast Asian Sources</u>

There are common themes in Southeast Asian life that confers an overall unity to the diversity of life found there. "Unity in diversity" is the predominant theme of Southeast Asian Studies.

A vegetable culture, a bamboo culture, a rice and fish culture, a monsoon culture, a Riverine culture—Southeast Asia can be characterized by its commonly shared traits that have helped to shape its life-ways.

But also recurrent in the region are other general themes:

- The importance of maritime trade.
- The Chameleon-ness of identity.
- The dialectical tension between the peoples of the highlands and the peoples of the lowlands.
- The role that great religions and indigenous spirituality has always played in the daily life of its people.
- The proximity and cultural appreciation of the natural world.
- The unifying role that the rivers and streams have long played in the integration of its diverse areas.
- The outward looking orientation of its peoples.
- The periodic waves of acculturative change that have occasionally swept through the region.

    And,

- The autochthonous origins and deep sense of cyclical, rhythmic time of ancient, traditional civilizations, even into modern eras.

Such common themes amount to no more than the reiteration of trite truisms whose substantive basis is not apparent until one has lived and traveled within Southeast Asia among its many people.

In claiming that the Southeast Asian setting, its nature, its geography, its climate, has had an important shaping influence upon Southeast Asian culture and character, is to risk falling back into an old argument about environmental determinism.

But the influence is there, and has been remarked upon in reference to the use of space and geographical orientation among the Balinese; the ritual ecologies of New Guinea highlanders or of the *Rhade* of the Vietnamese highlands; the thematic recurrence of nature symbolism in Vietnamese literature and poetry, art and music; the spiritual animism of the *Dayaks* of Borneo; in the cultural ecology of highlanders throughout the region; in the ecology of rice among the Thai and the Javanese, etc.

Many other examples can be found to attest to the direct symbolic role and value that nature and the natural environment has played in influencing the aesthetic sensitivities and religious sensibilities of the many different people of Southeast Asia.

Perhaps it is because nature in this tropical setting is so intrusive in virtually every part of one's life. Whether it is a morning parade of ants through the halls of one's home, a snake in one's kitchen, a resident gecko in one's kitchen sink or six inch long centipede in one's outhouse sink, the encroaching jungle growth that appears in every crack of the sidewalk, the torrents of rain that fall endlessly from the high clouds, or the monitor lizard in the parking lot of a major university, one cannot easily escape the direct contact with nature that living in a Southeast Asian setting brings.

Not all Southeast Asians are equally and unequivocally lovers of nature or conscientious conservationists of the region's natural resources. The region has long been witness to irreversible destruction of many primeval forest habitats that continues at a ceaseless and alarming rate.

Many people in their daily activities and attitudes evince little concern or appreciation or sense of empathy for their natural environment. And yet many of the most basic cultural patterns that predominate in Southeast Asia can be found to have direct linkages with the natural tropical habitat.

What is commonly referred to in the literature as the traditional, interregional system of Southeast Asian civilization, must be seen as a structurally and socially persistent pattern, constrained by its ball and chain mountain backbone, maritime and tropical cultural geography, of the organization of diversity—an intrinsic sense of diversity that is all at once ecological, economic and ethno-cultural.

The style patterning of Southeast Asian Civilization is best characterized by its synthetic nature, and by its synergism in integrating a broad diversity within a common thematic unity.

The genius of Southeast Asian Civilization can best be thought of as its capacity for syncretic creation of new forms based upon the borrowing and modification of previous forms.

The complexity of pattern and the broad diversity of its components require that any Southeast Asian scholar must adopt a cross-disciplinary approach and a synthesizing attitude that allows the dialectical integration of many contrasts and contradictions.

No single perspective, idea, or fact is by itself sufficient for understanding the history and culture of Southeast Asian civilization.

No one point of view is by itself complete or correct. Multiple points of view tend to cancel out what is incorrect by mutual exclusion and contradiction. Inferior or false points of view will tend to be selected out. An axial center becomes robust that remains highly credible unless refuted by specific counter evidence. Peripheral portions become identifiable as primary research problems.

Rather than building theory from the ground up, it attempts its "substantiation" by means of bringing into clearer focus particularistic data of individual lives from the framework of the most comprehensive perspective possible.

The credibility of any such construction has depended as much upon its thematic architecture as upon the source of data used as support.

It is somewhat misleading to speak of Southeast Asian Civilization as a single, integrated phenomenon. There have been and are many different and distinct Southeast Asian civilizations and often the possibility of their comparison is a rather moot point.

But all of Southeast Asian peoples and their traditional cultures share certain basic structural themes that are related to a common Southeast Asian geography, a common Southeast Asian ecology, and a common Southeast Asian socio-historical context as a crossroads.

These themes have been important in the structuring of the long-term patterns of Southeast Asia as distinct and unique in the world. Within these broader outlines we can frame a better understanding of Southeast Asia.

As a region of exchange, we can say that for the most part contact and acculturation has been extremely creative in giving rise to new forms in the Southeast Asian scene. It can be taken as a mark of the strength of Southeast Asian civilization to be able to successfully adopt and integrate new and foreign forms, to appropriate and modify alien symbols and to successfully reemerge in a vital unique new way.

At the same time, there are long-term continuities that survive the onslaught of the different and the distant threads that link the most modern with the most ancient in Southeast Asia.

<u>Southeast Asian Sources</u>

These old forms are not merely anachronistic survivals of a bygone era; rather they remain a vigorous substrate and source of vitality for the synthesis itself.

In the clash between the new and the very old, the familiar and the foreign, Southeast Asian civilization always emerges as a more complex, more structured and more chaotic cauldron of civilization than before.

We might speak of the emergent forms of the diachronic processes of civilization and acculturation, caught within an historical dialectic, producing a hybridization of Southeast Asian civilization as a mixture and a mosaic of many different cultural patterns.

Two long-term structures of dialectical contrast have always been apparent in Southeast Asian Civilization, fostering fundamentally different kinds of adaptations and styles of life. This is the contrast between the highlands and the lowlands, and the contrast between the land and the sea.

These sets of contrasts are entangled in one another in virtually every way, and have provided the basis of the civilizational development of Southeast Asian peoples in which the outside world has increasingly intruded upon, and altered one side of their life, while leaving virtually unchanged the other.

We can refer to the basic dialectical dynamics underlying the rise of human civilization and development of regional integration in Southeast Asia, as the central axis of contrast about which the patterns of history have unfolded from the remotest of times.

It provided a regional continuity of character, as an historical structure of the long run that has witnessed unchanged the coming and going of many peasants and the rise and fall of many Princes.

These factors remain in the background as pervasive constraints and limits to the possibilities of human action and development, and have set the stage for the enactment of many Southeast Asian dramas.

Several broad phases, or stages of the historical emergence of Southeast Asia can be recognized. These stages did not come to replace one another so much as one became layered upon the other, with the consequence that with each next layering a growing complexity of overall pattern resulted.

> **Early Prehistoric I.** First, there is a long and deep early prehistoric stage in which the Southeast Asian Mainland and islands became increasingly peopled until people came to occupy a diverse range of sparse settings across the mountains, valleys and coastlines. Foraging subsistence based upon a bamboo and stone tool adaptation (Chopper-Chopping Tool complex) that grew in sophistication formed the basis of this way of life.

> **Late Prehistoric II.** Second, there emerged at the end of this long phase a late prehistoric phase that corresponds with the Neolithic. It is a phase that witnessed the domestication and cultivation of many species of plant and animal, combined with a more sophisticated tool and pottery technology, and that allowed long-distance extension and "detachment" of culture groupings from their natal homelands.

> **Early Protohistoric I.** Third, there emerged at the end of this phase the technological basis for metallurgy: first copper, then bronze, then followed by iron. There was also achieved during this phase the "agricultural revolution" in which cultivating patterns were replaced by sedentary patterns of planting and harvesting. Socio-political organization also emerged in greater "central place" complexity during this phase, which speaks for the importance of controlling markets and long-distance trade connections.

Late Protohistoric II. Fourth, early "Mandala" states emerged at the end of this phase with the full use of iron tools and weapons, wet-rice agriculture, long-distance trade networks, formal markets, and a state religion combining priests and political symbols of people-hood.

Early Historic I. Fifth, contact with foreign powers, primarily from the Northern Mainland and then the West, ushered in a phase in which written records of these contacts was left, usually by the foreign peoples, but indigenous accounts are later found increasingly. We can include in this the very early contacts with Chinese, Indians, even Romans, and later with Arabs. This is the phase in which we can speak properly of the emerging interregional integration of Southeast Asian civilization in which a completely local orientation gradually began receding from the forefront.

Late Historic II: This phase properly commences with the first contacts by the Europeans, starting with Portugal and the Spanish, and followed by the Dutch, French and English, and ending with the Japanese and the gaining of independence from neo-colonial interference by the newly emergent modern nations of Southeast Asia.

Early Modern I: This phase commenced with the rising of Western oriented and anti-colonial nationalistic movements in Southeast Asian colonies, following the achievement of independence, and then followed the post-independence eras characterized by chronic problems of poverty, underdevelopment, totalitarianism, local institutional deformations, corruption and criminal organization, political conflict and war, and non-democratic, social authoritarian organization.

We might only speculate about what a late modern or post-modern phase might mean, because if we are there yet, we still don't quite know it. The phases are not clear-cut, and it is obvious that there is a great deal of overlap between them.

It is possible that there may have been critical transition periods marking off this overlap—periods that may have actually been quite brief from the longer point of view, during which major structural transformations might have occurred.

What is perhaps important to recognize is that these phases may also have been marked by a gradually emerging process of regional integration, as well as an emerging overlay of complexity of interrelation upon previously established and newly existing patterns.

I: The "Waterways Hypothesis"
The Maritime-Coastal-Riverine Cradle of Southeast Asian Civilization

Scientifically conservative continental archaeologists have shied away from synthetic reconstructions of the past, especially those focusing upon human maritime and waterway adaptations.

The cumulative consequences of these tendencies toward methodological conservatism are the implicit undervaluing in inductive, ground-up reconstructions as well as chronic underestimation of the potential human capacity for civilization.

Besides the chronic underestimation of the human capacity for culture implicit in such conservatism, there is also an a-theoretical rejection of counter-factuality as a heuristic means of hypothetical reconstruction of the past.

Strictly speaking, counterfactual reconstruction of prior events may be logically impossible, but may still be historically plausible.

The insufficiency of evidence alone, especially if this insufficiency is due primarily to a lack of research or evidence in an area, is not enough to reject competing alternative hypotheses, as long as an hypothesis:

a) Can reasonably account for available data.

b) Provides reasonable alternative conclusions.

c) And is not explicitly contradicted by any specific counter-evidence.

The Orthodox Conservatism of Conventional Archaeology

The conservatism of conventional archaeology is expressed in several ways:

1) Its "nothing but" analytical orientation.

2) Its "data-boundness."

3) Its "as late as" evidentiary caution.

4) Its spatial "locationalist" and "localist" bias.

5) Its "Great Tradition/little tradition" dichotomization.

6) Its lumping/splitting tendencies in categorical constructions.

And, finally,

7) Its exclusive "territoriality."

The cumulative consequences of these tendencies are its implicit undervaluing of the potential human capacity for civilization in its inductive, "ground-up" reconstructions, and the professional devaluation of the logical role of counter-factuality in hypothesis construction.

It is argued that the orthodox rage of "scientific" consensus in the professional identification of the field systematically precludes the historical role of Archaeology as a heterodox "humanity."

1) Jacquetta Hawkes delivered a critique of the encroachment of scientific reductionism in archaeology in her 1971 John Danz Lecture "Nothing But or Something More," based upon her sense of distrust in the systematic narrowing of the rational "beyond its true meaning of the

> reasonable until it excludes subjective experience, a great
> part of what it means to be a human person..." (Pg. 3.)[3]

Against this urge to "nothing but" reductionism, Hawkes posed the "something more" of a "universal reality of hierarchy" in which multiple levels of organization that are "two-faced" and that are structured both from below by its component elements and above by its relationships with higher levels of integration, and from which new properties emerge at each level not present at lower ones. Furthermore, such universality of hierarchy can be demonstrated experimentally as well as theoretically.

Her critique of reductionism, when applied to "analytical archaeology" that restricts itself to graphs, statics and histograms, is the attempt to define humankind as nothing but technical, material and economic—as next to a "mosquito" in evolutionary terms and without the free will or consciousness which has played such a determining role in history. Left out is the sense of the "human will to meaning" and value that has been such a part of the human creation of civilization.

Hawkes summarizes a trait list of shared characteristics of the independent pristine civilizations of the old and the new worlds, noting that while the Mesoamerican civilizations had developed a ball game with score keeping, mathematics and a calendar, they had not developed technological features of a wheel, an arch or a metallurgy.

These are such that a materialist hypothesis would logically lead one to suspect as being the point of convergence between civilizations. (Ibid. pg. 25.)

---

[3] The analytical emphasis of such reductionism represents the single minded extension of a methodology of the physical sciences to more humanly problematic enterprises of anthropology until it becomes a worldview...." (Hawkes, pg. 6.)

2) "Data-boundness" is a general bias of attitude and orientation that I have noted especially among many archaeologists and physical anthropologists whose primary researches are concerned with the minutiae of analysis of bones, teeth, and, in the case of archaeologists, chipped stones and potsherds.

It is an attitude of near exclusive preoccupation with the analysis of the artifact or the physical specimen rather than with the conjecture of the history that these material items may represent.

There is an a-theoretical method-bound fear of counterfactual conjecture and restrictiveness of interpretation—focus often becomes concentrated on the development of componential analysis aimed at establishing the internal/external provenience and validity of the *objet d'homme*.[4]

There is a predisposition to view the hidden history behind the material data with the same general sense of material objectivity as is embodied in the data itself.

History is firmly rooted to the ground. Perhaps this kind of theoretical caution is safe (especially when it comes to setting confidence limits), perhaps too safe, and therefore perhaps it is also inevitable and unavoidable.

When we hold an ancient flint chopper or scraper in our hands, we can conjecture how its maker may have held and used it. We

---

[4] The consequence is that when and if they do generalize, they end up taking a grand leap of faith and falling off into a chasm…There is a consequence of theoretical naiveté and historical blindness in the superimposition of the researcher's own values and preconceptions upon the "origin" story of the data—the classic case is the interpretation of all "Venus figurines" as cult fetishes and fertility symbols. (S. M. Nelson, "Diversity of the Upper Paleolithic 'Venus' Figurines and Archaeological Mythology." in <u>Archaeological Papers of the American Anthropology Association</u> 1990: pg. 11-22.)

can turn it over in our hands to find the most suitable grip and the clearest cutting edge.

We might even go so far as to try to make one our selves, or to attempt to use it in various tasks—and if we did this enough we might even become good at it and develop a "feel" for the object that we would not gain through the microscope.

3) "As late as" evidentiary caution, versus "at least by" evidentiary conjecture, has an understandable reason in archaeological interpretation. The peopling of North America can only be as old as the oldest fossils yet discovered, the stratigraphic level of a site can only be as early as the latest artifact found at that level, unless it is known to have percolated from a higher or lower provenience.

From a scientific standpoint this is supremely sensible. We are wed to an empiricist tradition which holds that an unseen, unsounded tree fallen in the forest could not have fallen. It is also extremely safe—let someone else stick their professional neck out on the block to build mansions on ground that is not there. Ever since Piltdown and Lysenko, the scientific community loves to "falsify" and chastise.

The problem with this general attitude is that it is extremely conservative and entangled in a long tradition that wishes to confer upon humankind only the most shallow and recent history possible—"perhaps no later than the flood." (Margaret T. Hodgen Early Anthropology in the Sixteenth and Seventeenth Centuries, 1964.)

The general trend of evidence has been to push in unprecedented fashion our sequences and reconstructed trees and dates back further and deeper into the past than anyone would have been daring to admit. It was thought incredible that humankind could have an origin of several hundred thousand, or even a million years, but when Lucy was found to have a tentative history of 3.5

to 4 million years, it all seemed astonishing. Even in the archaeological and paleontological record, things eventually fall into place, and dates, sequences and trees eventually stabilize—at least enough to permit more confidence and consensus of reconstruction, or at least until something unexpected is dug up.

"At least by" daring should not be so much a mark of professional incompetence, as it should be a measure of the willingness to search beyond what exists to see that even the artifacts themselves must have had precedents and a history other than what we ascribe to them.

The human capacity for culture that led to the creation of the artifact must have been in place and preceded its creation and humankind making its own history must have been more of a continuous process than a single stratigraphy may show.

    4) The spatial "locationist" bias is the tendency to see cultural processes of the past as self-contained groupings, segregates, as units or as little culture gardens that can be clearly demarcated on a map and thus studied. This bias tends to underemphasize the importance of human movement, migration, trans-cultural communication and transmission and of regions of great cultural overlap, interaction and multiple diffusions.

The consequence of this kind of bias inherited from the gemeinschaft culture area approach is the implicit tendency to see groups as locally rooted and embedded in time, as fossilized artifacts standing for distinctive peoples, cultures, phases and horizons whose boundaries are clearly marked and exclusive. (Jacob Pandian, The Other in Us: An Essay Concerning the

Southeast Asian Sources

<u>Function of Anthropology in the Western Intellectual Tradition</u> [unpublished manuscript] 1982.)[5]

We can imagine the original owner of this skull, standing here in this place, ten thousand years ago when this place was not a hole but a hill, surveying the boundaries of his property—the same land of his ancestors and of his progeny. History has significance because it is continuously and contiguously linked with the here and the now.

This tendency to isolate "segregates" in time and space on the historical map of the world overlooks both the likelihood that the greater part of Human prehistory must have been marked as much by human movement and people getting around and going places and mixing it all up, as it was by the archaeological stasis implied by stratigraphic provenience, and by the fact that the earth itself, and everything on it, has had its own dynamic natural history marked by erosion, evolution and bio-geophysical processes.

We have no good idea how far "primitive man" must have traveled or the distances spanned during seasonal peregrinations or over a brief life-span of survival, but there seems to be little sound reason for presupposing that the more ancient the people, the more local and homebound their travels and orientation.

5) The "Great Tradition/little tradition" dichotomy is perhaps rooted in the secret desire to discover the last lost pristine civilization of the world, buried somewhere in the vast emptiness of a desert or underneath a tropical rain forest canopy or in some hidden mountain valley.

---

[5] Time is implicitly frozen in this view of the past as static, predictable, and linear measure of absolute distance from the present—historical and cultural distance is directly translatable into geographical distance. (Johannes Fabian <u>Time and the Other: How Anthropology Makes its Object</u> 1983.)

We end up with a stratified pyramid of sites hieratically ranked from high to low and from grand to little. The archaeologist is as local a figure as the site s/he can claim. We tend to see in the stratigraphy the same sense of site stratification—rather than a continuum of process and change. There is a clear spectrum of categories and prototypes ranging between the poles of Grand and local.

Of course, ancient monuments and high art are always crowd pleasers while pot shards and fragments of bone or stone are at best boring museum pieces, though the latter type of artifact may in fact be more informative about a bygone era than the former.

What can we really say about this "Great Divide" except to see in it the romantic reflection of our own "Core-periphery" prejudices and selective perception, and a tendency to see in the "primitive mind" of the makers of the latter types of artifacts the cultural and civilizational deficit of the "Genius" of the makers of the former type.

If this is true, then we must conclude that the original artists of the Lascaux caves constitute the first clear evidence of pristine human civilization that antedates state-development in all other regions by some ten millennia.

> 6) "Lumping/Splitting" tendencies are perhaps as much the consequence of a spotty and incomplete record, in which the number and size of gaps far outweigh amount of available evidence, as it is our own categorical predisposition to label everything we find. Splitting comes from the tendency to recognize in every newly discovered artifact a new type, a new category, a new species, rather than merely a variant of previously known groups.

Thus we get a proliferation of periods and peoples in direct proportion to the number of discoveries and discoverers. Lumping is the reverse tendency to reduce all variation down to a single common theme—to have one basic archetype, one type-site for all cases unearthed. Either way we can only really guess at ranges and limits of variation.[6]

The question underlying these tendencies is how much variation of a small sub-sample is enough to be theoretically predictive or historically significant of the true population. Our small sub-sample may be skewed, or else the original population may have been skewed in ways not evident in our sample.

What lumping and splitting does indicate is a preoccupation with the relations between the data rather than with the relations between the data and the gaps in the record. Any gap, of whatever size, can become the basis for splitting the sample into two or more sub-samples, or else it can become the basis for filling in between two samples to create a union, for lumping differences under a single category or continuum.

The gap is either absolute and unbridgeable, or else nonexistent and easily spanned by the imagination. Either way, we tend to systematically exclude the unknown and perhaps the unknowable as well, from our analysis of what is little known. This represents a somewhat anal preoccupation with boundaries and a fear of the unknown as something uncertain, to be covered over or cast out.

It also represents a preoccupation with being knowledgeable and expert on one's chosen topic.

Lack of evidence should not be counted as counter evidence but as space available for plausible hypothetical counterfactuals.

---

[6] The problem is not the continuous record or relative lack of one, but the relative, intrinsic and extrinsic limits of our symbolic linguistic descriptions of discrete and discontinuous rational interpretation of the records. We use terms and terminologies of today to talk about worlds of yesterday built of forgotten knowledge.

7) Territoriality is perhaps directly proportional to ego—my site, my area, my people, my specialty, my provenience, my phase, and my horizon. We seek to monopolize and drive out competition such that our authority can be seen as the final authority. The borders we mark out around the material manifestations of our work the boundaries of our own interest, character, and professional investment.

We possess the ideas, the knowledge, the data, the history, the authority, as these things possess us. We must defend them at all cost from any threat or contradiction or error that looms upon our horizon. In so doing we seek consensus that comes from perfect order and stability, and drive out all sense dissonance, uncertainty and difference. A period in history, a place in time, and a people becomes our own private preserve.

Perhaps such territoriality is rooted in a need for control, which itself may be rooted in deeper needs and insecurities. Such control manifests itself in two kinds of way—the need to control the site, the type, the data, the artifact, the conclusion, for the sake of "science" and the need for political control over the information, the understanding, the resources of that part of the profession.

The combination of these kinds of biases is symptomatic of a sense of conservatism in archaeological interpretation. Besides the chronic underestimation of the human capacity for culture that is implicit in such conservatism, there is also an a-theoretical rejection of counter factuality as a heuristic means of hypothetical reconstruction of the past.

A model of rational parsimony of explanation is not necessarily the most reasonable or realistic rationale for representing the phenomenal complexity of human historical patterning—we cannot systematically reduce these complexities to the level of first principles or component parts without a loss of fidelity to the "facts" in place.

<u>Southeast Asian Sources</u>

Furthermore, general confusion exists between the deterministic strength of historical cause-effect relations and the inference strength of logical conditionality, and this tendency underlies the consistent over-rating of material datum and the under-rating of interpretive counter factuality.

Modus tollens-type fallacy that cannot strictly apply in logical argument—arguing from the consequent to the antecedent—may apply in a known historical relationship. The difference in this case is between strictly deductive inference, and abductive and inductive methods of inference. The latter types of reasoning are not strictly provable from a logical standpoint, but they are useful ways of deriving inferences when dealing with especially complex causal multi-determination (i.e., history).[7]

Strictly speaking, counterfactual reconstruction of prior events may be logically impossible, but may still be historically plausible.[8]

The "Waterways" Hypothesis

An alternative "waterways" hypothesis is proffered regarding the culture ecological role of human adaptation to marine

---

[7] In inductive inference in which generalization is based upon a limited sub-sample, the conclusion may be falsified by a single contradictory case. In Abductive logic, unlike deduction, there may be more than one conflicting inference derived from the consequent, though only one conclusion may actually be true. (James L. Noyes, <u>Artificial Intelligence with Common Lisp: Fundamentals of Symbolic and Numeric Processing</u> 1993: pgs. 296-303.)

[8] The insufficiency of evidence alone, especially if this insufficiency is due primarily to a lack of research or evidence in an area, is not enough to reject competing alternative hypothesis—as long as the hypothesis: a) can reasonably account for available data; b) provides reasonable alternative conclusions; c) is not explicitly contradicted by any specific counter-evidence. (Giles Fauconnier, <u>Mental Spaces: Aspects of Meaning Construction in Natural Language,</u> 1985: pgs.81-142.)

environments as a "primary mover" and possible interregional catalyst to the systemic development of early human civilization.

This hypothesis represents a general extension and revision to Karl Wittfogel's "hydraulic hypothesis" as a prime mover in early despotic states, to encompass the entire range of human relationships to water and its resources as a primary environmental constraint in the multivariate "systemic circumscription" of early civilization.[9]

The paucity of evidence due to the weathering and poor preservation effects of exposure to water, the shifting of coastlines and river-courses, the rising and falling of water levels, and alluvial flooding, have precluded the formulation of any major hypothesis regarding the role of human lacustrine, riverine and marine adaptations in the development of early civilizations.

An ethno-historical reconstruction of human marine adaptations must take into account the vital role which rivers, lakes, coast-lines and seas may have long played in interregional cultural integration as channels of communication, control, and transmission.

Such maritime reconstruction must also take into account possible periods and processes of three analytical phases—prehistoric, proto-historic and historic, as well as the interregional "trans-local" character of the processes of contact, acculturation, diffusion, migration and stimulus generation underlying the development of human civilization.

The adaptation to exploitation of aquatic resources may have provided an important resource base in the promotion of population growth and social-environmental circumscription

---

[9] Karl Wittfogel, <u>Oriental Despotism: A Comparative Study of Total Power</u>, Yale University Press, 1957.

stimulating early human social formation, development and migration.[10]

Bodies of water may have long provided important barriers which may have served as "thresholds of integration" in the early development of human civilization—overcoming the barrier presented by water required optimal levels of social organization and technological sophistication, while mastery of the waterways has always conferred a tremendous power and strategic advantage.

The model of the "waterways" hypothesis is a systemic one in which the relative availability and control of water is both a "resonance dampening" and a "resonance amplification" mechanism in the development of human social organization and integration.[11]

The consequence is that the control of water has been a primary mover in the development of human civilization. This model may be summed up by the following set of hypothetical postulates. It has served both as a "first-order" resonance dampening mechanism (A) of social-environmental circumscription, and as a "second-order" resonance amplification mechanism, (B) leading to the systemic, interregional organization:

---

[10] Fishing-Farming cultures have been closely associated in the archaeological record with the beginnings of agricultural development. (Carl O. Sauer <u>Seeds, Spades, Hearths & Herds: The Domestication of Animals and Foodstuffs</u> Cambridge, Mass.: The M.I.T. Press 1952: pgs.24-5.)

[11] Kent Flannery "The Cultural Evolution of Civilizations" in <u>Annual Review of Ecology and Systematics"</u> 3, 1972: pgs. 399-426, and "Archaeological Systems Theory and Early Mesoamerica" in <u>Anthropological Archaeology in the Americas</u>, Washington D.C.: 1971: pgs. 67-87.)

A. Waterways have provided an important set of factors contributing to the systemic circumscription of local and regional human populations.

I. Periods of Glaciation and rising/falling sea levels and accompanying climactic fluctuations may have created the early demographic/environmental circumscription which lead to the evolution of modern humans and their cultural complex.

a. Advancing and retreating coastlines may have had a consequence of facilitating adaptive radiation and then divergent isolation—leading to a "founder effect".

b. Rising water levels and advancing glaciers may have induced intense periods of environmental/social circumscription in some areas, resulting in rapid selection.

II. Water, its availability or scarcity, has always served as a critical constraining factor in human social patterning.

a. Control of water as a critical resource, as an unpredictable menace, and as a strategic advantage, has long been a primary preoccupation of and impetus for human social organization.

1. Natural precipitation has always been an uncertain and undependable source of water.

2. The collection of a stable supply of fresh water, in either natural or artificial reservoirs, has long been a primary social preoccupation of human groups.

3. The earliest vessels served the function of containing water.

b. Large bodies of water and concourses have provided an important relatively stable protein resource pool upon which large and healthy human populations can be supported.

Southeast Asian Sources

1. Specialized adaptations/technologies/techniques in the cultural ecology of aquatic resource exploitation was an early, and important, extension of the human resource base.

c. The production or abundance of a stable supply of food has always depended upon a predictable and stable supply of water.

1. Assurance of a stable, steady supply of water stimulated the development of artificial water control technologies and techniques.

III. Large bodies of water and concourses have long been both obstacles to human movement and communication that have always challenged people to overcome.

a. Overcoming the natural obstacles imposed by large bodies of water and concourses have required a minimal degree of technical invention, cooperative social organization and political integration.

1. Irrigation and flood control projects required the mobilization and coordination of large numbers of people.

2. Shipbuilding, fishing, and trading required craft-role specialization.

b. The challenge of overcoming the obstacles posed by waterways provided a "springboard" for more complex social organization and development.

B. Mastering the challenges presented by the obstacles of waterways conferred important strategic adaptations and advantages in transportation, communication, command and mobility that allowed groups to extend their range of exploitation and control to encompass a broader spectrum of environments and resources than otherwise possible.

I. Gaining control of waterways made possible trans-local, regional integration and interregional contact and diffusion.

    a. Waterways provided a fast and efficient route of transportation and communication.

II. Maintaining control of waterways required the development of secondary social institutions to manage and mobilize people in construction projects, in trade and commerce, and to protect the strategic lines of communication afforded by waterway traffic.

    a. Control of piracy became a major preoccupation of many states, providing the basis for interstate cooperation, and for the organization and mobilization of navies to protect the waterways.

III. Development of waterways made possible the growth of a cosmopolitan way of life based upon interregional trade and water-born commerce.

    a. There occurred a transformation of cultural adaptations that led to increasing interregional interdependencies upon waterway trade and traffic—in both basic commodities and in sumptuary and symbolic goods and capital.

        1. Sociocultural institutions were rapidly modified in adaptation and dependency upon access to non-local resources most readily available by waterborne transportation.

        2. There occurred a secondary patterning of competition and conflict that led to a pattern of imperial "rise and fall" development of states, chronic warfare and increasing incorporation of peripheral regions into the nexus of traffic and trade.

IV. Mastering maritime transportation stimulated and facilitated diffusion and intercultural contact, providing:

  a. An escape valve for relieving of population and environmental pressures.

  b. A maritime "frontier" for early pioneers.

Early periods of glaciation and the accompanying rising and falling of sea levels, accompanying shifting of coastlines and climactic fluctuations may have created the early demographic/environmental circumscription which stimulating development of modern humankind (non-Archaic Homo sapiens) and their cultural complexes.

Advancing and retreating coastlines may have had a consequence of facilitating adaptive radiation and then divergent isolation— leading to a "founder effect."

Rising water levels and advancing glaciers may have induced intense periods of environmental/social circumscription in some areas, resulting in rapid selection.

Water, its availability or scarcity, has always served as a critical constraining factor in human social patterning. The control of water as a critical resource, as an unpredictable menace, and as a strategic advantage, and the collection of a stable supply of fresh water in natural or artificial reservoirs, has long been a primary preoccupation of and impetus for human social organization.

Natural precipitation has always been an uncertain and undependable source of water. The earliest vessels served the function of containing water. Larger vessels made mostly of wood came to increasingly serve the purpose of floating and travel in water with streamlined features like oars or paddles, a rudder, and sails.

The production or abundance of a stable supply of food has always depended upon a predictable and stable supply of water. Assurance of a stable, steady supply of water stimulated the development of artificial water control technologies and techniques.

Large bodies of water and concourses have provided an important, relatively stable protein resource pool upon which large and healthy human populations can be supported.

Specialized cultural adaptations, technologies and techniques in the cultural ecology of aquatic resource exploitation were an early, and important, achievement extending the human resource base.

Large bodies of water and concourses have long been obstacles to human movement and communication. Overcoming the natural obstacles imposed by large bodies of water and concourses have required a minimal degree of technical invention, cooperative social organization and political integration, the challenge of overcoming these obstacles posed by waterways providing a springboard for more complex social organization and development. Shipbuilding, fishing, and trading required skill and experience.

Mastering the challenges presented by the obstacles of waterways conferred important strategic advantages in transportation, communication, command and mobility that allowed groups to extend their range of exploitation and control to encompass a broader spectrum of environments and resources than otherwise possible.

Gaining control of waterways made possible trans-local, regional integration and interregional contact and diffusion. Waterways provided a fast and efficient route of transportation and communication.

Mastering maritime transportation stimulated and facilitated diffusion and intercultural contact, providing an escape valve for relieving of population and environmental pressures and a maritime frontier for early pioneers.

Maintaining control of waterways required the development of secondary social institutions to manage and mobilize people in construction projects, in trade and commerce, and to protect the strategic lines of communication afforded by waterway traffic.

Control of piracy became a major preoccupation of many states, providing the basis for interstate cooperation, and for the organization and mobilization of navies to protect the waterways.

Development of waterways made possible the growth of a cosmopolitan way of life based upon interregional trade and water-born commerce. There occurred a transformation of cultural adaptations that led to increasing interregional interdependencies upon waterway trade and traffic—in both basic commodities and in sumptuary and symbolic goods and capital. Sociocultural institutions were rapidly modified in adaptation and dependency upon access to non-local resources most readily available by water-born transportation.

There occurred a secondary patterning of competition and conflict that led to a developing pattern of imperial rise and fall development of states, chronic warfare and increasing incorporation of peripheral regions into the nexus of traffic and trade.

The net consequence is that the control of water has been a primary mover in the development of human civilization. It has served both as a "first-order" resonance dampening mechanism (A) of social-environmental circumscription, and as (B) a "second-order" resonance amplification mechanism leading to the systemic, interregional organization.

Many regions are candidates for such a hypothesis. For instance:

- The circum-Mediterranean region including the reaches of the Nile throughout the early history and prehistory of Europe and Western Asia.
- The North Atlantic during the period of the "Red Paint Peoples" and later during the era of Viking conquest and settlement.
- The "Sea of Sunrise"/Tigris-Euphrates region in the early civilizations of Mesopotamia and Dilmun.
- The Gulf of Mexico/Caribbean region during the periods of the pristine Meso-American Civilizations.
- The central role of lakes in the development of many early civilizations—Olmec/Toltec/Aztec.
- The Bugandan state in Africa.
- The role of rivers in others—the Indus-system of Harappa, the Red-River in North Vietnam, the Yang-Tse in early China.
- Early maritime-riverine-delta "Mandala" civilizations of proto-historical Southeast Asia.
- The Niger in the early development of African Nok Civilization.
- The Nile in the case of Egyptian Civilization.
- The Northeast Coast complex in native North America extending from Alaska down to the coasts of California.
- The development of riverine cultural complexes throughout Amazon and Orinoco riverine systems.
- The Missourian-Mississippian Mound-building complex, the transmigration, trade network.
- And high Island/low Island tributary complexes of Melanesia, Micronesia and Polynesia.
- And even the circum-Polar (Arctic) adaptations of the Inuit peoples.

Though many early civilizations may not necessarily have developed in such a way, Incan civilization, Aztec Civilization,

<u>Southeast Asian Sources</u>

Southwest Amer-Indian civilization, and the very early role of a single ocean in the regional and interregional development of Southeast Asian civilization, cannot be ignored.

The Southeast Asian Maritime Context

A few scholars have emphasized the importance of a "maritime" perspective in Southeast Asia—the early work on trade in Southeast Asia by <u>van Leur</u> (1955) deserves recognition for its originality, and the work of O. W. Wolters (1982: pg. 40; pages 60 and 178 in this text) and his "single ocean" perspective deserves special attention.

Donald Emmerson, in his appeal for a Maritime perspective on Southeast Asian civilization, notes the paucity of research in this regard—"The disappearance of the seascapes in the way Westerners view Southeast Asia is more than a curiosity of maps. It is symptomatic of the general invisibility and underestimation of the regions maritime side."[12]

This maritime perspective of Southeast Asia as a region has been underrepresented in archaeological research, despite evidence that points to the early domestication of rice, agriculture and civilization along coastal perimeters. It is proposed that interregional integration and development via human mastery of surrounding waterways has been a primary impetus behind civilization in this region for a period much deeper in time and to

---

[12] Donald K. Emmerson "The Case for a Maritime Perspective on Southeast Asia" <u>The Journal of Southeast Asian Studies</u> March, 1980 pp. 139-145. "There are, it seems to me, two subjective impediments to seeing the centripetal role of the seas in Southeast Asia…The first and most obvious is to think that bodies of water, especially waters as shallow and near land as Southeast Asia's, are obstacles rather than invitations...Less generally overcome is a second hindrance: to regard the sea in Southeast Asia as merely a medium for traffic rather than a resource in its own right...these two uses of the sea—as medium and resource—will not always be compatible." (ibid. pg. 142)

a much greater extent than most pre-historians would generally acknowledge—perhaps as early as 30,000 years BP.

Southeast Asia has long been referred to as a crossroads of interregional trade, migration and acculturative contact between many civilizations of East Asia, the Pacific, South and West Asia, and Europe. Without doubt this region has figured time immemorial in the traffic of certain region specific tropical goods—nutmeg, rhinoceros horn, birds nests, kingfishers, gold, exotic woods, gums and resins.[13]

Maritime trade and traffic was regulated by the seasonality of the Monsoon climates. Such trade included exotic tropical woods, resins, gold, precious stones, spices, silk yarns and batik fabrics, Chinese tea and clay and porcelain vessels, glass objects, rugs and tapestries from West and Central Asia, as well as objects of art and religious objects.

These patterns of trade and traffic were subject to shipwreck, piracy, transient markets, relative lack of political security or stability, and "the availability of convenient entrepôt centers…throughout the trading arc extending from India to China. It can nevertheless be assumed that the character of the trade itself, intended as it was for princely and patrician consumption, changed but little from century to century."[14]

---

[13] "Trade was a perennial influence in the historical development of Southeast Asia. In association with agricultural and human resources, commercial currents influenced the rise and fall of political units, institutional changes, and the appropriation of alien religious and art forms." (J. Cady, The Development of Southeast Asian Civilization, 1964:21.)

[14] "The transient peddlers, the temporary beach and market bazaars, the more permanent shops and warehouses, the eternal haggling of merchants with each other and with peasant producers, plus the activities of wandering adventurers were the universal and timeless

Southeast Asian Sources

Evidence also points to the suggestion that the patterns of many of its basic exchange networks and interregional contacts may have been as complex in the deeper prehistoric phases as they were in the later proto-historic era. These were relations that have undoubtedly left an indelible mark upon the character of Southeast Asian civilization.

The Analytical Framework

This hypothesis requires an analytical framework within a set of broad, overlapping historical periods. Three phases will be considered: the prehistoric phase from the late Paleolithic and Neolithic, the proto-historic phase, encompassing the rise of early civilizations until the end of the middle ages, and the fully historic phase beginning with the European "Age of Discovery" and the role of Western colonial imperialism in the rise of the capitalist world system.

Several distinct periods will be briefly considered. The first prehistoric period (Phase I & II) is the long presence of early Hominids in the Southeast Asian Archipelago.

The second proto-historic period involves the evidence for an extensive "coastal culture" during the Neolithic throughout Southeast Asia, emerging in the later sub-period with the development of early trade networks and local political integration throughout the region based upon riverine-delta Mandala kingdoms (Phase III & IV).

The third Historic Period (Phase V & VI) includes the trade sojourning patterns of Chinese, Indian, Arabian and European merchants and continuing until today.

---

characteristics of port centers. The commercial impact of neither India nor China became historically significant until the second century A.D." (J. Cady, The Development of Southeast Asian Civilization, 1964:21.)

The beginning of the next phase did not necessarily signal the end of the previous phases, but rather the embedding of processes and patterns one upon the other, such that today in Southeast Asia it is possible to find the presence of living stone age people next door to people who dwell in sky scrapers—easily spanning the full range of historical and cultural diversity.

Generally, the Paleolithic may be divided into several sub-phases.

The earliest one is the prehistoric land-bridge phase, up to 45,000 BP, in which population movements of early hominids must have depended for the most part upon the presence of critical land-bridges that allowed the crossing from Continent to island, or island to island or Continent to Continent.

Such early land bridges may have existed during glacial periods in which there was a significant drop in global sea levels, the Bering Straits in the early peopling of the Americas, the Sunda Shelf in the Paleolithic peopling of the Indonesian archipelago, Melanesia and Australasia.

We may speculate that during this formative early period the advance and retreat of glaciers and the corresponding advance and retreat of coastlines and of altering climactic patterns may have been important circumscriptive elements in the emergence of human culture and the evolutionary development of modern Homo sapiens.

A broad and critical transitional phase from the upper-Paleolithic through the Neolithic is hypothesized (45,000-4,000 BC) during which decisive archaeological evidence for maritime adaptations (fish hooks, harpoon heads, weights, shell-middens, and lacustrine habitations and settlements) begins to emerge in increasing complexity and abundance.

This period must have witnessed the increasing frequency of contact and migration of peoples across water-barriers and along water-edges by means of pre-constructed boat-float devices—that meant the broader extension of habitation along coasts and previously inaccessible insular regions than before permitted. This phase culminated in a late-prehistoric phase that witnessed the rise of the first pristine civilizations (4,000-1,000 BCE).

In all areas, the proto-historic phases might be referred to as the "classic period" of human maritime migration and expansion— the age of Homer during which even European annals of history and Asian history remained for the most part local, homebound "intra-regional" histories with but few exceptions.

Admiral Grand Eunuch *Cheng Ho* was sent out to pacify and map the distant regions off the shores of China in the mid-15th Century, during the period that the Portuguese were rounding the cape and several decades before Christopher Columbus. But the exceptions were significant—Herodotus, Tacitus, and Marco Polo were early examples of the European Explorer who presaged the later Age of Discovery by several centuries.

This phase witnessed the growing civilizational linkages throughout the world such that few if any significant barriers of communication or transportation existed except perhaps the huge oceans separating the New World from the Old world, such that no major region of the earth was without significant, complex human civilization.

Few areas were during this phase absolutely isolated from outside, ultimately global, or interregional civilizational influences. Practically everywhere on earth a sophisticated riverine-maritime cultural ecological complex of adaptation had taken root.

This phase witnessed the peopling of the Pacific, over the limits of the Western Arctic and the western coastline of the Americas, the migration of Siberian peoples down the coast of the Northwestern and Western North America, the discovery of the

New World by the Vikings, and the rise of pristine civilizations upon almost every continent of the world.

The historic phase is better known and well documented, and witnessed the global incorporation of almost all the earth's people into the world system. The proto-historic and historical phases did not begin everywhere at the same time.

What was significantly historical at fairly early periods (1,500-500 BC) in a few regions, like East Asia, Egypt, Mesopotamia, and the Mediterranean, showing patterns of dense, precocious civilizational activity, remained largely prehistoric or proto-historic regions in most of the rest of the world. History proper began two thousand years earlier in Europe than it did in the New World, and even a thousand years earlier in the Orient.

It is this broad unevenness of the record of historical development across many regions of the world that the phase between the end of the Neolithic and the beginning of the "Age of Discovery" is to be construed as proto-historical whatever the region, and that the fully historical phase begins with European maritime exploration and colonization of the nonwestern regions of the world and rise of Great Pristine Civilizations in South and East Asia

Phase I—Early Prehistoric

At the point of maximal drop in sea levels, there existed no land bridge between Australia and New Guinea and the Island mass then referred to as *Wallacea*. It is therefore most likely that between 50-30,000 BCE, people ancestral to the Papuan speakers or to the Australian aborigines had crossed the narrow straits separating *Sahul* from the mainland by means of some kind of water-borne craft—perhaps primitive "boat-float" devices powered by wind or paddle.

Southeast Asian Sources

The only viable alternative explanation to this would have been that people en mass swam across these straits, though this seems less likely because not every individual would have had the same swimming skills. In any case, the ability to swim across these straits must have meant a previous existence alongside of water and extensive contact and swimming experience in the water.

Forging the 65 km. wide straits on a rough raft or crude boat is the most plausible explanation. Whether this was a well-executed boat design or not, it must have been built well enough to transport a viable community, and probably to have made more than one crossing.

If this was the case, then there is no reason not to presume that these people and some of their coastal descendants were using water craft ever since, and that subsequent to this time but still very remote, extensive travel and settlement along coastal and riverine reaches had already occurred.

Though it was unlikely that these early craft would have been seaworthy enough to carry people across wide and uncertain expanses of water, they probably did allow short excursionary movements along coasts and up and down streams under suitable conditions.

Extant research done on early Southeast Asian boats includes an article by Pierre-Yves Manguin focusing upon the trading craft of the protohistoric period, from which it surmises the Chinese may have inherited certain features in the later designs of its ocean-going junks. (Pierre-Yves Manguin "The Southeast Asian Ship: An Historical Approach" Journal of Southeast Asian Studies. Sept., 1980.) He summarizes the early design of these craft:

1. Their large capacity, carrying upwards of 1,000 people and 250-1,000 tons.

2. Their lack of iron in joinery—either pegs or external bindings.

3. A hull consisting of several layers of planks.

4. The use of quarter rudders for navigation.

5. Rigging with multiple masts and sails.

6. A lack of out rigging. (Pg. 275-6)

I would add to this the possibility of certain unique construction techniques, such as the use of dripping hot-oil and continuous pressure to bend the central hull keel beam at about 3/4-2/3 its length into the appropriate shape described to me by a Vietnamese fisherman.

A very plausible candidate for building material would be bamboo, a vegetable item of culture that was surely already widely used in a number of ways. It is also probable that if they relied on water-bearing craft to transport them in any one direction, they had to have a means of propelling and steering the craft. In shallow waters poles are commonly used. The only other alternatives are by paddling or by wind.

Possible early boat designs may have been by wood, bark, hide, clay, rattan or reeds, bamboo. They may have been rather like floats or rafts, or more streamlined. Streamlining yields various prototypical features of boats—maximum length to width, relative flatness to depth of keel in the water, of composite materials or of a single piece, high bow and stern or relative flat profile in the water, single person size or large enough to carry several or many people.

People of the early prehistoric were probably playing around with such craft for a long time before a streamlined and prototypical hull design became fully developed, and before a means of locomotion became a standard part of its design.

The earliest evidence of boats is hieroglyphic designs of boats at least 6,000 BC. By this time, boat building must have become a stable and common trait of many different cultures throughout the world. Locomotion would have entailed such streamlining, and would have been square sails made of *Bata* material, basketry, skins, and/or rough-cut paddles or oars.

At any rate, basic boats and boat-sized trade goods must have quickly become one of the earliest and most widespread characteristics of early prehistoric civilization—perhaps only next to fire in its order of importance. Not only was it a thing that rapidly diffused, but also it was a primary vehicle for the diffusion of culture.

How streamlined these boats had become by the time of the recession of the coastline remains impossible to determine, but undoubtedly they would by then have acquired their prototypical hull-like shape, rather than being a raft-like platform, and they would have gained some kind of rudder, keel and sail as a means of stabilizing them in the open seas.

By the time the Islands of Indonesia became isolated, humans probably had acquired the capacity for traversing long distances between the islands, and probably did so with great regularity (Maximum rise in sea-level is given as 4,000 BP.)

Before this time also, we can speak of the likely integration along the coasts and river accessible interiors via the reliance upon rafts and canoes. Rafts of bamboo can easily be floated down stream, but it would have required a more streamlined design and paddles or poles to maneuver a vessel upstream. And if a canoe with paddles had been developed at some early point for traveling up streams, these vessels would have also been carried down stream and out into the open seas.

The early development of dependable and seaworthy boats would have meant several important things. First, areas separated by a relatively short distance as the crow flies but by an unfordable body of water, would have been subject to increasing contact, and integration.

In many cases traveling a few of miles across a body of water would have been much faster and perhaps less hazardous than traveling along the coast or by an inland route.

Secondly, extensive areas of coastline, or of inland regions along river routes and tributaries, that would otherwise have been out of reach and effectively cut off, would have become brought within a widening zone of contact and integration.

Third, protein rich and dependable resources of the sea that would have otherwise been inaccessible would also have been brought within a zone of increasing exploitation. An important, protein rich, resource base would have been added to the ecological adaptation of not only those people living along the coasts and river-banks, but those peoples inland within a zone of contact and trade.

Fourth, the sea afforded new routes of immigration and movements of people that might otherwise have been blocked by either geographical or social obstacles.

Phase II—Late Prehistoric (12,000-1,000 BC)

How extensive or well developed this form of traffic was by 8,000 BC, at the dawn of the agricultural revolution, we may never know. We can imagine small pockets of such development in protected or bay areas that featured shallow harbors, calm waters with little wave action, few strong currents, and short stretches of shoreline settlement featuring the same or very similar maritime or riverine ecological orientations. We can

<u>Southeast Asian Sources</u>

imagine a much more infrequent and irregular movement of boats along most shorelines.

Archaeological evidence of the "*Quynh-Van*" cultural sequence consists of coastal shell-middens. First discovered in 1963 north of *Vinh* in the *Nghe-An* province, it was the first and earliest evidence of lowland occupation contemporaneous with the *Bac-Sonian* sequence, marks a cultural sequence distinct and separate from that which gave rise to the *Phung-Nguyen* sequence.

Thirty-one flexed inhumation burials from *Quynh Van* have been found, with an absence of polished stone implements, and radiocarbon dated to the mid-fourth millennium BC.

Where these "Proto-Austronesian" peoples originally came from is not well established, though linguistic evidence points to South China.

Whatever their direction of movement or rebounding, there is evidence of coastal shell-middens of early Neolithic occupations along the coasts of central Vietnam. The people of *Quynh-Van* ate seafood as well as vegetables and used seashells as cutting and shaping tools was well as stone implements.

The most distinguishing feature of this culture are the shell mounds (or "heaps," also called kitchen middens) that yielded not only the discarded shells of edible mollusks, but also fragments of stone and pottery, animal and fish bones, charcoal and ash. Some of the pottery showed crude basketry impression. Beneath the shell mounds were found several human burial sites. (Whitfield, 1973, pg. 244-5)

Higham (1988) notes the long tradition of coastal archaeology in Vietnam—there are four groupings of such sites—known as *Bau Tro, Hoa Loc, Ha Long* and *Cai Beo* "cultures." The earliest sequence at *Cai Beo* on the island of *Cat Bo*, 40 km. from the shore of the Gulf of *Bac Bo* is a stone tool assemblage with strong "*Hoabinhian* affinities," as well as pottery with basketry impressions.

Above this is found the shouldered axe of the *Hoabinhian* variety with cord-marked and incised pottery, dated to about 4545 BC. The final assemblage includes shouldered, polished stone axes and adzes parallel in type to the *Ha Long* culture. Burials were in a flexed position. The association of axes, adzes and hoes suggests an agricultural orientation.

Higham predicts that trends towards the establishment of food production may be found among the growing number of sedentary coastal groups who may have initiated settlement of the Middle Country—"the name given to the lowlands immediately above the confluence of the Red and Black rivers."

These sites are ascribed to the *Phung Nguyen* culture. "The obstacle to testing this possibility is the rarity of well-provenanced biological remains and the consideration of inter-site relations through the exchange of goods...a model for a similar situation is available for the *Chao Phraya* valley" (Higham. Pg. 45.)

These sites are very similar to sites further north in China such as "*Ch'eng-Tzu-Yai*" which suggests the possibility of a "fishing-shellfish gathering culture" existing along the coastal regions and primarily dependent upon fishing for subsistence. Shellfish and harpoon heads suggest at least partial dependence upon the products of the rivers and seas.

Such a fishing-shellfish gathering culture might possess also the polished stone tools of Southeast Asia and the cord and mat-marked pottery of northern Asia. Its conversion to agriculture would lead to movements inland, particularly along the rivers, where fishing would still be a source of supplementary diet.

<u>Southeast Asian Sources</u>

The distribution of cord-marked and mat-marked wares from Siberia to Southeast Asia and Japan indicates a coast route and accordingly material traits for a fishing economy might perhaps be added. (Fairservice, 1959: pg. 97.)

Fairservice notes in his "Stage 4B (3,500-2,000 BC) the development of a coastal-riverine culture that depended upon fishing and its economy. "It probably diffused from Southeast Asia and is best represented by a variety of polished and ground stone artifacts, particularly the Celt. Rice cultivation, rude handmade pottery, basketry and net making, and possibly pole houses along with such traits as tattooing and canoe building." (Fairservice, 1959: pg. 139.)

These early shell-middens are associated with one of the earliest forms of "cultural sedentarism." "As such, it is felt legitimate to consider their culture within the general framework of complex sedentary and increasingly domesticated hunter-gatherers." (Higham, pg. 84.)

Certainly by 3,000 BC, and possibly much earlier if we are to believe the evidence of coastal settlement sites, extensive waterway networks and maritime civilizations had already been developed in many regions of the world.

We can suggest the existence of fairly extensive and effective shoreline networks of waterborne traffic and trade that formed the basis for regional or interregional integration that was one of the first precursors to the rise of the pristine states.

Between 4,000 and 2,000 BC, Austronesian speaking peoples; must have begun their "fanning out" upon the seas of Southeast Asia that culminated in their maritime feats of navigational prowess in Polynesia. The point of origin of these peoples is not known.

Though linguistic concentration suggests somewhere in the Northeastern Melanesia, it remains strongly plausible that their earlier point of origin may originally have been northeastern Southeast Asia and Southern China. By this time, Chinese civilization had just emerged out of its mythological mists.

Undoubtedly a coastal fishing/trade network had become well developed stretching from Japan to Southeast Asia. From somewhere along this expanse, Austronesian-speaking peoples settled Formosa, the Philippines, Micronesia, Polynesia, the coastal regions of New Guinea, Indonesia, and Malaysia, and even reached across the Indian Ocean to Madagascar.

Excavations by Higham and Bannanurag (1991) at *Khok Phanom Di* (2,000-1,500 BC) in the Gulf of Thailand reveal irrefutable evidence of a well developed, pre-bronze age coastal dwelling culture whose primary diet was from the muddy banks of the sea. Such a region would have been pristine for the cultivation of wet rice, the development of which may have been stimulated by the gradually changing coastline.

"It is self-evident that the origins of rice cultivation are of critical importance to an understanding of the processes involved in the massive expansion of human settlement now documented for the period 3,000-1,000 BC." At least two models for the origin of rice cultivation are feasible. One resembles that formulated for the Near East by Louis Binford and the other by Kent Flannery.

It has the following principal features: coastal settlement in the few rich coastal/estuarine enclaves was sedentary. The occupants used pottery vessels, maintained cemeteries and exchanged goods with inland communities. Their economic base was the exploitation of marine resources.

Sedentarism fostered population expansion, and settlements fissioned at critical population thresholds (a figure of 300-400 people is a common ceiling for autochthonous communities).

Southeast Asian Sources

When all suitable coastal terrain was taken up, new settlements
were founded in the more marginal zone behind the seashore. It
was in such areas that rice manipulation from a shy seeding
perennial to an annual variety was undertaken, a process which
made possible the expansion of the human settlement which has
been archaeologically documented.

An alternative model seeks stress in the actual coastal/estuarine
sites, particularly as fluctuating sea levels impaired predictable
food resources. This stress made the manipulation of rice a highly
adaptive strategy, particularly as the sea level fell and coastal
resources became increasingly remote.[15]

We should not need to hook the rise of a maritime complex in
Southeast and East Asia to the domestication of rice. It is clearly
evident that the Polynesians may not have originally had rice as a
staple carbohydrate, but relied instead upon what has been
referred to as the "Yam-Taro-Sago" complex. The planting of
root cultigens may have preceded the domestication of cereal
grains.

Surely such a complex had been well established throughout the
Pacific and, as is evident in the highlands of New Guinea,
permitted large, but unstable population densities. "These crops
do not in themselves provide a balanced diet for they provide
little protein; if, however, the thesis that this early agriculture was
developed from a fishing culture is correct, these protein needs
would have been supplied by fish and shell fish." (Keith
Buchanan 1963? [1967]: pg. 63.)

Associated with this complex are also the domesticated dog,
chicken, ducks and geese and pig, all of which are rather small

---

[15] C. F. W. Higham and R. Bannanurag, The Excavation of Khok
Phanom Di: A Prehistoric Site in Central Thailand Vol. 1 London: The
Society of Antiquaries of London 1990: pg. 10-11.

animals (boat-worthy) of the household or farmyard that are known to have had an early presence in Southeast Asia.[16]

Carl Sauer has suggested the "cradle area" of agriculture lay in the Bay of Bengal area of Southeast Asia, "comprising Burma, the adjoining areas of Siam and Indochina, and parts of the coast plain of eastern India."

This region "meets the requirements of high physical and organic diversity, of mild climates with...abundant rainy and dry periods, of many waters inviting to fishing, of location at the hub of the Old World for communication by water or by land. No other area is equally well suited or equally well furnished for the rise of a fishing farming culture." (Sauer, 1952: pg. 24.)[17]

The picture that emerges from this is the previous widespread presence of the "yam-taro-sago" complex throughout Southeast Asia and the Pacific. It is one in which maritime trade networks and maritime resources were an important platform for regional integration.

Then came the gradual introduction of a new rice-cultivating culture, bringing with it a more stable sedentary settlement pattern, the need for plough-draft animals, larger local population densities, a strain on local protein resources, thus the need to extend the range of fishing/trading networks, and the eventual rise of centralized states to control these networks based upon hierarchical exploitation of the rice-cultivating peasant.

---

[16] Carl Sauer Agricultural Origins and Dispersals: The Domestication of Animals and Foodstuffs 1952: pg. 24-34.

[17] "Farming and fishing were initially closely associated, and it is here that we can find the beginnings of the domestication of animals, the development of planting techniques and for the improvement of plants for vegetative reproduction." (Sauer, 1952: pg. 24.)

<u>Southeast Asian Sources</u>

This rice-cultivating complex overlaid, and to some extent partially supplanted the previous yam-taro-sago complex, but nowhere totally replacing it.[18]

Phase III—Early Protohistoric Period (1,500-1 BC)

Though the ecology of rice is old, we can distinguish, as J. E. Spencer does, four "hierarchies of mixed cultivation."[19]

This development may have been preceded by the rise of a cumulative regional population density and distribution over lowland-coastal areas of Southeast Asia that made the ease of migration to a new uninhabited area a less likely prospect. Wet-

---

[18] "At the earliest stage of settled agriculture in the region, then, man was dependent on the yam-taro-sago complex of plants with domesticated animals of local origin and fishing to provide his protein needs. The subsequent agricultural history of the area centers around the progressive 'rolling-back' of the northwestern frontier of this early crop-complex as a result of the advance of the rice-complex...The general picture that emerges is one of a progressive but uneven retreat of the earlier yam-taro-sago complex in the face of the newer wet-rice complex. The beginning of this retreat dates back far into the early history of the region but because of the ecological problems involved the processes by which the earlier cropping system were replaced were extremely slow." (Keith Buchanan <u>The Southeast Asian World: An Introductory Essay</u> London: G. Bell & Sons, Ltd. 1967: pg.65-6, in reference to J. E. Spencer, <u>Shifting Cultivation in Southeastern China</u> 1966.)

[19] J. E. Spencer, <u>Shifting Cultivation in Southeastern China</u> Berkeley and Los Angeles: The University of California Press 1966: pgs. 136-165. Or as Lucien Hanks does, between broadcasting, harvesting, wild-gathering, and lowland cultivation of rice. (Lucien Hanks, <u>Rice and Man: Agricultural Ecology in Southeast Asia</u> Arlington Heights, Ill.: AHM Publishing Corporation 1972.) We must place the development of lowland wet-rice cultivation in Southeast Asia, along with the development of early bronze-iron metallurgy, in the perspective of the rise of the early "Mandala" kingdoms.

54

rice cultivation; made possible the rise of local population densities and a need for wider, trans-local integration.

The form of migration associated with the "agricultural involution" of wet-rice cultivation was essentially a different, slower, steadier process than earlier inland/highland swidden slash and adaptations or estuary coastal fishing-planting orientations.[20]

This adaptation can be associated with the spread of the Thai, the Vietnamese and the Cambodians, which eventually displaced or absorbed numerous local Mandalas within their arc of influence.[21]

The Red River delta region of North Vietnam was fairly early incorporated into a more fully historical phase with its colonization by the Chinese in 111 BC, but rice cultivation and irrigation had already been well established in the region.[22]

Evidence of Mandalas suggests a basis upon yam-taro-sago complex as well. Nevertheless, this must be seen as broadly a transitional period in the rise and development of early state organization, and is reflected in the transitional character of these Mandalas as well.

What is apparent is that inland riverine civilizations may have developed relatively early along the Red River Delta of North Vietnam, and that peoples from the inland and peoples along the

---

[20] Clifford Geertz Agricultural Involution Berkeley: Univ. of California Press. 1963.

[21] Whether or not early Mandalas depended directly or primarily upon rice-agriculture remain open to question. (C. F. W. Higham "Prehistoric Rice Cultivation in Southeast Asia" in Scientific American April, 1984, and The Archaeology of Mainland Southeast Asia Cambridge: Cambridge University Press 1989.)

[22] Jennifer Holmgren Chinese Colonization of Northern Vietnam, Australia: Australian National University 1980.

sea eventually amalgamated and produced a new Southeast Asian synthesis.

This contact was presumably with early "mandala" communities, tribes, chiefdoms and kingdoms across the seas and along adjacent coasts—evidence of *Dong Song* cultural artifacts is found in South China, Burma, Borneo, Indonesia, Vietnam, and even in New Guinea.[23]

As such early prehistoric Southeast Asian civilizations grew and developed, routes of exchange followed paths of exploration and settlement. Interregional articulation and variation constituted a growing environmental/ecological mosaic, an indigenous framework of reciprocal interdependencies of resource exchange against which later exogenous influence must be configured.

Later traders followed already established local and interregional networks of exchange. Indigenous inland commodities were carried down stream to local coastal foci of exchange.

The existence of such early loci of exchange stimulated the development of mutually beneficial exogenous trade that was probably not the result of external contacts alone. (Ibid: pg. 31.)

---

[23] These early polities were characterized, as later ones, by the theme of the organization and interdependence of diversity of almost every facet of life. "The mosaic of mainland Southeast Asian variability, especially ethnic and economic, is characterized by complex interdependence rather than discreteness..." (Jean Kennedy, "From Stage to Development in Prehistoric Thailand: An Exploration of the Origins of Growth, Exchange and Variability in Southeast Asia, in <u>Economic Exchange and Social Interaction in Southeast Asia</u>, edited by Karl L. Hutterer, 1977: pg. 23.

The most important characteristic of these early
"chiefdom/kingdoms" of trade-centered coastal states was their
relative ephemeral character.[24]

This early form of civilization is considered quite distinct from
what is found in other early instances of the rise of civilization.
"...The determining conditions of the Southeast Asian coastal
systems include not only a river-interrupted coastline but a
relatively unusual, almost neo-colonial, pattern of export trade."
(Bronson, 1977: pg. 51-2.)

Jean Kennedy recognizes a three phase pattern in the
development of these early "river-basin states" that corresponded
to three broad zones of ecological exploitation—uplands,
piedmont and coastal lowlands—with each zone corresponding to
a major shift or innovation in the major mode of production.

The rise of newer subsistence patterns did not replace earlier
modes of production, but the complementariness of these systems
resulted in an overall increase in the diversity and complexity of
the system. The early pioneer phase of the opening of each zone
is characterized by asymmetrical dependence of the pioneer
settlers upon the products of the parent society. Preexisting
relations of reciprocal exchange become extended by this early
pioneering phase—"by virtue of this exchange, the overall
spectrum is broadened."

---

[24] These early littoral chiefdoms or kingdoms formed "a single
hypothetical class of ancient exchange networks, one which involves
the control of a drainage basin opening to the sea by a center located at
or near the mouth of that basin's major river." (B. Bronson, "Exchange
at the Upstream and Downstream Ends: Notes Towards a Functional
Model of the Coastal State in Southeast Asia", in Economic Exchange
and Social Interaction in Southeast Asia, edited by K. Hutterer, 1977:
43.

Southeast Asian Sources

The spectrum becomes not only broadened and diversified, but is marked by a long-term tendency to shift within the framework of the old networks of exchange.[25]

Nevertheless, early prehistoric Southeast Asian civilization may have been marked by comparative isolation of groups with strong local identities, as well as by a gradual pace of communication, exchange and developmental change.[26]

Such features produced a cultural focus upon "men of prowess" accompanied by the mobilization of social networks within and between local settlements, and promoted characteristically regional attitudes of common expectation for achievement in public life as a means of acquiring prestige, as well as continuous public competition for pre-eminence.[27]

---

[25] "A series of successive steps carries with it the articulation of different modes of production by a proliferating network of exchanges...The increase in diversity and differentiation of productive modes is conducive not only to further economic specialization, but also to the development of intra- and inter-group controls and to the rise of central place exchange. In such developments, perhaps, lies the origin of the ethnic mosaic of modern Southeast Asia." (Jean Kennedy, 1977: pgs. 35-6.)

[26] "Cognatic kinship, an indifference towards lineage descent, and a preoccupation with the present that came from the need to identify in one's own generation those with abnormal spiritual qualities are, in my opinion, three widely represented cultural features in many parts of early Southeast Asia..." (O. W. Wolters, <u>History, Culture and Religion in Southeast Asian Perspectives</u> 1982: pgs. 4-9.)

[27] This competition may have led to "adventures into neighboring settlement areas...Finally, and very important in the extension of communications between networks of settlements, leaders in neighboring areas would recognize the higher spiritual status of a man of outstanding prowess and seek to regularize their relations with him by means of alliances that acknowledged the inequalities of the parties." (Wolters, 1982: pgs. 4-9.)

The prehistoric map of regional Southeast Asia is considered to have evolved from a complicated network of many small settlements into a hodge-podge patchwork of many overlapping spheres of power, or Mandalas or spheres of kings whose power, spiritually sanctioned, radiated out in concentric rings of lessening degrees of influence and prestige.

Boundaries existed only in the name of the ruler and the minds of his subjects, and peripheral regions, equidistant between two or more such centers, maintained a kind of ambivalent and chameleon identity between them both, leaning gravitationally to the bigger sphere of power.

Identity in such a context is not defined by geo-political boundaries, or by cultural hegemony, but by the relative distance traveled between such centers—identities and loyalties were shifting, contextually relative, and possibly even contradictory. Within each Mandala, one king claimed universal authority and personal hegemony over other rulers within his sphere who were his allies and vassals. (Ibid, pg. 16-17.)

Such early Mandala kingdoms were inherently unstable, often expanding and contracting in concertina fashion. Warfare and acculturation failed to define a stable structural core—authority was always in open competition—"The mandala perimeters continued to replicate court situations at the center. Centers of spiritual authority and political power shifted endlessly..." (Wolters, 1982: pg. 17.)

Wolters explains cultural diversity and regional variation by a consistent process of 'localizations' of exogenous elements to fit endogenous stylizations of meaning—the adaptation of foreign symbols to local needs and interests.[28]

---

[28] "...Materials tended to be fractured and restated and therefore drained of their original significance...the materials had to be localized in

<u>Southeast Asian Sources</u>

The proto-history of Southeast Asia is marked by a theme of unity provided by a shared, common sense of a 'single ocean' that both facilitated and hindered communication and transportation. The unity of a shared sea provided by the outward looking orientation as well as a corresponding sense of receptiveness, hospitality and tolerance to foreign influence, alien people and their cultures.

The need to maintain long distance trade ties brought with it the need to control piracy. The single ocean was a vast zone of neutral water that stable states sought to protect to maintain the mutual freedom of the seas. The linkages throughout Southeast Asia resembled a 'chain which would join together again even if one link were temporarily broken..." (Wolters, 1982: pg. 39.)

> "The single ocean is a significant fact of Southeast Asian historical geography, and continuous and lively commercial exchanges can be expected to have encouraged cultural communication that left a mark on Southeast Asian History..." (Wolters, 1982: pg. 40.)

In general, a regional model of early Southeast Asian state organization and civilization emerges whose boundaries were primarily the radii of its commercial influence and networks of exchange. Such states were numerous and ephemeral, leaving few traces of their history.

They developed to meet the need of control of conflict— protection of commercial and cultural interests—and for more efficient resource acquisition, management and utilization, and

---

different ways before they could fit into various local complexes of religious, social and political systems and belong to new cultural wholes. Only when this had happened would the fragments make sense in their new ambiences, the same ambiences which allowed the rulers and their subjects to believe that their centers were unique..." (Wolters, 1982: pg. 52.)

the need for "an organized approach" to foreign relations—
distant states demanded new local states.[29]

The prototypical Southeast Asian State was a kind of dual regal-
ritual and mercantile city-state that was capable of several
different directions of development. Such states formed a loose
network of commercial-tributary linkages described as a regional
interstate system that was traditional to the Southeast Asian
setting.

These systems were loose, relatively unstructured, without
internal recognition as a system as such, and became increasingly
economically dependent upon the existence of foreign trade and
foreign agents for this trade—externally, such systems were
recognizable as standing on their own.

The basic type of Southeast Asian state might be labeled the
subsistence, river delta kingdom. In the rough densely vegetated
terrain of much of Southeast Asia, the river systems offered the
best and frequently the only method of reaching inland areas.
Each river valley also offered a somewhat protected enclosure in
which to organize the state—the mountains watershed roughly
forming the boundaries.

Chieftains, once having established control over the mouths and
main trunks of these river systems by force, sustained themselves
and their positions by exacting tolls for goods and persons
traveling the waterways. Such subsistence kingdoms were largely
self-sufficient in food production and were active in international

---

[29] "...Thus interstate politics in traditional Southeast Asia were carried
out to enhance the state's domestic political philosophy, and the
division of the state into village and court components, with broadly
different purposes and constituencies, had an important impact in
foreign policy." (McCloud, Systems and Process in Southeast Asia:
The Evolution of a Region, 1986: pg. 93.)

trade and exchange only to the extent of filling for the population needs that could not be met internally.[30]

Phase IV—Late Protohistoric-Early Historic Period (1 AD-1500 AD)

It is at this point that we can begin to consider the historical period proper of Southeast Asia, and can talk about the various records of the Golden Chersonese, of Roman coins, of Chinese Eunuchs and Brahmanic trader/priests. Prehistory and history overlap in an extended proto-historical period of several millennia of sketchy and incomplete records and fragmentary artifacts. History of the region really does not come into its own properly until the arrival of the Portuguese in the early 16th century.

The Chinese had recorded a history of the region prior to that period, but most of it did not survive the later vicissitudes of Imperial dynastic politics when the Chinese suddenly became, once again, xenophobic to all that lay beyond its borders.

Thus the protohistoric period that lasted from around the Birth of Christ even beyond the Portuguese period until the Dutch arrived to take their place remains patchy and conjectural, indefinite in its time-line except for a few brief, but major, events.

In the main, the process of the regional and interregional integration of Southeast Asia continued with the rise and fall of the maritime oriented Mandala Kingdoms. What is important to

---

[30] "Referring to the natural drainage system of intermountain water systems as self-contained geographic units, Bronson hypothesized that control of a river artery or of one or more major tributaries provided opportunities to develop the 'lord-subordinate' relationships needed to expand kinship ties into political units by providing revenues from controlled commercial and other river traffic. These revenues were the critical economic surplus needed for expansion." (Donald McCloud, 1986: 67-8)

note here is the continuing into historical times, until even today, of patterns of a riverine-maritime orientation that are time immemorial in Southeast Asia.

We can speak, like Joseph Conrad, of the central importance that the rivers have played in the integration of life of Southeast Asia. "Beginning with the small rafts of bamboo or logs of the upriver people in the shallows and the gorges, we find lower down river hollowed out or plank rowboats, then sailboats, motor boats and, finally, river steamers."[31]

Rethinking Culture and Civilization as Historical Process

We are left to reconsider, and perhaps redefine, what we mean by culture and civilization in light of the evidence of the history of Southeast Asian peoples. Culture and civilization stand as "local/Grand" traditions, and suffer the same constraints as this kind of dichotomy.

A static, spatial view of culture has always considered it tradition-bound, well defined by its areal boundaries, primarily endogenous and well-integrated as an historical isolate and social segregate, as primarily conservative in its resistance to change.

Implicit in this view had been a paradoxical notion of change and conservatism and a sense of an ideal, non-relative baseline from which change and cultural evolution could be measured.

Both culture and civilization must be considered as the differential consequences of the same historical processes. In this regard, civilization as a process has always been occurring along

---

[31] "Near the estuaries we meet ocean-going steamers docked at the wharves of the bustling port cities. Technology, agriculture, and socio-legal organization also become increasingly complex as we voyage downstream..." (Colin Tweddel and Linda Kimball, Introduction to the Peoples and Cultures of Asia 1985: pg. 279.)

side the development and divergence of many cultures. Ideas were the currency of historical civilization—no society could keep a secret for very long, and thus no human group has ever long maintained an exclusive monopoly upon knowledge.

We can speak of the transformational, indeed revolutionary consequences of new ideas and their diffusion from multiple points of origin. Humankind, once having achieved fire, the bow, the boat, the wheel, the arch, was not likely to lose it again.

Civilization as process can be construed as basically a trans-cultural process that entailed the transformation of the exogenous cultural contexts in which local cultural developments became constrained and configured.

We may find the *Hoa Binhian* or *Dong Song* civilization widespread, but occupied or possessed by a wide variety of culturally distinct peoples, just as today the world possesses the artifacts and some of the symbolic accouterments of modern industrial civilization, though the cultural diversity remains great.

Once begun, the traffic in ideas and new things was usually, probably irreversible, if only because it was strongly motivated by human factors of interest and unrest. In time, such traffic knew few boundaries that could not be overcome. Civilization has always been rooted in an historical intercultural context.

Civilization can be considered to have existed a source of background noise or interference that was omnipresent for most cultures, no matter how peripheral.

The mere awareness of different peoples on the other side of the mountains, of the plains, of the seas, made likely, and therefore historically inevitable, contact, exchange, and exogenous change towards complex regional integration and interregional interactions.

Whatever any given culture may have been at any period, it always stood in complementary balance with the cumulative sum of what all other distant cultures were also. Not only had it been long occupied by very ancient people and their cultures, but strong evidence also supports the idea that Southeast Asia has been a seat of sui-generis civilization and the point of origin for the peopling of the Pacific.

Evidence also points to the suggestion that the patterning of many of its basic exchange networks and interregional contacts may have been as complex in the deeper prehistoric phases as they remained in the later proto-historic era. These were relations that have undoubtedly left an indelible mark upon the character of Southeast Asian civilization.

This leads to a view of historical processes and patterns of civilization as being not just chaotic but as being also complex. What may have stood as background noise in the form of destructive interference for one cultural grouping may have from the standpoint of other cultural groupings constituted information that served as constructive interference.

We may consider a "micro-system/macro-system" model in the regional integration and development of Southeast Asian civilization, as a dynamic, dialectical tension between locally oriented, tradition-bound cultures and open, regionally defined civilizational complexes.

This brings us to a systemic view of history as information and to a basic hypothesis that the historical structure of the long run will tend to always follow a normal distribution governed by the greatest background probability. If something is possible, no matter how unlikely, it will eventually happen if given a long enough frame of time.

A corollary of this is that the most probable course will tend to always outweigh the least probable, and, though events may be interdependent and conditional in probability, the main pathways of historical developments will tend to follow a rather stable and expectable patterns of change, whatever our local intentions or knowledge.

History as regulated by a principle of unintended consequences is only history from a biased point of view that does not know, and therefore cannot take into full account, the many factors and variables that have entered into its production.

Human civilization has time immemorial been a kind of background chaotic possibility in the context of any cultural grouping. For the longest time, it was probably for most people's minimum, and therefore a negligible source of noise.

But its presence was irreversible, and it would not go away. In the long run, it grew such that in came to incorporate more and more different peoples and traditions within an increasingly complex web of historical conditionality and entailments, from which few if any peoples could really escape.

The rise of human civilization has been the rise of a critical system of interrelated cultural elements—a self-organizing system that has reached and surpassed a critical threshold of systemic stability.

Civilization at any given period and place has been but a single historical moment of stability in the apparent transience of this vast historical river of time.

II: The "Crossroads Hypothesis"
The Historical Complexity and Chaos of Southeast Asian Civilization

Biological, linguistic and archaeological evidence is considered in the reconstruction of the historical evolution of the *"Austric"* peoples. The Austric peoples are held to have been the earliest progenitors of Austronesian speaking peoples of the Pacific, as well as the *Tai-Kadai* and Austro-Asiatic speaking peoples of the Southeast Asian Mainland, who were a culturally related civilizational complex centered in South China and Northeastern Southeast Asia and who fanned out and diverged across the Pacific regions sometime after 10,000 BC.

This reconstruction will be considered from the point of view of a crossroads hypothesis that takes to task some basic biases and fallacies that are intrinsic to our tendency to taxonomically classify and to construct evolutionary trees based upon relative differences within our sample data. An alternative "evolutionary network" is offered as a viable, if non-parsimonious solution to some of the basic problems of taxonomic hierarchy.

The Taxonomic Tendency

It is argued that such biases in our evolutionary reconstructions represent oversimplifications of the actual historical complexity of past events and processes, and are largely the product of our own inherent limits of "depth perception."

There are many problems with the construction of evolutionary trees representing human culture historical development. It is clear that our theory or data will precondition the kind of evolutionary tree we construct because of our taxonomic organization of the data and at least tacit labels, and the kind of tree we build will therefore also reflect to some extent our ideas and biases.

Several criticisms of taxonomic reconstruction of evolutionary trees are pertinent:

First, it has nowhere been proven that there is any necessary or tight linkage between cultural and genetic traits. In fact, more evidence points to the relative independence of language and culture from biological underpinnings. Thus the changes that occur in the patterning of a language or a culture may in no necessary way reflect changes that occur in the genetic composition in a group of people.

Second, unlike speciation in biological evolution, language and cultural change is influenced phenotypically by the diffusion of traits across boundaries. These processes and sources of exogenous change; are not well understood and are extremely variegated and complex, such that few simple one-to-one correspondences or simple cause-effect principles hold.

Furthermore, such exogenous influences have been continuously present in language and cultural change, and cannot be simply accounted for or factored out of our equations for such change.

Third, constant rates of change for language, culture and biology have been presumed but never proven. Rates of change in language and culture are likely to be much more variable, and the patterns of divergence much more complicated, than is usually posited for biological evolution. Because of the lack of constancy of historical change, we cannot calibrate our clocks by a non-relative standard.

Fourth, and finally, lacking a non-relative standard, we have no common ancestral baseline by which we can measure and compare changes in cultures, either through time or across space. The baseline we arbitrarily establish is more likely the reconstruction of our own biases and preconceptions than it is any actually valid representation of the past.

Our scientific preference for clear, exclusive taxonomic classification and for direct causal determination renders problematic and usually biased our interpretation of the past as:

1) A movement from simple to complex.

2) A continuous rate of endogenous divergence.

3) A derivation from a single common ancestor.

4) A de-emphasis of exogenous factors of change.

A consequence of such bias is to seek and see in the record a homogeneous versus an heterogeneous origin—a single, finite, prototypical baseline from which all subsequent change is to be traced.

There is an underestimation of the possible degree of variance and complexity of patterning of the original ancestral population, as we simply do not have a satisfactory measure or knowledge of the full range of variation in the remote past.

Such biases in our evolutionary reconstructions represent oversimplifications of the actual historical complexity of past events and processes, and are largely the product of our own inherent limits of depth perception.

Different techniques of analysis confer different capacities for calculating time depth. In the case of glottochronology and lexicostatistics, the depth of time that can be inferred for change is not completely known, though few scholars would believe that we could see back in linguistic time much deeper than 6,000 BP or at most 10,000 BP.

The depth perception of the genetic record is held to be much greater, and virtually unlimited. Archaeological records seem to be limited only by the paucity and kind of datable material in the deposits.

But the greater the span of time that must be accounted for, the greater the relative paucity of available data and the greater the gap that must be filled—the more inherently uncertain and vague become the outlines of our historical record.

There is a tremendous exponential difference between the amount of change that occurs in one year, ten years, a hundred years, a thousand years, ten thousand years, a hundred thousand years or a million years. With each decrement, we have a corresponding level of the relative improbability such that, whatever our evidence, our knowledge is that much less representative of the time frame it encompasses.

But there also occurs an effect of fusion upon the horizons of our field of view, such that at great distances differences of time of hundreds of thousands of years become equivalent to what in more proximate points may be a matter of hundreds of years. Past that threshold, something that is 1,000,000 years old might just as well be 2,000,000 years old, though the absolute difference is almost twice.

Thus there is also an inherent theoretical limit to our depth perception such that given whatever information is available governing a period; we must accept its fragmentary character and the greater improbability of seeing accurately and clearly into the distant past.

The net consequence of this historical myopia is that it confounds our attempts at taxonomic construction. Lacking a stable basis in knowledge, such trees therefore tend to be unstable.

This inherent instability of our gap-laden taxonomic frameworks have been marked by their great proliferation, their theoretical preconditioning, and their overall ephemeral quality, becoming reconstructed almost with each new piece of evidence.

After all a well ordered framework is the epitome of scientific presentation. One single piece of new material evidence can overturn or upset years of taxonomic reconstruction.

The depth blindness of our reconstructions renders these trees subject to a critical "taxonomic tendency" and deterministic fallacy that precludes either the possibility of alternative complex, multivariate models of change or the possibility of ever capturing the real complexity of the past with any reasonable accuracy.

The taxonomic tendency can be regarded as our proclivity to see things we label in terms of exclusive, non-overlapping categories. The deterministic fallacy follows from this in the tendency to rank order and hierarchically categorize relations. Temporally this translates into a linear progression of time in which things that came before predetermine those things that follow. The net outcome of these pre-dispositions is the spatial diagram of the "Evolutionary Tree" that stands for change in time.

We get a sense of set-piece stability and stasis that is illusory when we consider the real fluidity of time and change. We get Zeno's paradox, and a stratigraphic conflating of temporal depth as a two-dimensional plane surface—a sounding into the well of the past. We get the inevitable convergence of the curve of variation towards a common ancestor.

It is one thing to reconstruct a prototypical ancestral form from several descended forms. Our depth of view allows this much. It becomes more problematic to reconstruct a super-prototype from presumably related prototypes, and even a fourth-order super-super-prototype. The problem is that we can only push our reconstructions back so far before the evidence upon which we base our reconstructions becomes too flimsy.

We can reconstruct part of the prototypical core of a common stock, but not the ancestral form, because it is mostly likely that the languages from which we base our reconstructions did not have a directly ancestral form, but only an indirect ancestral stock.

We can reconstruct only from what we know, not from what we don't know. What we don't know always outweighs the little we do know, such that each time we learn something new, our representation of the past becomes overturned.

There is a tendency each time we do this to augment our uncertainty and decrease our empirical foundation. Each time we achieve a more normal shaped curve of distribution, but each time the degree of variation in the curve becomes narrower and narrower.

The artifact of our effort is that we come up with a strong sense of a shared central tendency, but one that revolves around a narrow axis of only a small subset of invariable forms.

Building evolutionary trees from this perspective will always have the same result of yielding a common, narrowly defined ancestor, losing the sense of original variability and the range of variation. Evolutionarily we know that divergence has been a continuous process.

It is unlikely that two forms branched off from one another at the same time, though branching occurred through time. Many more offshoots were formed than are available now to our senses. The clean tree with the same point of divergence, the same ancestor rather than a related stock, is the deception of our own treelike representations—historically or evolutionarily a highly improbable event.

An evolutionary tree based exclusively upon the principle of irreversible divergence is bound to look symmetrically balanced and uncomplicated in its representation.

In human cultural evolution, development has never been only irreversibly divergent, but possible processes of re-convergence related to borrowing has meant that we can speak of an evolutionary network of entangled shoots leading away and back to one another.

Finally, in our culture historical reconstructions it is probably unnecessary to try to extend our phylogeny past the super-family to some earlier proto-language.

We may say that if Indo-European, Austric and Sino-Tibetan may be remotely related to some ancient ancestor—the original form or rootstock is nonexistent except perhaps as the barest shadow on the surface of the sand.

By any working definition, we can still maintain that these three language phyla are essentially, for all intents and purposes, unrelated—or rather that the hypothetical relationship is irrelevant because its reconstruction cannot be demonstrated. Another way of putting this is that their relationship, or degree of correspondence, is so indirect as to be meaningless.

It is not necessary to belabor the convolutions of the physical relativity of space-time to recognize in such tree construction the gross oversimplification of complexity and simplistic reification of order that is the outcome of reductionism.

And yet, we would be very hard pressed indeed to come up with viable and satisfactory alternatives in the modeling of the complexity of our past. There is perhaps only one principle that we can be sure of—whatever period we are talking about, the past had probably never been as orderly as our present representations of it.

The Crossroads Hypothesis

The attempt to construct an evolutionary model of human cultural biological evolution tends therefore to exclude the problems of historical process. Unlike species, languages, cultures and peoples may mix in productive ways. The borrowing between peoples, languages and cultures has been a constant source of exogenous change upon the historical developments of people.

In an especially complex historical context such as Southeast Asia, that has long served as an interregional crossroads of trade and migration, historical processes may be inherently problematic, especially if we take into account the very plausible hypothesis of repeated re-convergence and subsequent back-borrowing from distantly related languages, cultures and peoples coming back into contact after a considerable period of separation and divergence.

The hypothesis entertained in this paper is that Southeast Asia has been the origin point of a single super family of remotely related languages, cultures and peoples, and the host to the intrusion of a second super family.

The crossing-over and back-crossing between languages, cultures and peoples within this region has resulted in a complex, variegated and virtually unsolvable jigsaw puzzle of what and who are related, and what has been borrowed, lost and returned.

The "Crossroads" hypothesis that Southeast Asian civilization, though possibly sui generis to somewhere in the Northern reaches of the Southeast Asian Mainland, may have actually had multiple points of origin and many different beginnings, is entertained in terms of a comparison of linguistic and biological and archaeological reconstructions—alternative "time-lines" and "trees" may be considered on the basis of different theoretical interpretations.

The crossroads hypothesis is presumably based upon the notion of the continuous existence of a widespread and relatively stable "root stock," or common civilizational "trunk" in Southeast Asia, from which at various periods separate branches diverged and frequently intertwined and re-converged, and toward which other alien influences intruded.

In considering this model, we must separate processes of linguistic and cultural divergence that represent the limbs and branching structures of the tree, from the presumably more basic processes of aging that are affecting the development of the structure of the main trunk (as well as the entire tree) from which all related languages are divergent.

There is little reason to presume that the social landscape which existed before 10,000 BC in Southeast Asia was any less inherently complex in terms of its branching and variegation, and, from an analytical standpoint, any less problematic than what subsequently emerged during the proto-historical and historical phases.

As a crossroads region, Southeast Asia has always been a great mixing pot of different peoples, languages and cultures. The capacity for Southeast Asian civilization to absorb the new and the alien and to maintain a sense of cultural continuity and identity with the old and familiar is nothing less than remarkable.

We can lay the foundation of our crossroads hypothesis in positing a basic core of civilization, of cultural, biological and linguistic traits which are inherently conservative and highly resistant to substantial change over time, and in the excoriation of multiple outer layers which are more peripheral and therefore ephemeral products of historical influences.

We must distinguish between exogenous and endogenous sources of change, such that, by definition, we may claim that exogenous change, among other things, tends toward assimilation, or synchronous substitution and replacement, whereas endogenous change tends toward drift—or diachronic modification and alteration. We may further say that whereas exogenous change tends to be disintegrative and random, endogenous change tends to be more nonrandom and integrative.

Replacement of the core will proceed at a much slower and more constant rate and will remain less complete than replacement of the peripheral layers. The likelihood of survivals of basically unchanged elements from thc very earliest times is highest in the core.

Though both the core and the periphery will be subject to drift, the likelihood remains greatest that remotely related groups will share a few core characteristics which are not the result of diffusion, and that the more closely related in time, the greater the likelihood of shared core characteristics. In other words, people of a common heritage will most likely possess a common core.

Core characteristics may be most visible, and most conservative, among those groups that are the most outside or isolated from the crossroads of historical change and happenstance.

Drift can be referred to as natural historical divergence that is the result of endogenous factors of change and alteration. Though drift results in diachronic replacement, such replacement is always one of homologous derivation through continuous modification rather than of analogous conversion, or the substitution of one trait or complex for another.

Rates of drift will be variable and be partially dependent upon outside influences, such that those groups that are from the exogenous point of view peripheral to the crossroads, possess cores which are also most peripheral and therefore subject to the greatest amount of drift.

As a consequence drift and assimilation are not completely independent processes. The region of their interdependence defines an intermediate zone in which change is definable as amalgamation—the fusion process between the new and the old, the familiar and the foreign.

The very factors that contribute to the great external conservation of forms upon the periphery and the rapid assimilation of forms at the crossroads also tend to contribute to processes of greatest internal drift at the periphery and greatest internal conservation at the crossroads.

A consequence of this may be something of an evolutionary paradox—peripheral groups may always have core characteristics that are more re-constructible, but cross-road nodes or cores may be more likely to retain survivals of characters that do not need to be reconstructed—closer to the original prototypical form.

The greatest variation is not likely to be found in the oldest core, but in the intermediate region in which those core characters merge with the peripheral. These are the non-primary core characters.

Another factor is the saltational nature of the overall process. Short-term stability may belie long-term fluctuation, while long-term stability may be based upon short-term transitional periodicity.

Another way of seeing this is that a group may not always remain at the crossroads or the outlands, and that to some extent; one group's crossroads may be another group's periphery.

Structures of the long run are not always predictable by the patterns of the present, and the current unfolding or stability is not always governed or predetermined by the long-term pattern of change.

Southeast Asian Sources

The problem remains to locate the core of a group. In this case of detection and discovery, several minor hypothesis may be presumed.

First, the most basic core (primary core) is common to all groups and all peoples who are related by common definition, no matter how remote the actual relationship. A corollary of this is that if cores are discovered which seem basically unrelated, this is evidence of a lack of remote relationship and evidence for a multi-lineal evolution of unrelated groups.

Second, interregional and regional distributions of cores may be identified which are unique for one branch of people or another. A corollary of this is that such secondary cores may be the diagnostic features of that branch or sub-grouping, and may locate that group to a common prototypical form.

A third principle is that two or more cores cannot occupy the same space at the same time, such that if there is evidence of one core intruding or taking over another, it must be construed as an event of assimilation, possibly involving the ethnocide or even genocide of the previous group, or an instance of amalgamation.

A corollary of this is that when two cores do come within proximate contact, conflict and chaos is likely to ensue—whether destructive or constructive in its consequences.

A fourth principle is that multiple non-primary cores may be added over time, and the historical pathway of a distinct group's development will be marked by the temporal accretion of such non-primary cores.

A corollary of this is that the history of a distinct local group is embedded in a complex stratigraphy of layering of non-primary cores about some often hidden heart.

We may speak of the superseding of old cores by the emergence of newer cores, as the covering over of the older heartwood by the newer sapwood. Though the developmental history of this process may be quite variable for different groups, the capacity ("growth") and course ("age") of embedding, remains equivalent and the same for all groups.

A corollary of this is that all complexes are at core equally old, though some cores may be more embedded than others, and, regardless of the absolute age, all complexes still have the same capacity for growth.

Another way of putting this is that more primitive forms though relatively older, may have more relative potential whereas more derivative forms, though relatively young, may have less relative potential.

We are still left with the problem of locating the core of all complexes, and the crossroads hypothesis anchors this common core to those forms and functions that are the most basic, prototypical or necessary, and the most shared by correspondence between all groups.

Linguistically, we might locate the basic core as those traits that are most basic of the human body, the elements of the environment, those relative markers or dichotomies, and those relationships that are most socially basic. Basic core characters are likely not to be conceptually abstract or based on anything able to be borrowed. They are unmarked, unelaborated and nonspecific concrete referents well rooted in basic forms of expression, perception and conception.

There is a sense of neoteny (developmental primitivism) about these basic core characters. A child's detailed recognition of the forms of animals, faces, natural designs, insects, and basic man-made objects lends credence to the notion of natural categories, a level of intellectual sophistication preceding the formal acquisition of color terms, of numbers and mathematical manipulations, etc.

Similarly, the child's natural language and its structure also reflect this basicness—a bee as being the basic form, for both a distant bird, a fly, a bee and a spider.

Core characters share a feature that might be referred to as a high rate of correspondence of prototypical form and function. Correspondence derives its value from its associational context with the character complex in which it takes part and in which it is embedded. Correspondences can be said to be something more than mere analogues, but not quite completely homologous structures.

Correspondence might be taken as the measure of proto-typicality or "basicness" of a trait or trait complex—it is that set of characters for which there is the greatest likelihood of common correspondence with other sets of traits, and therefore the greatest likelihood (or ratio) of genetic, non-convergent relationship.

Correspondence can be taken as an indirect measure of the degree of relatedness between two complexes. More directly, it is a measure related to complexes, or to its constituency, more than to its individual components.

It is a measure of the basicness of its constituency structure, a measure of its degree of internal coherence or strength of integration—the linkage between its components is relatively stable and unbroken—as well as being a measure of its equivalence of value or function

Indirectly, correspondence measures the degree to which similar traits in similar complexes perform similar kinds of functions. Correspondence as an indirect measure of relatedness is rooted in the "structural covariance" of its basic factors, even across different forms and sets of data.

Biological Evidence

Bones of early modern Homo sapiens have been found in association with *Bac Sonian* contexts in Northern Vietnam and Malaya (Burling, 1967: pg. 19) But without doubt earlier modern humans ancestral to the Australian Aborigines must have passed through, and perhaps occupied, the regions of Southeast Asia between 50,000 and 30,000 BP, as evidenced by the early remains at *Niah* Cave in Sarawak.[32]

Burling speculates that later mongoloid groups coming from the north pushed back, displaced and partially absorbed the earlier *Negritoid* and "*Australoid*" races that are held to have unique physical features that can be found occasionally among some contemporaneous Southeast Asians.

The Negritoids survive today as the *Semang* of Malaysia and the *Aeta* of the Philippines, and the indigenous peoples of the Andaman Islands off the tip of Burma. "When these characteristics are shuffled among a large population, an occasional individual is likely to turn up who looks rather Negritoid...." (Burling, 1967: pg.19)

Next in this conjectural sequence are the "*Veddoids*" resembling the people of South India and Sri Lanka, who are held to have either descended from or mixed with *Australoid* elements in Southeast Asia.[33]

---

[32] Even earlier evidence of modern hominids have been found since Tom Harrison's report of Niah Cave (estimated 27,000 BP) remains. *Leong Tebo* (IB1) Cave in Kalimantang dates to 31,000 BP.

[33] They were presumed to be represented by the *Senoi* of Malaya "wavy-haired, narrow headed, dark skinned agriculturalists practicing shifting cultivation. And, as in the case of the Negrito type, this type has varying degrees of dilution over much of Southeast Asia..." (Buchanan, 1967: pg. 27)

<u>Southeast Asian Sources</u>

The "*Melanesoids*," ancestral to the Melanesians, are held by some to have come next to Southeast Asia, but if so, then they were only a transitional type. They were succeeded by the Austronesian or "Indonesian" type who spread throughout the Western Pacific as well as venturing into peninsular and insular Southeast Asia. Arriving perhaps earlier than 3,000 BC, perhaps concurrently with the arrival of the more "*Mongoloid*" (*Sinodontic* versus *Sundadontic*) peoples from the north.

There is even held to be an infusion of a "*Nesiod*" group, or "Brown Race" who were "olive-skinned" with wavy hair and narrow noses and originated in Western Europe, through the Mediterranean and the Middle East to northern India.[34]

But the latest group held to have arrived in Southeast Asia were the "*Alpine-Mongoloid*" peoples—broad headed, black straight hair, epicanthic folds, prominent cheekbones. They are held to have moved slowly and steadily southward from the Second Millennium BC, spreading down the river valleys of the Irrawaddy (600 BC), the *Chao Praya*, the Mekong and the Red River, and down the coastlines, "being deflected from Yunan by the solid group of *Nesiot* peoples established there."[35]

Constructions of such racial sequences are dubious at best, and unenlightening at worst—they remain essentially unproven. New genetic sequencing data should provide over time more

---

[34] "The group appears to have diffused into Southeast Asia from the northwest and may have been the bearer of the megalithic culture of *Assam* and *Chota Nagpur*. Today its extent is from Southern China (many of the minority peoples are non-Mongoloid and belong to this group) to the Indonesian Islands...." Buchanan, 1967: pg. 28.
[35] "This southward drift of Mongoloid peoples has continued up to the present time and the migration of Chinese into the area in the last century in response to the demands for plantation and mine labor and the new commercial opportunities, can be regarded as merely the continuation of this thousand-year old overflow towards the tropics." Buchanan, 1967: pg. 29.

empirically and historically accurate sequences based upon haplo-grouping and degree of shared genetic profiles,

The aspect of the genetic and cultural diversity and heterogeneity of Southeast Asia is more informative—we would expect with a deep history of migration and mixing, a broad and pervasive "Southeast Asian base" to have formed characterized by such diversity and heterogeneity, among which exist perhaps isolated pockets of "purer" forms.[36]

It would be expected that the range of variance within and between local and regional populations is much greater than the differences separating regions.

One must legitimately ask, when given the lack of complete objectivity of such racial data and its analytical interpretation, whether the racial sequences inferred about the past in Southeast Asia were not as much the product of our own prejudices about racial progression and superiority rooted in a Great Chain of Being, with the most primitive black Australoids and Negritoids coming first, followed by the brown *Veddoids* and *Nesoids*, and then by the yellow Alpine Mongoloids, and the concomitant advancement of civilization (and finally the Europeans.)

One criticism of this approach is that we do not have at any point in time a good idea of the genuine total genetic variance of human populations. We cannot simply assume that at some arbitrary point, 10,000 or even 30,000 years ago, there was less overall genetic variance than there was at some later point, 3,000 BP or even today. Not being able to assume increasing racial variance with time, or the original lack of variance, means that

---

[36] "The general result of these movements is reflected in the great diversity, racial and cultural, of Southeast Asia's population. Mixing of peoples of the most diverse physical types has been taking place over many, many millennia; so, too, has the inter-weaving of many diverse cultural elements." Buchanan, 1967: 27.

<u>Southeast Asian Sources</u>

we cannot say with any legitimate certainty which "race" came
first, based alone upon extant evidence of "types."

Luigi Cavalli-Sforza has been the most sophisticated proponent
of the consociation of genes and culture in history, and he has
given us a rough map of the Southeast Asian populations based
on relative differences in blood alleles.

His work is more interesting and more empirically valid that the
previous taxonomies shown, and therefore warrants consideration
before building his taxonomic scheme. He has dealt
quantitatively and mathematically both with the problem of
genotypic distribution and change through time, as well as with
the issue of cultural transmission, the Neolithic transition, and the
question of the relationship of language, archaeological, cultural
and genetic characteristics.

First, Cavalli-Sforza has posited a definite correlation between
genetic heritage and cultural heritage, based upon the way that
both have depended upon the same factors of isolation and
migration, themselves the function of history, ecology and
geography. (1986: pg. 14)

The main factor of this correlation, beyond isolation and
migration, are the adaptive radiations of various groups at various
times, and the alleged cultural conservatism "so that people
settling in new areas will retain much of their culture even for
long periods of time." (Ibid.: pg. 14).

In this association he emphasizes the role of "demic diffusion" of
people who displace others rather than of the cultural diffusion of
cultural characters, evidenced by the relatively slow and steady
rate of the spread of the Neolithic revolution in Europe from its
origin area in the Middle East.

Relying upon "principal component" analysis of genetic
composition of various populations, his genetic map of clinal

variation almost exactly corresponds to the map of the spread of the Neolithic. The picture that emerges agrees with the prior existence in the area of expansion genetic variation, the capacity of farmers to increase to high densities, a slow migration rate and the assimilation of local hunter-gathers—either by marriage or acculturation.

Cavalli-Sforza also deals with the geography of the distribution of cultural complexes, and the "fine clustering" that is related to the greater local versus broader areal or local affinities that are probably nonrandom in distribution if only slightly disturbed by random movements of mobility.

Again, assuming the inherent conservatism of cultural complexes, such distributions could be achieved by "demic diffusion."[37]

Cavalli-Sforza correlates demic descent with a certain cultural complex of characters, especially family, kinship and house-building style, which were traits least correlated with environmental adaptations and the complex associated with such adaptation—subsistence strategies, technology and house-building materials.

His correlation in this regard is indirect though, because he first correlates language differentiation, as highly conservative, with

---

[37] "...In the complex history of the settlement of Africa, some groups have expanded much more than others, and inevitably split a number of times in tribes that have occupied different areas, split again, moved again and so on. A highly conserved cultural trait will then spread with the people...Naturally there cannot have occurred only fissions, but also fusions, which will generate greater complexity; but with groups rapidly expanding in relatively unpopulated areas, fissions are likely to have been more numerous than fusions..." (L. Cavalli-Sforza "Diffusion of Cultures and Genes" in On Evolutionary Anthropology: Essays in Honor of Harry Hoijer, 1983. Edited by B. J. Williams 1986: pg. 24.)

genetic differentiation, and then language distribution with the previously mentioned trait complexes.

The factors of whether these correlations are by demic descent or "reciprocal interaction between the traits" (Ibid: pg. 27) is not clear, but such correlations provide evidence of slow rates of evolutionary change, either during movement or fission.

In conclusion, he supports the high correlation between some cultural traits, language, kinship and family, and genetic transmission, because of co-transmission—"that is, people carry both with them. The vagaries of demographic expansions associated with new cultural developments, permitting rapid demographic increase in some groups, can only magnify the geographic variation of genes and culture while retaining their essential associations, i.e. their co-variation." (Ibid: pg. 33)

In another work, Cavalli-Sforza makes the case for the close association between genetic and linguistic transmission, and the relative stability of language change over time.[38]

He creates an evolutionary tree in which 42 groups are related, showing close association with the linguistic and genetic data for time of splitting and sub-grouping.[39]

His reconstruction of Southeast Asian groups contains an original super-cluster that splits into mainland and insular southeast Asian groups, "a fairly tight cluster of six populations...on

---

[38] L. L. Cavalli-Sforza and M. W. Feldman Cultural Transmission and Evolution: A Quantitative Approach; 1981.

[39] He correlates genetic data derived from the study of 120 alleles (Luigi Luca Cavalli-Sforza, Alberto Piazza, Paolo Menozzi, and Joanna Mountain "Reconstruction of Human Evolution: Bringing together Genetic, Archaeological and Linguistic Data" in Proceedings of the National Academy of Sciences, USA. Vol. 85: pgs. 6006-4, August, 1988) linguistic data based upon evidence for "super-families" and Archaeological evidence.

bootstrapping, Filipinos are lost 29% of the time, Malaysians 23%, and Indonesians 7%" (1988, pg. 8004) Pacific Islanders clustered into a loose group of three, and New Guineans and Australians which "remain together more than 50% of the time."

His phylogenetic reconstruction of genetic evolution in Southeast Asia records an early split of Southeast Asians with New Guinea and Australian populations at a genetic distance of about .017 at a time estimate greater than or equal to 40,000 BP.

A subsequent split separated the New Guineans and Australians 25-30,000 BP, and later Mainland Southeast Asians from Pacific peoples between 15,000 and 30,000 BP.

Subsequent divisions of Polynesians and then Micronesians and Melanesians, including later South Chinese, Austro-Thai, Indonesian, Malaysian and Filipino groups, and then finally the Austro-Thai into the Mon-Khmer and Thai groups.

Though the linguistic evidence does not exactly fit this model, it is apparent that the *Austric* superfamily, with a possibly earlier relationship with Indo-Pacific and Australian families, supports the view of the grouping of Austronesian languages with *Austorasiatic* and *Daic* languages. The only misfits are the South Chinese languages (*Miao-Yao*) that are grouped with the Sino-Tibetan but which at least one linguist, Benedict, has associated with Austro-Thai.

Ethno-linguistic Evidence

Unfortunately, there is very little nonrelative, clear-cut stratigraphy in language, and no method as absolute as radiocarbon dating. Linguistics does have a small arsenal of techniques of comparative linguistics, the age-area hypothesis, lexicostatistics and glottochronology, which are of some precise value in determining common genetic relationship and in hypothetical reconstruction of prototypical ancestral languages.

Southeast Asian Sources

Unfortunately, it is the thesis of this paper that such techniques remain relative, cross-linguistically problematic, and of a relatively shallow parallax or depth perception.

In general, they are based on some set of presumptions about a constant rate of replacement of basic cognates, the inherent conservatism of language, and the continuous rate of divergent, endogenous morpho-phonological conditioning of words and structural change in syntax.

The ethno-linguistic map of Southeast Asia is as obscure and confusing as the physical evidence, though on firmer ground than the former. I have come across at least five different phylogenetic trees of the historical relationship and classification of the different languages found in Southeast Asia.

What this represents is the lack of thorough linguistic description and comparison of the languages. Each tree perhaps rises from and gives rise to a different picture of the historical development and sequences of Southeast Asian peoples. The pattern is confused, because it is not known which pattern of movement, in which direction, obtained for each language group.

There are of course, with any classificatory problem based upon the lack of complete evidence, the lumpers and the splitters. Splitters might see as many as eight or more language families.

Robbins Burling divides them into eight families—*Miao-Yao, Tibeto-Burmese, Thai, Vietnamese-Muong, Mon-Khmer, Malayo-Polynesian, Kadai*, and *Andamanese*.

LeBar, Hickey and Musgrave have as many as eleven different language families just for the mainland region, including *Mon-Khmer, Viet-Muong, Semang-Senoi, Cham, Malay, Thai, Kadai*, Chinese, *Tibeto-Burman, Karen, and Miao-Yao*.

Shorto lumps the languages of the mainland into five families: *Indonesian, Mon-Khmer, Tibeto-Burman, Thai,* and *Miao-Yao.*[40]

Buchanan's picture is somewhat different, recognizing three major families—the *Austro-Asiatic,* including the *Mon-Khmer,* the *Malayo-Polynesian,* including Indonesian and Cham, and the Sino-Tibetan, including Vietnamese, Thai and Burmese.

Grouping at the next higher level of the superfamily is also variable. Buchanan's Austro-Asiatic and Malayo-Polynesian speakers were the original inhabitants of the region, followed by the Sino-Tibetan Languages which came to predominate and push the others of the Mainland into the highlands of the Annamite Cordillera except for the Lower Mekong region which remained Mon-Khmer.

According to Shorto, Thai is the most recent, widespread and least differentiated language, whose introduction is a matter of historical record, driving like a wedge down the center of the peninsula, shattering the formerly continuous communication network of localized cognate speech groups, spreading from a point of origin somewhere along the Vietnamese-Chinese border—the area also representative of the greatest linguistic diversity.

Burling notes that the *Kadai* language is found in the same general region, giving credence to the notion that they may be both historically related.

LeBar, Musgrave and Hickey identify four super-families—*Thai-Kadai, Sino-Tibetan,* incorporating Chinese, *Tibeto-Burman,* Karen and *Miao-Yao, Austro-Asiatic,* including *Mon-Khmer,*

---

[40] Missing reference, see Shorto, 2008, this bibliography.

Southeast Asian Sources

Viet-Muoung and *Semang-Senoi*, and *Malayo-Polynesian* including Cham and Malay.[41]

Tibeto-Burman languages are concentrated in the northwestern region of Southeast Asia and are attributed to a late migration into the region. Because they are much more diverse, they are considered to have had a longer history than the Thai language. Malayo-Polynesian, though highly dialectically differentiated in the insular regions of Indonesia, represented by only a few languages in South Vietnam, and shows greatest diversity in Melanesia.

Mon-Khmer is generally grouped as an Austro-Asiatic language and is held to be the oldest in the region, with age-area correlation supporting a central origin of the Mon-Khmer somewhere in the northern highlands of Thailand and Laos. These languages are related to the *Munda* languages of India.

Viet-Muong is widely regarded as a close relative, or cousin of Mon-Khmer, though it has been in an especially ambiguous category, assigned by some to the Thai or even the Tibeto-Burman languages.

At an even higher level, some linguists have related the Austro-Asiatic with Austronesian languages. Robbins Burling suggested the possibility of the remotest relationship of all the languages in one great super-family.[42]

---

[41] Frank M. LeBar, Gerald C. Hickey, and John K. Musgrave <u>Ethnic Groups of Southeast Asia, Vol. I & II</u>. Human Relations Area Files, 1964.

[42] "Such an hypothesis should probably not be dismissed completely, though it seems more likely that the similarities can be explained by mutual borrowing through out the long course of history of these languages.... As a result, languages can come to resemble each other in many ways, even though they go back to different antecedents."

More recently, linguists have come to believe that Austro-Asiatic and Austronesian were the respective continental and maritime descendants of a common *Austroasian* ancestor.

Joseph Greenberg has traced a single ancestor "*Austric*" for Austro-Asiatic, Austronesian, Daic and Miao-Yao, all of which diverged fairly early. Thai diverged more recently from Austronesian.

The Austric Hypothesis was first proposed by Schmidt, and has recently been revitalized by the work of Benedict on Austro-Thai and Headley, and has been more recently picked up by Greenberg and Meritt Ruhlen.[43]

Ruhlen does not trace the structure back to the earlier Austric, but has two main families of language—Austro-Asiatic and Austronesian. Austro-Asiatic comprises four branches—*Munda, Mon-Khmer, Malaccan* and *Nicobarese.* Mon-Khmer, the most widespread and diverse branch, consists of sub-branches— *Palaung-Wa, Monic, Khmuic, Viet-Muong, Katuic, Bahnaric,* and *Pearic.*

Proto-Mon-Khmer, from which all the sub-branches descended, is held to have constituted a unified language during the second Millennium BC.

Austro-Thai is the hypothetical super-family that embraces all of Kam-Tai and Austronesian languages. Next to Indo-European, it is the most widely dispersed language family in the world.

Ruhlen divides Austro-Thai into "*Kam-Tai*" and "Austronesian" some time before 5,000 BC, and traces its origins to south central

---

Robbins Burling <u>Hill Farms and Paddi Fields: Life in Mainland Southeast Asia</u>. 1963: pg. 26.
[43] Merrit Ruhlen, <u>A Guide to the Languages of the World</u>, 1976.

China. Kam-Tai is further subdivided into "*Tai-Kam-Sui*" and *Kadai*.

From *Tai-Kam-Sui* the Tai language families split off from the *Kam-Sui*, the former giving rise to Thai in the Southwest, *Nung* in the Central and *Yay* in the north, and the latter leading down to *Lakkia*. *Kadai* has lead down to *Laqua*.

The Austronesian family is divided into two major branches, the Western or Indonesian, and the Eastern or Oceanic. Austronesian dispersal across the Pacific began sometime after 5,000 BC, with the occupation of Formosa, by which time the *Kam-Thai* languages had already diverged.

Proto-Austronesian speakers found Micronesian and Polynesian Islands unoccupied, occupying the Philippines, and the presence of Melanesian and Indo-Pacific speakers who originally occupied a wide area of the Indonesian Archipelago. Austronesian speakers demically displaced and obliterated the Melanesian peoples.

The greatest area of diversity today of Austronesian languages is bi-focally situated in Western New Guinea into Eastern Indonesia and Eastern New Guinea until neighboring New Britain.

By 3,000 BC the original Austronesians had diverged into several distinct groups. One group constituting the "proto-Oceanic," made its way to the area of east New Guinea-New Britain. The other group went southward to somewhere near the Celebes and became the eastern branch of Austronesian.

It is hypothesized that the age-area hypothesis belies the original homeland of Austronesian peoples because of a backward expansion during which the original north to south expansion was followed by a south to north movement, obliterating traces of the original languages. The present diversity of these languages is held to represent only a portion of the total diversity that originally prevailed.

Evidence for this "double dispersal" hypothesis lies in the presence of Austronesian of great antiquity lying upon the periphery of the central focal area of Western Austronesian. From here, subsequent to 3,000 BC, these languages spread westward through southwest Indonesia and Borneo and northward back to the Philippines, obliterating the previous Austronesian languages.

Formosa today is split into two branches of Austronesian, the ancient *Atayal* descended from the original proto-Austronesian form, and the rest belonging to the second northward expansion. Indonesian subsequently split into Western Indonesian and *"Hesperonesian"* that subsequently split into Eastern Indonesian and Northern Indonesia, comprising the Philippine and Formosan languages.

The eastern branch of Austronesian began to disintegrate in about 2,500 BC into separate language groups that came to disperse across the entire Pacific region. By 1,500 BC, Fiji was occupied by Eastern Oceanic speakers, who several centuries later became the first "Proto-Polynesians" occupying Tonga.

 The settlement pattern of Polynesia is a textbook case of historical linguistic methods. Tongans settled Samoa, then the Samoans inhabited the Marquesas Islands by 300 AD, as well as the Tokelau Islands, the Ellice Islands and other Islands in Micronesia and Melanesia. By 500 AD, Easter Island and Tahiti were settled by the Marquesans. New Zealand was settled from the Cook Islands by 800 AD, and Hawaii from the Marquesas by 1,000 AD.

Archaeological Evidence

Robert Blust, in his paper on Austronesian Culture History, uses the comparative method in the corroboration of archaeological evidence in the reconstruction of the culture history of the proto Austronesian peoples.[44]

Despite a major disconformity between Archaeological and Linguistic evidence relating to iron and a number of other material items, including rice, which has been attributed to the inherent complexity of the regions involved, there are a number of areas in which both lines of evidence point to similar conclusions.

An early paper by Hendrik Kern (1889: pg. 417-432) presented lexical evidence of an original Austronesian speech community inhabiting an environment of "sugarcane, coconut, bamboo, rattan, cucumber, stinging nettle, deriss root, taro, banana, pandanus, yam and such animals of the dark-haired langur were found."[45]

He argued that this homeland must have been insular or littoral, otherwise there would not be so many far-flung cognates relating to the sea, marine life and maritime technology. He attributed to these speakers the domestication of the dog, pig and fowl, and knowledge of rice and iron. "In this way he was able to limit the class of possible homelands to the coastal zone of the South-East Asian mainland.

An alternative view was developed by Murdock who, based on the great concentration of these languages in Eastern New Guinea, believes their presence predates the borrowing of these

---

[44] Robert Blust "Austronesian Culture History: Some Linguistic Inferences and Their Relations to the Archaeological Record." in World Archaeology, Vol. 8, No. 1, 1976: pp. 19-43.
[45] Hendrik Kern, "Linguistic Theories about the Austronesian Homeland" Brill, the Netherlands, 1889.

cultural traits from "peoples of a different language and superior culture" on the South-East Asian mainland.[46]

This hypothesis shows remarkable disregard for the wide sharing of basic cognates related to many of these cultural items that would require assignment to Proto-Austronesian of these items.

Blust (1976) outlines Proto-Austronesian culture history as follows: they occupied settled villages containing houses and public buildings, "an unwalled or low-walled building where people met, public business was transacted and strangers spent the night;" a "boat house;" a "house of retirement for women during menstruation and after childbirth;" a yam shed; and a small shrine house on poles with only one side of roof only."

Houses were made of stilts and entered by a ladder. A gabbled roof contained a ridgepole, covered by an inverted log or bamboo rain shield, thatched with sago leaf. A hearth was built on the floor to one corner, with one or more storage shelves for pots, firewood, etc. above it. Inhabitants slept with a wooden headrest or pillow.

They had the pig, dog, fowl and hunted, made pottery, plaited mats and baskets, wove true fabrics on a simple back loom, mended torn materials with needle and thread, tattooed themselves, chewed betel, and drank a kind of intoxicating beverage. Some form of native script may have been invented and used on perishable materials.

Evidence suggests they possessed a well-developed maritime technology, cultivated a variety of root and tree crops, rice and millet that they pounded with a wooden mortar.

----

[46] George P. Murdock "Genetic Classification of the Austronesian Languages: A Key to Oceanic Culture History" in Ethnology 3.2, pp. 117-26.

Bow and sharpened bamboo spikes were used in hunting and warfare, and headhunting is associated with a complex of religious ideas that must certainly have existed as early as 2000 BC, they may have had slavery and some degree of social stratification.

Various tropical skin diseases were prevalent. The resulting mixed picture suggests a somewhat "polymorphous economic base incompatible with the somewhat rigid notion of 'progress' from one exclusive level to the next." (Blust. 1976; pg. 37)

The pig, as evidenced by skeletal and dental remains and by similarity of cognate form, is an example of striking corroboration between linguistic and archaeological evidence.

The disconformities of this picture relate to the apparent cultural loss of iron and rice, supplanted by sago, and the loss and subsequent partial reacquisition of the back loom, as these peoples fanned across the Pacific.

The likelihood of distant groups referring to iron and to a "knife/sword" by the same cognate by chance or borrowing remains small, unless the borrowing was simultaneous from the same apparently widespread source.

The early origins of Austronesian, dating the separation of the *Atayalic* from others between 4,500 to before 6,000 BP, makes it unlikely that the original referent of these words were to "iron," or even the earlier "bronze."

Later separations occurred between the *Batak* and *Iban*, (3,500 BP) and the Northern Sarawak languages, (3,000 BP). Other cognates, notably "blacksmithing," "anvil" and "rust" support this picture of a major disconformity.

Similar kinds of contradictions appear with rice ("Rice plant, unhusked rice, husked rice, pound rice and cooked rice"), millet/barley, weaving ("Loom, weave, cloth, weavers "sword", 4000 BP), writing systems ("Write, paper, book, letter, write."), headhunting (4,000 BP) and the blowpipe. All show evidence of an early common origin in the language.

Rice, in the form of *Oryza sativa*, the Asian cultivated species of rice, shows greatest diversity of varieties in a belt "extending from the Assam-Meghalaya region of India to the mountain ranges of Southeast Asia and southwestern China." Early maturing, drought resistant varieties probably emerged between 15,000 and 10,000 BP along the Northern and Southern Slopes of the Himalayas.[47]

While it seems highly unlikely that so many different groups would share by accident or even borrowing the same complexes, it is also highly implausible that a common proto-culture 6,000 BP would share an advanced iron working technology and a writing technology.

Some other kind of explanation must be sought, either an intrinsic bias in lexicostatistic methods, or a complicated history of simultaneous widespread diffusion and subsequent migration, involving possibly "back migration." This is a clear instance in which the parsimony and logic of our methods is contradicted by the complexity of archaeological and historical evidence.

It is in this regard that we can consider the kinds of trees we can build with more substantial archaeological evidence. The evidence from *Niah* Cave can be taken as a type-site for the prehistory of the region. Tom Harrison's 1967 progress report put

---

[47] Annual ancestral forms of O. Sativa emerged along the periphery of wild annual progenitors… Alternating periods of drought and pronounced temperature variation accelerated the development of the annual forms of O. Sativa in northeastern and eastern India, northern Southeast Asia and southern China..." M. S. Swaminathan "Rice" in Scientific American, Jan. 1984.

Southeast Asian Sources

the presence of early Stone Age and the earliest modern Homo sapiens at 40,000 BC, and evidence of occupation until about 30,000 BC.[48]

A second "Mesolithic" period evidenced by an extensive burial complex dates "prior to 4,000 BP and not earlier than 20,000 BC. This cultural complex is characterized by presence of advanced flakes, edge-ground pebble tools at the lower levels. In strata prior to 2,025 BP, are found Neolithic burials in wooden or bamboo coffins, with pottery, quadrangular adze, mats, and nets.

By about 1,200 BC, there is evidence of bronze, elaborate pottery vessels and urn burials. This was soon replaced before 700 AD by iron technology, import ceramics, glass beads, and death ships. Site looting and Malay texts are found at 1400 AD and glass bottles, indicative of Europeans, by 1860 AD.

By this evidence, and associated evidence from other sites, we may speculate that an early occupation of Southeast Asia occurred around 40-30,000 BC of peoples remotely related to the Australoid peoples. A second clear phase of occupation occurred between 20 and 10,000 BC. We might suggest people remotely related to the Negritos.

A third phase of occupation commences within the fifth millennium BC, and continued until the middle of the second millennium. This Neolithic culture is characterized by round axe, pottery, mats and nets, and undoubtedly reached Borneo by sea. From then on continuous contact by sea lead to successive phases of bronze (1200 BC) and iron technology (500 BC-500 AD.)[49]

---

[48] Tom Harrison "Niah Caves: Progress Report to 1967" in The Sarawak Museum Journal. XV, 1967 pp. 95-6.

[49] If we compare this with Higham's chronological table for sites of Mainland Southeast Asia, (Charles Higham The Archaeology of

Early Hunter-Gatherers, for example at Spirit Cave, before 10,000 BC, are associated with a limited range of stone tools, wooden implements for hunting and gathering, fishing and trapping.

Shellfish and gathering wild plants were important to these small band sized groups. Between 5,000 and 1,500 BC there is evidence for extensive coastal settlement at *Khok Phanom Di* that culminated in a complex maritime cultural orientation, rice, exchange, ranking and elaborate mortuary ritual.

There is overlap with settlement sites from General Periods A (3,000 BC) and B (2000-500 BC) along the interior regions of the major streams and valleys (*Ban Chiang, Phung Nguyen, Samrong Seng*) with small settlements and weak ranking, stone implements and shell indicating exchange with coastal communities, and giving way to bronze working sites with mines in the hills, casting in lowlands, ranking in small communities, signified by jewelry and bronze implements and cultivated rice.

There is then General period C beginning from 500 BC and characterized by iron-working, interregional contacts with China and Indian Civilizations, social ranking, agriculture. Bronze drums, body plaques, bowls and drinking vessels, and chiefly burials in boat coffins. From AD 200 until AD 1500, General Period D corresponds to the rise of Mandalas in Northeast Thailand, the Chao Phraya valley, coastal Vietnam, the lower Mekong, with court centralization, Indian inspired religions, statecraft and Sanskrit.

The "Evolutionary Network"

Given these alternative trees, what conclusions can be drawn from the data that would allow a viable reconstruction of the

---

Mainland Southeast Asia: From 10,000 BC to the Fall of Angkor. 1988: pgs. xv-xvi,) we see a very similar agreement.

long-term history of Southeast Asia? From the standpoint of chronology and sequence, the archaeological data is the most dependable.

The problem with it is the lack of knowledge of the total range of variation of the original population. For instance, are the samples we possess representative of the full range of variability present at the time of their deposition, much less of what existed in the time periods between our radiocarbon dates?

On the other hand, there is a certain modicum of complementariness of the linguistic and genetic record with the archaeological record.

Comparative reconstruction of proto-language families, allow us to backtrack and gain some knowledge of the range of linguistic variation during previous periods. The genetic evidence provides us with some sense of the most conservative rates of change and the degree of "absolute" differences separating current groups.

Things to be considered in each record:

Genetically, there is always some degree of biological intermixing of gene pools such that the dominant population will tend to absorb the minority population

Population flow will go in the direction of the downward gradient of the asymmetrical power differential. Great radiation of human complexes occurred because of the adaptive advantage that they conferred to those who possess them.

In the Archaeological record, periods of temporal overlap in cultural horizons are those transitional eras of spatial-historical contact which signal the inauguration of a new set of developments in the integration of the region.

Linguistically, the odds of widely dispersed language families sharing a common set of cognate complexes by accident or simple processes of borrowing are highly unlikely, and thus constitute the analytical basis for the reconstruction of their shared root.

It is also apparent that entire complexes such as iron working, weaving or writing, may be borrowed from a single source at one point in time and subsequently rapidly and widely diffused across the spatial network as part of a common trade language that is far-flung.

These complexes will become subsequently embedded in the distribution of the families to be indistinguishable in the reconstructions from earlier, original complexes. Such introduced complexes may come to occupy the positions of the complexes that they have displaced.

It is also apparent that we must take into account certain important discrepancies and occurrences in each of the different kinds of records.

First, we must consider the possibility of culture loss considered earlier—the dropping out of a rice complex or a writing complex among the Polynesians such that their basic cognates would be retained though no archaeological evidence may be found. Such cognates would represent anachronistic survivals.

Second, is the notion of the backtracking of a culture such that there occurs subsequent re-convergence of previously divergent cultural complexes. This is akin to an evolutionary tree in which the branching may be seen as spatially reversible, if not diachronically reversible.

The consequence is that the long term spatial distributions and patterns may not accurately reflect the complexity of the temporal patterns of diffusion and distribution. Re-convergence is a possibility always to be considered in human cultural evolution, while by definition it is impossible in biological evolution.

In this regard, the question of the differential likelihood for convergence of different trait complexes must be entertained—such that homologous trait complexes which are similar in form and function may enjoy a higher rate and more complete re-convergence (or else replacement), and it is precisely in these trait complexes that we can expect the highest rate and likelihood of re-convergence to occur.

When re-convergence occurs, we are left with either a telescoping of the history of divergence and the consequent contradictions of the side-by-side presence of very old and newer forms.

We end up with a patterning of cultural evolution that resembles more of a directional transition network of interconnecting branches than a branching tree. We might speculate on what kind of surface patterning such a network would yield:

1. A shattered and variegated distribution in which very new and old elements were peripheral and central, widespread and isolated.

2. A pattern in which the greatest distribution of related languages may not be indicative of the greatest age.

3. A pattern in which the nodes with the greatest number of interconnections may be the most derivative, confused and least historically indicative.

4. Boundaries between groups will tend to be fuzzy such that the dominant group will be marked by the absorption of the characteristics of the subordinate group, and the subordinate or peripheral groups will become characterized by borrowing from the central groups.

5. On borrowing or diffusion, versus divergence, character complexes will undergo adaptive modification that is similar in form to endogenous processes of divergence.

The primary characteristic of an evolutionary network that distinguishes it from the more conventional tree is that any single offspring may be the actual descendant of more than one ancestral parent. It can be shown that in the cases of multiple geneses, the dominant and proximate parent will be the most apparent and probably associated.

The second corollary is that though many languages may show direct divergence from a single common ancestor, and only few will be genuine Creoles, all languages will be, probabilistically, at least indirect offspring of such mixed marriages. One theoretical consequence of such networks is that, depending upon our primary inferences, alternative trees may be reconstructed for any given set.

There are two sets of related theoretical issues that we must deal with in regard to such evolutionary networks. The first is the issue of analogy and homology, which will be taken up in the following section, and the issue of historical dependence and independence, which will be taken up in the next chapter.

Analogy and Homology in Historical Reconstruction

The problem of analogy (convergent or parallel affinities not of common origin) and homology (similar affinities of common origin) has received some debate in anthropological theory, and centrally concerns the problem of comparison and control.[50]

---

[50] See, for instance, Richard A. Gould and Patty Jo Watson "A dialogue on the meaning and use of analogy in ethno-archaeological reasoning" (in Journal of Anthropological Archaeology I: 355-381,) and Alison

Southeast Asian Sources

To what extent can analogy inform us about our past, and what is the role of analogy in reconstruction, and then how much is our science predicated upon the inferences of homology?

There are few textbook cases of an evolutionary tree of unmuddled divergence that would make a classic case for homology.

One of the few is the history of Polynesia proper and the strong congruence between archaeological and lexicostatistical data showing clearly the evolutionary pathways of the human settlement of this area.

On the other hand, there are few clear and uncomplicated cases in which the reverse case of analogy in the effect of borrowing upon a single language. One of the few of these that stand out is the history of English and its several successive phases of borrowing from outside languages.

The historical reality of most languages, cultures and peoples, if we go back far enough, is one of a mixed analogical/homological patterning. The further back one traces one's ancestry, the stronger the probability will become of analogical borrowing which created the basis of the rootstock of the complex in question.

The point is that we can rarely clearly and cleanly separate the problem of convergence by borrowing and divergence by endogenous change, and in most cases of complexes of characters, this is usually the case. Even in cases of individual characters, we may have the dual effect of both borrowing and refashioning that accompanies inheritance and reproduction.

Wylie, "The Reaction against Analogy" in Advances in Archaeology: Method and Theory, vol. 8, 1985: pp. 63-111.

We are left with several basic principles that we must contend with in our model building and reconstructions.

The first is that we are always dealing with polythetic sets, asymmetrically stratified samples, fuzzy boundaries and prototypical effects that must always be somehow accounted for in our formulas of relative distances.

Second, space and time may not necessarily be directly translated into one another, such that distances in space may not be equivalent to actual temporal distances, and vice versa, spatial proximity may not be the equivalent of temporal shallowness.

The consequence of this is that we are dealing with a ratio variable of space/time. For every quantum of space we are dealing with, there is a corresponding nonequivalent quantum of time that must be inferred.

Third, we must deal with the conditionality of analogous/homologous relationships such that for any given character, set or complex of characteristics, we have a probabilistic ratio of the relative analogous versus homologous features to contend with.

Fourth, neither analogy nor homology are defined clearly in terms of either identity or difference, but also by a ratio of the degree of similarity/difference. Likewise, we can imagine forms of relationship that are inherently intermediate. Borrowing is a kind of homology that has analogous implications, and convergent evolution is a kind of analogy that has homologous implications.

Though all this seems to run against the grain of simplifying solutions of our science, there may be a measure of sanity in our approach to the inherent chaos and complexity of our history.

Southeast Asian Sources

In modeling our evolutionary networks, we can simulate the consequences and test the effects of various combinations and sets of presumptions and inferences that dictate alternative pathways through the system.

Furthermore, we can minimally anchor such a system to a finite database derived from absolute archaeological data by which we can perform our tests and increase the precision and plausibility and probability of our inferences.

III: The "Autochthony/Heterochthony Hypothesis"
The Promethean Origins of Vietnamese Civilization

A more realistic picture of Southeast Asia may eventually emerge from the synthetic corroboration of data from alternative sources, bringing to focus the questions of the ethno-historical comparability and commensurability of different and alternative data sources.

Human proto-history the world over provides common, widespread evidence of different people periodically converging and diverging, coming together in conflict or constructive competition or cooperation, from which human development on both individual and social levels occurs, often in an accelerated and chaos-producing manner.

We cannot discount mythological claims of autochthony as but evidence of essentialist, primitivist ethnocentrism or chauvinism vis-à-vis other people, and as symbolic religious justification of contemporary social structural systems, but at the same time we must seek multiple lines of different forms of evidence and explanation to better inform us of a possibly more realistic and complex picture of the dynamics of human systems.

We must look to the socio-structural, push-pull dialectical dynamics of these broad human forces of key change in the shaping of human systems upon the earth, especially in inter-regional, crossroads contexts like larger or local Southeast Asia.

Southeast Asia has been a proto-historical laboratory of the social structural dialectics that has informed its regional demographics and its developmental dynamics through time and across many spaces.

Southeast Asian Sources

Two sources of data are considered, archaeological and folkloric or historical, as fitting candidates for the degree of congruence in a hypothesis of the sui-generis origins of Vietnamese civilization in the Red River Valley of North Vietnam.

Systematic Corroboration and the Calculus of "Confidence"

What we know is always probabilistically conditioned by what we do not know. This relationship between the known and the unknown is not one of a simple dichotomous complementariness: "not known" is not synonymous with the unknown. Rather the complementariness between known/unknown can be said to be complex and governed by dynamic relations of conditional equivalence.

This non-dichotomous relationship underlying our information systems permits us the flexibility to search, construct, simulate and test alternative hypothetical frameworks from the standpoint of a variable calculus of confidence.

The known and the unknown are not mutually exclusive subsets of the total range of possible knowledge—rather they are intersecting sets with overlapping complementariness and fuzzy edges. Thus there is a chaotic interaction between knowledge and the unknown, and there is a proto-typicality effect of both the known and the unknown such that some kinds of knowledge are "better known" and less conditioned by the unknown than others.

A lower level of significance for one set of data may lead to higher corroboration with other sets of data, thus a cumulative optimization and reduction of the net differences between data sets, while a higher level of significance may actually decrease the corroboration with other data sets.

If subsequent trials tend to randomly skew the known sample, this will be an indication of conceptual bias, or symbolic reification of the data. In a random sample, the least likely in a normal curve will be as improbable as the most likely.

This is because all knowledge is known and must therefore follow a normal curve of distribution. The failure of such data to do so will reflect a bias in the primary dimensions of relation rather than in the sample itself.

The presumption of the system of calculating confidence in the corroboration of fundamentally incommensurable data sets presented in this paper rests upon several premises.

1) The subset of the known tends to fall into a normal curve of distribution of variation.

2) The subset of the unknown is a complex set composed of the noise of the unknowable that is totally random and follows no normal distribution, and a subset of the knowable "unknown" that will tend to fall into a range of normal distribution—one that tends to be proportionately complementary and skewing of the curve of the known.

The gaps in our record of knowledge, and how we deal with these gaps, have a critical influence upon how we inter-relate our information and construct our hypothesis. There is a biased tendency to deal with such gaps in a "mythological" manner, which will have an affect upon how we conceptually frame and interpret our knowledge.

The larger the gaps the more "random" the unknowable and the more skewed the likely relation between the known and the unknown. These gaps between knowledge points can be evaluated as relative "distances" in hypothetical, multidimensional space, upon which we can construct an operator-goal difference table.

Plausible alternative hypothesis should work to reduce these differences in a complex, multidimensional way—the most probable set of hypothetical inferences being the optimal composite value that minimizes this distance.

This is offered as a viable, systematic substitute to the loose application of Occam's famous razor. The discovery of subsequent data should work to confirm or disconfirm alternative hypothesis by predictably or unpredictably increasing/reducing this net distance.

The greater the "skewing" effect of subsequent data is, then the less plausible the original hypothesis. The smaller the subsample, the higher the limits of confidence must be set and the lower the level of significance obtainable.

Corroboration in the lack of empirical evidence does not have to depend upon the researcher's own biased preconceptions, philosophical premises and rationalizations based upon the application of Occam's razor—human history has rarely taken the most direct course in its development.

When multiple sources of information are available, even if the net cumulative information is insufficient, then a systematic approach based upon the relative distance between cumulative data points for each source will allow a less biased means for the construction and selection of alternative hypothesis.

It is apparent that we must separate the issue of the relative arbitrariness and non-arbitrariness and relativity/absoluteness of data of data from the related issue of discrete/continuous or qualitative/quantitative scales of description.

In general we may say that an arbitrary category is necessarily a relative or non-absolute category, but is not necessarily a qualitative as opposed to quantitative category. In general, quantitative categories may be relatively arbitrary and qualitatively categories may be relatively non-arbitrary.

Though this systematic quality suggests that the complexity of the problem of commensurable quantification of alternative sources of data may even be entered into a computer, the problems of counting, sampling, statistical description, and comparability, remains essentially qualitative problems of "confidence" in the normative decision-making and judgment involved in the assignment of discrete, absolute values to continuous, relative data sources.

At some point in the decision-making process, a trade-off must be made between the empirical accuracy of the data and the rational reduction in the inherent complexity of the problem.

This point may be reached when the etic grid of arbitrary "tesserae" of measurement cross-cut the "natural" or basic boundaries of the aggregation of data in a minimally random manner, and this can be represented by a proportional ratio of fit between the grid and the data set.

This "measure of confidence" can be used to combine and compare alternative sources of data by means of weighted and ranked averages.

The weighting and ranking of these proportional ratios of confidence may be done paradigmatically and alternatively, and sets up a systematic search-solution space for the comparison of different data sets, by means of the multi-dimensional scaling of the different ratios of confidence—the best choice being the solution set with the minimal net distance, or the maximal proximity, between combined data points, and the range of variation being the best boundary of plausibility for alternative solutions.

Abductive historical logic arguing backwards from the effects to the cause makes possible alternative plausible hypothesis that would not be possible in forward deductive logic. The selection of alternative hypothesis in historical reasoning therefore depends critically upon the estimation of likelihood and weighting of probabilities of alternative antecedent events.

Though ultimately a relative procedure, the assignment of values is anchored in the relative availability/paucity of evidence, and in the degree to which alternative, and relatively independent sources reveal consensus or support one hypothesis versus another.

Abductive historical reasoning is a modified version of inductive inference. Such inference is guided by the most likely values available in a given sub-sample, and permits alternative inferences that are defined by only one basic constraint—as long as an inference is not definitely contradicted by counter evidence—the criterion of falsifiability—that all swans are white until one black swan is discovered.

Hence, inductive reasoning is inherently tautological, or internally unfalsifiable. Abductive reasoning is internally false, as it involves a *modus tollens* fallacy of arguing from the consequent. But both modes of reasoning are very useful and indispensable in scientific and empirical research, especially with super-complex problem sets.

When given gaps in the record, and no firm idea of the total population or the relative size of the sub-sample, we tend to fall back upon internal arguments of non-contradiction and parsimony, i.e. Occam's razor, in construction of our hypothesis.

But the chaotic complexity and multi-determination of historical patterns and processes tends to undermine the value of applying Occam's razor and tends to obfuscate the "mythological" filling in the gaps with arbitrary and alien frames of reference/inference.

A systematic substitute for this process of accounting for the "gaps" in the record is outlined as a way of coming to terms with, rather than implicitly denying, the inherent complexity and problematical quality of the phenomena involved.

This method relies upon the development of measures and a calculus of "confidence" that relies upon the relative weighting of alternative sets of data and the cumulative summation of the relative distances of alternative sources of data when plotted in multi-dimensional space.

This method relies upon the observed fact that the curve of distribution of any sub-sample tends toward a normal Gaussian distribution, whatever the overall skewing of the original population, and with the Bayesian conditionality of the relative cultural consensus of multiple data points that is robust with even a relatively small sub-sample of elements.

This entails that the multidimensional correlation of different sets of data in a common space will tend to reflect the strength of interdependent historical relationship, and that the greater the clustering of these points in multidimensional space, the greater the strength of correlation between them.

Furthermore, on the basis of this kind of scaling, it becomes possible to construct a set of alternative reference/inference frames in which the probable direction of determination is based upon the relative inference strength, or confidence value, of arguing in one direction versus any other plausible direction.

It is possible to further systematize this process of inference frame construction and exploration by means of setting up a discrimination and operator-difference table based upon the probabilistic calculation of the total paradigm of alternative possibilities of inference.

The most likely pathways through the resulting N-K network graph can be summarized as an inferential rule, which in turn can be used to build an inference engine for driving a computer based system of knowledge.

The conclusion to be drawn from this combination, if it can be implemented, is that inferential confidence can be probabilistically based upon systemic coherence that is in turn based upon a limited, given set of information, and that relative coherence can be based upon estimations of conditionality and consensus of alternative sets of data.

Such an approach, while complicated and ultimately arbitrary in the determination of its initial values, would permit the systematic exploration, simulation and comparison of alternative hypothetical frameworks that would clarify the process of filling in the gaps in the record and that would thus reduce the likelihood of external subjective bias in the construction of frameworks.

The success of such a system would depend upon the relative weighting of the initial values, a process which itself can be anchored in empirical data and tests, and rendered systematic in a similar fashion, such that a range of alternative weightings can be calculated and compared.

Each set of initial values will generate a search space of alternative solutions, which can be narrowed to the most probable pathways based upon the presumption of a normal distribution. Alternative sets of inputs will thus generate multiple spaces. It is argued that these spaces will them selves be normally distributed, and that this distribution will constitute a basis for the estimation most plausible values.

An extension of this approach would be to "frame" the gaps and to plug in alternative "additional" evidence to generate alternative "scenarios." This would allow the investigation of the "gaps" that would allow us to make predictions, again based upon the presumption of a normal distribution, about which lines of research should be pursued and which kinds of evidence would support what kinds of hypothesis.

The Autochthony/Heterochthony Hypothesis

Archaeological and historic-folkloric sources of evidence are compared for the case of the sui-generis origins of Vietnamese civilization. Evidence suggests patterns for a few, successive, gradual and periodic mass-migrations of groups over the Southeast Asian region along a North-South axial gradient, overlaid by a greater cumulative frequency of many, omnidirectional mini-migrations of smaller groups.

The net consequence of this pattern of human movement in the region presents a picture of surface complexity overlying and obscuring larger regional and structural continuities.

This suggests a relatively deeper history for many Southeast Asian cultures than is apparent when considering its surface character as an historical and interregional crossroads.

We can conclude that Southeast Asian civilization is not so much a hybridization of South, Oceanic and East Asian civilizations, as it consists of its own autochthonous core rooted in its peninsular-insular regional character, periodically shaped by convergent and divergent heterochthonous influences from acculturative and trans-culturational sources.

Furthermore, we may speculate that Southeast Asian civilization may have been at least an early source influence upon the development of South Asian, Oceanic and East Asian civilization as the reverse case.

The notion of autochthony has certain implications of a long-term continuity and embedded quality of identity in a certain region, a notion of precedence that underlies one's sense of attachment, and belonging, rooted to the geography of the region.

It might also imply a form of congruence of different kinds of data in the confidence of relating divergent or different forms to the same origin point in both time and place. It is a presumption that the degree of cultural ecological integration and adaptation will be high, and will tend to be posited in certain basic and recurrent forms that are highly elaborated.

The Autochthony hypothesis has certain other implications of the originality of Southeast Asian civilization—perhaps a place for the domestication of rice, pigs, dogs, chickens, perhaps one of the first centers of the Neolithic revolution; perhaps a place of early origin of boats, and perhaps the location of the invention of bronze, and maybe even iron metallurgy.

We can legitimately refer to the original and seminal achievements of Southeast Asian civilization, an hypothesis that looks beyond the more conventional, Western point of view that regards Southeast Asia as largely a passive recipient of foreign influences, a crossroads of perennial acculturation, and that neglects to consider either the originality or the deep rooted sense of unity which may well characterize many Southeast Asian peoples.

What does it mean to be deeply rooted as a cultural tradition and as a people to a fixed place time immemorial? What does the claim of autochthony, if genuine, imply for our understanding of such peoples and their culture?

An autochthonous civilization implies sui-generis cultural continuity in a local region from a very early point in time. The question of autochthony may very well be an impossible one to answer because of its inherent relativity.

We are forced to ask how old, compared to whom and at what point in time that the sui-generis birth took place. Probably few extant cultures on earth can claim the prehistoric depth and undisturbed cultural continuity and conservatism as the Aborigines of Australia. We must also always ask who came before.

It is clear that before the Polynesians arrived in Hawaii, these islands were probably always uninhabited by humans. And yet the depth of the Polynesian presence on these islands is sufficiently shallow that if we wish to find the origins of the Hawaiians, it would not reach too deeply into humankind's proto-history.

A claim of 1,000 years BP does not have the same magnitude of a claim of 10,000 or 40,000 years, though the sense of local connection may be as deep and as strong in the former as in the latter case.

This is a difficult claim to make in light of the prehistory of movement and settlement of so many peoples. The genetic stability or transitivity of local human populations must always be held in question—replacement of earlier groups by invading peoples may have been total or partial, and acculturative influence always uncertain of chaotic outcomes.

There should always be presumed some minimal degree of miscegenation between populations. But the question is not one of racial identity with the remote past, but rather of cultural continuity—the cultural life-ways, values, customs, folklore and symbology are all connected and interwoven with the region in which it is found.

The people may not be of exactly the same genetic frequencies as the original founders of the tradition, but they will be the legitimate native inheritors of that tradition.

The linguistic roots may remain somewhat anomalous, as the connection with other far-flung languages may be tenuous and the result of extensive borrowing, or evidence of linguistic dispersion and divergence from a point of origin. The argument for an autochthonous civilization stemming from a deeply rooted cultural tradition would in most cases be a difficult, if not impossible one to make.

Many indigenous populations may in fact have a very shallow history in an area, or else may be the original, but only very recent inhabitants. Another important factor that needs to be taken into account in our formulas for autochthony are the vast cultural changes that have also been continuous time immemorial.

Just as the present culture-bearers may little resemble their primitive fore-bearers in many physical characteristics, it cannot be expected that the language or the cultural patterns will actually have many deep connections or unaltered survivals. We could not really say that the culture that exists in the same region today is very much similar to its ancestral varieties.

What core features would characterize the peoples of an autochthonous civilization? Several candidates come to mind.

- A deeply rooted but difficult to pinpoint sense of the people of their connection with a remote past.
- A natural region and sense of place tied to local and regional features.
- A firm but unmarked pride in their cultural heritage.
- A strong and deeply rooted connection to a sense of the homeland.
- An elaborate symbology that is intricately enmeshed with the features of its regional homeland.
- A deep tradition of mythology and folklore which points to local features, and that are lacking in foreign features.

- A mosaic patterning of different cultural adaptations side-by-side that encompasses a broad spectrum of the very old and the very new.

From a linguistic point of view, there is a tendency to view a point of origin as most highly fragmented and dialectally varied. There is a local complexity of patterning that does not exist in surrounding regions, and that is indicative of a long history of local divergence, borrowing, invasion and amalgamation.

Peripheral to these centers may exist pockets of extremely conservative and changeless isolates. A recent historical record of dramatic, possibly violent cultural upheaval is the result of strong acculturative and developmental pressures.

The picture of what an autochthonous peoples look like becomes clearer by contrast with peoples whose culture has been definitely dislocated from its point of origin. Local adaptations may be accompanied by the presence of modified core cultural value that was rooted in another place and time.

There is likely to be a biological, cultural and linguistic boundary separating it from neighboring groups. But in both cases of clearly autochthonous or non-autochthonous groups we should have some sense of a geographical/historical isolate surrounded in a sea of foreign cultures.

Perhaps the only way of firmly establishing autochthony of a people to a region, as the birthplace of an ethno-nation, is by means of the cross-corroboration of multiple lines of evidence all of which may seem to point to the same place, or at least in a similar direction, and which shows some sort of an emergent picture—a chronic collage—of the sequences and periods of emergence and development of the people.

Various lines of evidence must corroborate in a clear and unambiguous way. We can look to evidence from archaeology, physical anthropology, from language, from cultural values and patterns, cultural ecology, symbology, mythology and folklore, and the more these alternative lines of evidence seem to indicate a similar point of origin, the greater the inference strength of an autochthony hypothesis.

Exceptions and discontinuities that appear to occur should not necessarily contraindicate an autochthony hypothesis, but rather should point to the presence of some kind of foreign influence.

We can hypothesize for autochthony that:

1) A people have never been entirely supplanted or displaced from their native birthplace.

2) A people have never distantly emigrated from their point of origin.

3) Subsequent infusions of foreign peoples and cultures never entirely erased or supplanted their local identity or identification.

4) The culture should be characterized by a very conservative core of linguistically, traditionally and culturally embedded values, views, beliefs, and symbolisms, surrounded by a sheath of an extremely flexible hodge-podge of characteristics that were the result of cultural amalgamation and acculturative borrowing.

5) The ecological patterns and knowledge of the local region will be detailed, intricate, and deeply interwoven with unique cultural, religious and linguistic patterns.

6) That the people will have culturally a deeply rooted sense of ethno-national identity that is firmly rooted to the local region, expressed through their folklore, mythology, and aesthetic and religious symbolism.

<u>"Autochthony/Heterochthony Hypothesis"</u>

From the standpoint of a definition of civilization as opposed to cultures, civilization as an inherently transcultural phenomenon, it is perhaps self-contradictory to speak of an autochthonous civilization with the implication of the birth of a pristine high tradition.

We must recognize that an autochthonous civilization may not have had to be an imperialistic one, extending its self in distant directions. An autochthonous civilization may have been a passive recipient of foreign influence, imbibing such influence in a creative fashion to produce its own unique concatenation.

What marks a civilization from a culture is the amount of contact it may have survived from other cultures, as the Brits survived and eventually incorporated the Romans, despite the fact that being a Briton during the Roman Empire meant being little more than a slave-animal. Such contacts provided stimulus for the local development and elaboration of the culture.

We must refer back to Alfred Kroeber's definitions of civilization as being characterized by the relative frequency or presence or absence of unique cultural genius, and of distinctive style-patterns that were the tidewater-marks of cultural development.

To count as "Civilization" in any significant sense, such stylization and realization of the human capacities for culture must have been disproportionate to the average.

In archaeology we inevitably associate such civilization with some degree of focal involvement, artistic elaboration or craft-specialization.

There is also a sense that socially and historically a people with a shared culture achieve a sense of a regional identity as opposed to just a local identity—that local totemism and tribalisms are somehow transcended in the imagination of the people to look to a broader cultural horizon.

<u>Southeast Asian Sources</u>

Such a distant horizon becomes most visible in the worldview of a people only when a sense of foreign presence looms largely upon that horizon.

What are the factors that lead to some civilizations becoming "hot" and other cultural traditions remaining "cold?" The peoples of the New Guinea highlands are possessors of an autochthonous cultural tradition, but they have never apparently achieved the level of cultural development that we would call a "Grand Tradition" of civilization.

We are left to consider a basic historical dialectic in which civilization as the process and consequence of foreign acculturation comes to interplay either neutrally, destructively or constructively with autochthonous processes of local cultural traditions and ethno-cultural identification to produce a unique synthesis of style patterning.

Corroborative Evidence of the Sui Generis Origins of Vietnamese Civilization

The hypothesis of Autochthony is evaluated in reference to the hypothetical sui-generis origins of "*Dai-Viet*" civilization in the Northern Highlands of Southeast Asia and Southern China.

Evidence for the autochthonous origin in South China-North Mainland Southeast Asian highlands will be considered, as possibly a contiguous area of settlement for "*Austric*" speaking peoples; more recent origins in the highlands of North Vietnam and Laos for the Dai-Viet civilization.

Multiple lines of evidence will be reviewed and reconsidered in light of this hypothesis of the autochthonous origins of the Dai-Viet speaking peoples in the northern highlands of the Southeast Asian mainland.

The cultural and linguistic map of peninsular Southeast Asia presents a very complicated and confusing picture that suggests an extended history of cross-cultural contact, migration, diffusion and intermingling in the region. Despite this historical complexity, there exists a surprising degree of corroborative evidence suggesting remarkable cultural continuities of indigenous peoples with the remotest past.

In trying to interpret the ethno-linguistic mosaic of mainland Southeast Asia, we are left with a number of questions. What are the motive factors that would propel one group, such as the Thai, to suddenly begin to spread out and take over the territories of other groups, when previously its residence among many other groups remained apparently dormant and unobtrusive?

We may ask this question not only of the Thai, but of the Burmese, of the Vietnamese, and earlier yet, perhaps of the Malays and Austronesian speaking peoples who spread out across the Pacific Ocean. Why do some groups wax while others seem to be on the wan, and why do others seem to maintain a "steady-state" time immemorial.

Archaeological Evidence

Evidence in the north of Thailand and from Northern Vietnam suggests the presence of early modern humans on the Southeast Asian peninsula (15,000 BP.) Wilhelm Solheim III has written of evidence for an independent Neolithic agricultural revolution in Southeast Asia, possibly as much as more than 5,000 years before present.

In archaeological sites in Northern Thailand and Northern Vietnam, evidence suggests a prehistoric continuity stretching back in time as much as 10,000 BP of a series of cultural sequences anticipating the arrival of the Chinese and the Sinicization of the "pre-Vietnamese."

<u>Southeast Asian Sources</u>

Excavations at Spirit Cave, *Ban Na Di, Non Nok Khe, Oc Eo* and *Khok Phanom Di* and *Angkor Watt* reveal the image of a prehistoric process of a gradual emergence of an indigenous Southeast Asian civilization based upon an early "planting-fishing-dog-pig" complex, and later upon the independent domestication and cultivation of rice and the independent invention of metallurgy.

Wilhem Solheim's model of the cultural sequences based upon the Archaeological evidence suggests and early "Lithic;" period, referring to thc early use of chipped stone implements, and ending around 40,000 BC.

The next period he calls "*Lignic*" (40,000-20,000 BP) and equates with the early "*Hoabinhian*" sequences. "*Hoabinhian*" gets its name from the early artifacts first unearthed in the 1920s in the mountains near the town of *Hoa Binh* in North Vietnam.[51]

These earliest sites between 10,000 and 5,000 BC yield at all the levels from this span a similar pattern of artifacts: simple stone tools "representative of a Southeast Asian hunter's and gatherer's culture."[52]

There are found throughout many of the levels of these earliest sites remains of pepper, butternut, almond, candle nut, betel nut, cucumber, bottle gourd, Chinese water chestnut, "and certain legumes: the pea (*Pisum*), either the bean or the broad bean

---

[51] "It is part of my hypothesis that during this period tools made of wood—particularly those made of bamboo—became more important to peoples of Southeast Asia than tools made of stone...." (Solheim, 1972)
[52] "*Hoabinhian*" culture is perhaps the earliest cultural sequence yet unearthed in Southeast Asia. It was a very stable cultural complex. Many such sites have been found in the northern mountain reaches of Southeast Asia—"almost always in small caves not far from streams..." (Ibid. 1972)

(*Phaseolus* or *Vica*), and possibly also the soybean (Glycine)." Some of these may or may not have been cultivated.[53]

The third period Solheim refers to as the "*Crystallitic*" that ended somewhere around 8000 BC. This is the phase when distinctive local cultures began to "crystallize" in Southeast Asia— containing cultural elements still found locally today.[54]

This cultural sequence is known as the "*Bac Sonian*." It derived its name as well from the region in which its vestiges were first uncovered in the Mountains North of the Red River.

This sequence is characterized by grinding and polishing of stone implements, possibly used in the clearly of forest. These bifacial "*celts*" (axes and adze-heads) are relatively more symmetrical than earlier implements and entirely smooth. They have neatly beveled edges and many have tangs for hafting to a handle.

Other noteworthy objects of this sequence include stone rings, ground by bamboo sections (possibly bracelets), square butted "bark cloth beaters," small shell or stone trinkets, and, last but not least, abundant pottery, characteristically incised, cord-marked or mat-marked designs on the surface.

---

[53] "...I suggest that what is called middle *Hoabinhian* was a culture or cultures whose adherents were experimenting with many different kinds of wild plants for many different reasons. At some point, probably around 13,000 BC, somewhere in the northern reaches of Southeast Asia, such experiments culminated in the domestication of some of these plants and the consequent appearance of horticulture as a new means of food procurement." (Solheim, 1972)

[54] "...I suggest that it was the late *Hoabinhian* culture, as it is represented in these levels, that achieved the transformation from horticulture to generalized plant and animal domestication and that also achieved the invention of pottery. In different parts of the region different plants would have been selected for cultivation. The same was probably true of the animals involved: the pig, the chick, and possibly even the dog..." (Solheim, 1972).

<u>Southeast Asian Sources</u>

Most of these are wide-mouthed dishes or bowls, some with stands. These traits are usually associated with agricultural peoples and have been found throughout Southeast Asia.

There are indications of "rudimentary" agricultural development.[55]

There was a practice involving elaborate burial rituals. Numerous skulls have been found portraying "*Melanesoid-Australoid*" and Indonesian elements. These people settled in caves and grottos of the limestone formations but did not venture near the coast. *Bac-Sonian* culture is considered "transitional" between Mesolithic and Neolithic eras.

The fourth period Solheim calls "Extensionistic" (lasting from approximately 8,000 BC until the beginning of the Christian Era), referring to a major trend of migration out from the mountain slopes onto the neighboring plans and beyond into the river valleys and deltas.[56]

These inhabitants of the Sunda Shelf who retreated to the coast of South China and North Vietnam were possibly the ancestors of

----

[55] "Life in the Red River valley must have been that of a primitive agricultural people whose cereal diet was supplemented by hunting and fishing…The valley was still largely jungle, abounding in beasts such as elephants, rhinoceroses and tigers, and the no less dangerous insects that have survived. The rice fields were temporary, won from the jungle by fire, a practice that still survives among the *Mois* and other mountain people in Vietnam, but the fields already yield two crops a year under the care of a people that was slowly developing the qualities of physical and spiritual endurance characteristic of the peasantry of Asia...." (Joseph Buttinger, <u>The Smaller Dragon: A Political History of Vietnam</u> 1958: pg. 12.)
[56] "The Extensionistic trend...led the mountain peoples not only into the many other hospitable habitats of the mainland but also beyond them; the mountain peoples traveled by overland routes or by water in virtually every direction..." (Solheim, 1972)

126

the Malayo-Polynesian to the sea about 4,000 BC, and who eventually settled the entire Oceania.

During this phase, local cultures that were distinct from the earlier *Bac Sonian* evolved and people began fanning out. Mountain peoples began occupying the adjacent piedmont regions—enough of an environmental difference to lead to a shift in cultural ecological patterns toward a more sedentary settlement pattern. Such a transition is still underway. Even peoples in towns and cities collect wild plants and hunt and trap wild animals.

This cultural sequence is associated with the Phung Nguyen sites in Northeastern Thailand—cultural ecological adaptations on the middle courses of small tributary systems. Rice is found cultivated well before 2,000 BC on both sides of the Annamite Cordillera. Vietnamese Archaeologists have excavated more than fifty settlement sites in the "middle country" upstream of the Red River delta.

Three Thai sites in the middle Mekong River Valley, on the western slopes of the mountains, *Non Nok Tha, Ban Chiang* and *Ban Na Di,* also have been excavated and all these sites demonstrate the early occupation by agriculturalists, but real no evidence of earlier habitations by hunter-gathering peoples.

The earliest of these sites is dated to 2,400 BC, covering only a hectare in area and estimated to have held no more than a hundred occupants. The economic patterns of all these sites were similar—rice grown seasonally in flooded river valleys, cattle, pigs and dogs, augmented by hunting and fishing.[57]

---

[57] "...The pioneer farmers chose slightly elevated ground for their villages, locales with easy access to low, regularly flooded wetlands. The terrain inland from the Red River delta was ideally suited to such settlement." (Higham, 1984)

Southeast Asian Sources

The independent development of bronze metallurgy proceeded during this period.

This was superseded by a more advanced cultural complex referred to as the "*Dong S'on*," characterized by occupation sites that "covered tens of thousands of square meters and accommodated thousands of inhabitants."

These larger settlements consisted of the gradual aggregation of hamlets and clans, suggesting a communalistic social arrangement. There occurred a transition of rapid population increases and fissioning of smaller hamlets from larger settlements, the process demonstrated in historical times during the Vietnamese "march south."[58]

This period witnessed the development from an earlier social network of semi-autonomous settlements into a system based upon "a few large central places" and the rise of chiefly authority.[59]

"Numerous low hills command a stream that is tributary to the region's major waterway. The excavations at one of these middle-country sites, *Phung Nguyen*, show that the settlers combined rice cultivation with animal husbandry and hunting. They were also excellent potters and proficient workers in stone. The site's name has been given to the transitional Neolithic culture of the entire middle country region that extended from about 2500 to 1800 BC Only the most recent layers of a handful of Phung Nguyen sites hold small fragments of metal; they are bronze." (Higham, 1984.)

[58] "In any event, as seems to be the case around the world, the early farmers' settled way of life was followed by a period of population increase, the growth of hamlets into larger villages, and the establishment of additional settlements in a kind of continual fissioning." (Higham, 1984: 143).

[59] "...With one possible exception, the various cultures of the region seem to have shared much of the same kind of economic base and to have enjoyed contact with one another but to have remained politically

The earlier communalism broke up into a more hierarchically stratified society based on relatively small villages of family groups, culminating in the "*Dong Son*" that Vietnamese archaeologists date to the 7th Century BC, to First Century AD.

The graves of the elite are rich in bronze burial goods. "They show that the ruling-class people had by this time established a clear distance between themselves and the people they ruled." Bronze plowshares, Bronze drums, bronze weapons such as the pediform axe, symbolic of royal authority, were found in the graves of these elite.

It appears that the *Dong-S'on* may have been the result of the synthesis of two peoples, one from the highlands and the other a coastal people.[60]

The bronze pediform axe is depicted in an Austronesian artistic tradition, the same form, according to Vietnamese historical tradition, that was wielded by a lineage of kings bearing Austro-Asiatic titles.

Evidence suggests that the Dong Son economy was based upon the development of double cropping of rice for which the Red-River climate is ideally suited. (Higham, 1984: pg. 145.) It is at

---

independent. The exception is the culture of the region of what is now North Vietnam and the adjacent parts of China; during the Second Millennium BC, a centralized authority that was quite independent of the imperialistic dynasties of northern China may have arisen in these areas." (Solheim, 1972).

[60] "...*Dong-S'on* civilization was a cultural synthesis achieved by peoples inhabiting a single geopolitical environment. These peoples came from both the mountains and the sea. The society they shared eventually superseded their mutual differences. We can surmise that the Vietnamese people originated in a concerted human response by diverse peoples to a particular geographical setting, the plains of northern Vietnam." (Keith Taylor, The Birth of Vietnam, 1983)

this point that we have evidence of legend and history that will be considered in the following sections.

Mythological Evidence

The origin myths and historical legends of Vietnam are first considered, though it is likely that legends are available from a number of cultures that may help to corroborate or test the hypothesis of autochthony. Memories of pre-Chinese Vietnamese civilization survived, along with the language, the two Millennia of Chinese domination and acculturation.

Vietnamese tradition begins with the 15th Century compilation of lore "*Linh-nam chich quai.* "They begin with the ruler *Viem of Xich Qui* that was located somewhere south of the Yangtze whose son became *Lac Long Quan"* or "Dragon Lord of the Lac," who retired to "the Palace of the Waters" to leave his kingdom without a leader, and who founded the reign of the *Hung* Kings of the *Van-lang* kingdom, after he came to the *Hong* plain from the sea, teaching civilization, and rice cultivation, and then retiring back to the sea.

When invaders from the north came, the people of the Hong plain called for Lac Long Quan's help, whereupon he kidnapped "Au Co" the intruder's wife (or daughter), and took her to the top of Mount *Tan-vien*. Au Co gave birth to the first of the Hung Kings.

The Vietnamese origin myth has the story of the fairy queen, *Au Co*, of the mountains, and the dragon lord of the sea, *Lac Long Quan*, who married and gave birth to a sac of flesh containing one hundred eggs, which after five or six days hatched one hundred boys, 50 of whom went to reside with the mother in the mountain, and 50 who went to reside with their father in the kingdom of the Sea in the South.

Another legend has it that the dragon, associated with mountains and water, was the procreator of the Vietnamese stock. The dragon is vital symbolism not only of the geo-political integrity of the Vietnamese, but a synthesis of the basic antagonism between the land and the sea.[61]

Yet another legend describes the son of *Au Co* and *Lac Long*, known as the Mountain Spirit that dwelled on Mount *Tan Vien* after returning from the sea. One legend concerning the Tree spirit is held to be virtually identical with a legend from North Borneo.

Another legend about a three-year-old boy, *Ong Giong*, who grew into a giant after eating hoards of rice, ascending to heaven and returning to succor his people, is similar to a legend told in Indonesian Lore.

Battle happened between the lord of the mountain and the lord of the sea were once friends but had a falling out over a *Hung* princess over which the lord of the Mountain finally prevails and the Water Spirit unsuccessfully attacks the Lord of Mount *Tan Vien*.

Another legend of "*Nhat Da Trach*" or "One Night Marsh," comes from the southern part of the Hong River plain, a low swampy area near the sea.

A Hung princess named *Tien Dung* was exploring the deltaic plains when she met a naked young man named *Chu Dong Tu*. They married and the couple established themselves near the sea with luxuries of sea-borne merchants.

---

[61] This mythology is held to reflect a maritime cultural base with political accretions from continental influences. This idea was later elaborated by Vietnamese literati into a mythological "genealogy of *Lac Long Qua*n and *Au Co* that brought together the southern aquatic line and the northern continental line." This basic symbolic antagonism between the land and the sea can be found in many Southeast Asian countries." (Taylor, 1983)

<u>Southeast Asian Sources</u>

The Hung king sent an army against it, but the palace disappeared in a night into the swamp. This legend contains similar elements to the founding myth of what the Chinese called Fu-nan, in the lower Mekong.

The Hung Kings of the *Van-Lang* Kingdom are held to be descendants of the *Au Co* and *Lac Long*, and are a cherished tradition. "Hung" is derived from an Austroasiatic title of chieftainship that persists until today in the mountain dwelling Mon-Khmer speaking peoples, as well as between the *Muong* and even the *Munda* of northeast India.

The name "Van-lang" has been phonetically associated with similar words among the languages of minority peoples throughout the region bounded by the Yangtze and the Mekong that mean "people" and "by extension 'nation'." (Taylor, pg. 2-3)

Joseph Buttinger writes that the Muong called their feudal kingdom "*quan-lang*," the title of the sons of the legendary king Hong.

According to 14th and 15th Centuries Vietnamese historians, Van-lang was a decentralized feudal state whose inhabitants burned the forests and tilled the soil with hoes, lived on rice, used bronze, were fishermen and seafarers, and tattooed their bodies with pictures of crocodiles, dragons, snakes and sea animals. They chewed betel and blackened their teeth. (Buttinger, 1958: p. 116)

Though these legendary sources of the Hung Kings are controversial and unreliable, historical documentation locates Van-lang and its territory in the very heartland of the *Phung-Nguyen* culture complex (Davidson, pg. 113).

Henri Maspero to the Van-Lang Kingdom attributes the existence of the Hong-Bang and Hung-Vuong dynasties.

<u>"Autochthony/Heterochthony Hypothesis"</u>

According to Maspero, the customs of tattooing sea monsters by fishermen to confer protection against 'crocodiles', the chewing of betel nut, the blackening of teeth, were common customs of the kingdom of Van Lang. A mythical king ordered the fishermen to tattoo sea monsters upon their arms to protect them from crocodiles.

Throughout Oceania, fishermen tattoo themselves to achieve magical protection against drowning and sharks is a common trait throughout the Pacific. Vietnamese kings later had dragons, symbols of their royal authority, tattooed on their chests well into the second millennium, AD—as late as *Tran Anh Tong* (1293). The crocodile was the totem of the Chinese and Vietnamese, symbolic of the dragon.

Similarly, in old Vietnam, as until recently in Indonesia and Malaysia, betel nut played an important role in social and religious life. "A marriage proposal was always preceded by presents of betel nuts and leaves."(Buttinger; pg. 115.)[62]

Gia-ninh was a toponym referring to "the old *Me-linh* area at the head of the Hong River plain, where the Hong is joined by its three major tributaries." That Van-lang was an ancient Kingdom is attested to by Chinese sources as early as the Tang, and Hung as a royal title occurs as early as Chin in the Historiographies.

---

[62] The earliest source, <u>*Viet su Luoc*</u>, (VsU) reads: "In the time of King Chuang of Chou, [696-682 B. C.] In *Gia-ninh*, there was an extraordinary man who was able to cause the submission of all the aboriginal tribes by using the magic arts. He styled himself Hung King, established his capital at Van-lang, and named his realm the kingdom of Van-lang. He used simplicity and purity as the basis for customs and knotted cords for government. The realm was handed down through eighteen generations and each ruler styled himself Hung King." (VSL, I, IA, in Keith Taylor, 1983: pg. 309)

<u>Southeast Asian Sources</u>

This "golden-aged" affirmed by 14th century writers was probably based upon well-established, but poorly articulated oral traditions "rooted in the prehistoric culture of the Hong River plain." *Ngo Si Lien* of the 15th Century gives a much earlier date to the rise of the Hung Kings—2879 BC.

Me-linh on the Hong River plain is not far from the Vietnamese mountain of mythological origin "*Tan-Vien*" and "Mount Hung." This culture apparently had an early technique of irrigation— using the ocean tides to affect the water levels in the flat delta. Early irrigation and sedentarism lead to feudal stratification that was rooted in the disposition and control of the arable land, "a power always formalized as right, with a claim to some supernatural sanction."

The authority of the Chiefs of this region was symbolically represented on the famous *Dong S'on* bronze drums. According to tradition, the Hung Kings directly controlled the *Me linh* areas. Beyond this they were dependent upon the cooperation of the Lac Lords, whom they protected from invasions from the Mountains, while the Lac Lords supported the Hung Kings with their manpower and wealth.

According to Henri Maspero, this was a hierarchical society based on hereditary privilege, mutual obligation and personal loyalty. People lived in small kinship communities under the Lac Lords who enjoyed different levels of privilege and authority, from village headmen up to regional leaders who advised the Hung Kings. The Hung Kings maintained their prestige with a prosperous court life facilitating peaceful relations with neighboring mountain tribes (Taylor, 1983: pgs. 12-13).

The oldest descriptions by Chinese sources of the third and fifth centuries A. D. describing the Hong River plain supported by an economy based upon tidal irrigation of paddy fields known as "Lac fields." Lac Lords designated the ruling class.

According to Buttinger, "Lac" was the first ethnic denomination by which the Vietnamese became known to the Chinese. "*Lac*" is also the name of the "culture hero to whom Vietnamese tradition ascribes the introduction of agriculture." The name "Lac" may be derived from the Vietnamese "*lach*" or "*rach*" meaning "ditch, canal, waterway." The construction of drainage ditches was certainly the first step toward making the swampy plains of northern Vietnam suitable for agriculture.[63]

During the time of Lac Society, coastlines would have been inland more than ten miles and tidal influences may have reached much further inland. These influences may have been strongest in the *Tay-vu* area, downstream and beyond the pathways of the Hong River, between the *Cau* and Hong rivers "at the foot of Mount *Tam-dao*."

This would have been a fertile region of lakes, rivers, hills and plains, "bounded by mountainous terrain on one side and soggy delta lands on the other; it was heavily populated from a very early time." This area was also accessible to river valleys from the north. "A recent study of the ancient geography of this area suggests that this was where the Lac-field society was based. (Taylor, 1983: pp. 6-8)

Working eastward from the *Me-linh* area, the Hung kings would have gradually extended their authority over the *Tay-vu* area and Lac society. The Chinese associated the Vietnamese with the "Hundred *Yueh*" tribes of Southeastern China. The term "*ou*," a Chinese pronunciation of the Vietnamese word "*au*," as found in

---

[63] Canals and ditches with water gates would have been essential for using the tides for to control water. "The Lac fields, as described in the texts, were surely dependent on some kind of water-control system. We must nevertheless bear in mind that the Chinese texts cite the practice of tidal irrigation by way of explaining the name <u>Lac</u> and that Lac society may well have been based on a diversity of agricultural methods, of which tidal irrigation was but one." (Keith Taylor <u>The Birth of Vietnam</u> 1983: p. 10)

<u>Southeast Asian Sources</u>

"*au lac*" may have designated a "style of leadership" as well as a "borderland." The kingdom of *Van Lang* was superseded and replaced by the Kingdom of *Au Lac*.

The Chinese interpret the expression of "*Yueh*" roughly as barbarian or "uncivilized" and they applied it to all peoples towards the south who lay upon the perimeter of their Classical civilization. Thus "*Nan Yueh*" which is the early root of "*Nam Viet*" can be interpreted as the "Southern Barbarians." "The Chinese Historians referred to the Vietnamese as '*Lac Yueh*,' or merely 'Yueh,' or even "*Lac* is another name for *Yueh*."[64]

The mythology of Vietnam reveal themes that recur in the folklore of all Southeast Asian peoples who share a mythology based upon fundamental thematic motifs and dialectical contrasts between mountain and sea, winged beings versus water beings, men of the mountains versus men of the coast. But the dominant theme is that sovereign power came from the sea, a theme that shares elements found in Island and coastal Southeast Asia, and, according to Taylor, is the first evidence of the Vietnamese as a distinct people or nation.

Jean Pryzluski (1925) showed the idea that the king's power came from the sea is directly opposed to the continental cultures of the Indo-Aryans and the Chinese and attributed it to a prehistoric maritime civilization of Southeast Asia "whose hearth was not localized but whose force of expansion was considerable," which

---

[64] The Chinese assumed that the different 'barbarian' peoples who were fortunate enough to have been conquered would eventually be 'civilized'—in other words, would become Chinese. Any name expressing a people's distinctive identity, such as <u>Lac</u>, was diluted with broader terms, such as <u>Yueh</u>, which were employed as synonyms for "barbarian." (Keith Taylor <u>The Birth of Vietnam</u> 1983: pg. 42.)

spread into Southern and Eastern China and into the Indian sub-continent exclusive of the Indus Valley.[65]

Valerio Valeri notes a similar contrast between an autochthonous female authority connected to fertility of the soil, agricultural and natural rhythms, and an immigrant, noble and "male" authority found in many societies in the area, reflecting "a deeper contrast."[66]

A modification of the same theme dates with the rise of Indo-Aryan and Chinese civilization at their borders with the "central coast of modern Vietnam"—these myths have the theme of the marriage of a powerful newcomer with a local princess, thus founding a royal dynasty.

Vestiges of this theme come from the Former Han of China, the "*Yueh*" of South China, the *Nan-Choa* kingdom of Yunnan, the Viets of the Red River delta, *Champa*, *Fu-nan*, the *Khmer* empire, Laos, the Thai of the Menam basin, the *Mons* of Pegu and Thaton, the *Burmans* of the Irrawaddy Basin, the *Munda* of northeast India, the *Pallava* and Cola dynasties of South India,

---

[65] (See Keith Taylor's "Madagascar in the Ancient Malayo-Polynesian Myths" in Explorations in the Early Southeast Asian History: The Origins of Southeast Asian Statecraft edited by Kenneth R. Hall and John K. Whitmore, 1976: pg. 27.)

[66] That between the most fundamental, most unquestionable grounds for social existence (relative to which all are ultimately equal) and the noble values (wealth, military force, ability to attract, generative potency, etc.) are unequally distributed and which allow those who have them most to weave and reweave around their persons hierarchical networks defined by relationships of client-ship, alliance, descent, debt and even servitude." (Valerio Valeri "Afterword" in J. Stephen Lansing, Priests and Programmers: Technologies of Power in the Engineered Landscape of Bali 1991: pg. 137)
See: "La Princesse a l'odeur de poisson et la Nagi dans les traditins de l'Asie oriental" Etudes Asiatique, Publications, E'cole Francaise d'Extreme-Orient, vols. 19-20, 2:265-285. Paris, 1925.

<u>Southeast Asian Sources</u>

the *Srivijayan* traditions of the island world. Keith Taylor relates similar thematic elements of maritime origin, fertility and sovereignty in the myths of Madagascar and Easter Island.

The picture that emerges from the consideration of the various sources of data is that no single line of evidence is by itself sufficient or without major holes and discrepancies. When taken together, though the picture may be confusing and even at points contradictory, there occurs a process of non-parametric "covariance" that strongly suggests a common origin.

IV: The "Marketplace Hypothesis"
Priests and Traders in the Southeast Asian Marketplace

The case of the role of traffic and trade in Southeast Asia is considered in relation to a marketplace hypothesis in the regional integration of Southeast Asian civilization. More than a crossroads, many ports and places in Southeast Asia have been the location of trade entrepôts that have inter-regionally enmeshed the region in a worldwide network of economic and cultural relations that has long served to embed in local identity an outward orientation.

The Southeast Asian marketplace has long served as a central meeting ground between different ethnocultural groupings—a place for neutral exchange and reciprocities where conflicts are temporally set aside. The role of traffic and trade continues to be a vital intercultural linkage in Southeast Asia today.

In this marketplace hypothesis, the transaction was more than material, but cultural, social, religious and symbolic. Religion provided a forum for this transcultural interchange.

The presence of the petty, part-time trader and the full-time, long-distance merchant middleman has played a pivotal role in the economic integration of the region.

The role of the early trader, pioneer and entrepreneur, as the early forerunner of the modern capitalist, and the relationship of the trader with the role of religion in the interregional integration of Southeast Asia needs to be given the credit its due.

We like to think that the invention of capitalism was a strictly modern, post-feudal affair, but we might think that there may have been more than one invention of capitalism, and more than one kind of capitalistic enterprise in the world. There may exist in the world today several different forms of capitalism, and different forms of capitalistic interest and involvement.

"Corporate forms of organization along different principles have long been important factors in the trans-local organization of Southeast Asian society." (D. E. Brown Principles of Social Organization: Southeast Asia, 1976.)

Incorporation into groups that are larger than life, that survive beyond one's own lifetime, and that have as a principle concern the protection and maximization of shared group and individual interests, depends upon ritual-religious institutional integration. Southeast Asia has long been confronted by the challenge of ethnic diversity—a cauldron of ethnicity, it has always faced a common problem of integration and the organization of diversity.

This organization has long been a matter of self-organizing systems, one that has depended perhaps on a few basic and simple mechanisms of ritualized, customary equivalence structures for reciprocal interchange and transaction, and of spacing mechanisms that assured an optimization of resource acquisition and a minimization of conflict and competitive contact.

Social spacing mechanisms may have taken the form of ecological specialization and phase-transitions between pioneering, semi-sedentary and fully sedentary modes of subsistence, headhunting and warring practices combined with inter-local exchanges and tribal exogamy, formalized social etiquette and ritual, and a "live and let live" ethos of the tolerance and mutual coexistence of difference.

The problem of the organization of diversity of people and their differences in time and space begets the research dilemma of the organization of broad diversities of data types and of many different themes into a coherent pattern. The poly-thematic inter-translation of culture has depended upon achieving a certain presumed level of comprehensiveness—a panoptic perspective.

The likelihood and frequency of different peoples coming into continuous contact or coexisting within a shared context in Southeast Asia must have been great. "Rules of etiquette and engagement" must have, in such circumstances, been long worked out and more-or-less mutually agreed by all parties, which may have permitted a form of mutual coexistence and a kind of live and let live worldview that dictated tolerance toward and even strategic appreciation of socio-cultural differences.

Such a worldview would have been rooted in the reciprocities that tie different peoples into obligatory social transactions. A minimal knowledge of the other people with whom one can expect to come into contact, a willingness to take risks in contacts with strangers, a common trade language and mutually understood terms of agreement.

It may also have entailed the rise of central places—great marketplaces—where such polyglot meeting and transaction may have taken place. It seems that typically such central places were large markets that occurred at some dry location in the delta regions of the mouths of the main rivers.

There may have been many kinds of equivalence structures shared in Southeast Asia. Equivalence structures can be defined as those common, socially defined mechanisms that provide a high degree of information and a low level of randomness in interaction and mediation of complex and ever-changing events. They act as general behavioral and symbolic templates with which to organize and interpret varieties of data.

Among such equivalence structures we can identify alternating linguistic styles, religion, ritualized etiquette and social custom, common knowledge systems, conventions. Implicitly shared cultural rationalizations, fictive kinship and surrogate familial relations, shared cultural ecology, economic mechanisms of trade, pricing, and market exchange, technologies, cultural ecological practices and values, food and cooking, and basic divisions of labor. (Murray Leaf <u>Information and Behavior in a Sikh Village</u> 1972)

We may make a distinction between: 1. Sources of information that relative choice of informational value is high or low, and 2, the entropy of alternative information choices relatively is high or low. Though high entropy sources do not necessarily produce messages of high informational value; low-entropy messages necessarily produce low-value information messages. Different sources of information may vary considerable as to their informational structure, content and capacity.

Equivalence structures can be minimally defined as any relationship or set of relationships in which acts by some of its members will entail some predictable degree of expected response on the part of other members. (Anthony F. C. Wallace <u>Culture and Personality 2n. Edition.</u> 1970).

Such structures tend to reduce the entropy within the system, at the cost of reducing the informational capacity of the system. In general, within such structures, we may stipulate a tendency towards the maximization of congruence in such structures, one that is continuously counteracted by inherently chaotic tendencies.

We may also refer to the binding effect and the incorporating and obligatory nature of social relations based upon shared complementary symbolic structures or mutual interests and at least implicit commitment to maintaining the role-definitions of the relationship, from which emerges the mostly tacit social contract that is the foundation of the organization of diversity. Enmeshed in our webs of reciprocity and equivalence, we become bound to the maintenance of certain roles, standards, codes, customs and values that have greater social significance.

Regional integration of Southeast Asia has always depended upon the working out of such equivalence structures across a range of different groups of people. This regional integration has long had a history and distribution much deeper in time and extensive in space and intricacy than we might otherwise think.

Religion is one such set of symbolic-behavioral equivalence mechanisms, embedded through ritual operation and socio-cultural integration, that have served the purpose of regional integration and the organization of diversity in Southeast Asia.

The importance and role of religion in Southeast Asia cannot be overemphasized, nor can the part played by religion in the developmental dynamics of the historical processes of human civilization be ignored—civilization is never advanced in the vacuum of religious values, ideas, symbolism, or worldviews. There are many clear occasions of religious belief providing motivation in the face of uncertain adversity where no other kind of material incentive would prove sufficient.

Foreign traders brought with them important religious beliefs and symbolism that enriched and elaborated the inherently syncretistic orientation of the traditional Southeast Asian interstate system.

The role of religion in facilitating and legitimating state organization and stable trade contacts, under the umbrella of a common system of ritual belief and behavior, in providing a rational and motivational system for economic activity, has not yet been adequately studied. Different religious orientations, during different epochs, helped to confer stable, conservative symbolic forms sanctioning the traditionalizing process of developing Southeast Asian civilization.

Religion provides a cultural framework for the symbolic articulation of diverse groupings of people, a necessary basis for "ritual communality, cross-cutting ethnic, linguistic and ecological boundaries." It provides a common "ritual language" facilitating growth and diversification of "that very large part of culture which is concerned with economic action." (Edmund Leach, 1954: pg. 279)

"People may speak different languages, wear different clothes, live in different kinds of houses, but they universally understand one another's ritual. Ritual acts are ways of saying things about social status, and the 'language' in which these things are said is common..." (Ibid: pg. 279)

Religious worldview orients people around a common set of core values and a common attitude and framework for seeing the world, committing them to a shared course of social action. The introduction of religion into a region has always been a way of interregional consolidation of structural linkages that facilitates transmission across different boundaries.

Models of the rise of state civilization, whether prime mover or multivariate, are generally materialist-structural/functional in orientation. The role of religion is seen to be part of an ideological superstructure that is epiphenomenal, legitimating, reinforcing and, at best, secondary to the principle driving factors of social organization and development of civilization.

Similarly, systems models that also tend to be based upon functional and structural presuppositions, stress political-economic institutions, modes of production and social relations of production as the determining factors of such development.

The role of religion, seen to be dialectically complementary to materialist and functionalist mechanisms in the traditional, conventional, and familial based social construction of reality, has almost never been accorded much causal importance in this general process, in spite of a great deal of historical evidence which might suggest otherwise that such a dialectical complementariness and hence complex interdependency might actually be at the heart of such historical transformations.

Wherever we find evidence of trade, we find religious missions, and wherever we find religious missions, we find the encroachments of an alien civilization's values, worldview, a colonization of the soul, and we also find the first beginnings of a process of imperial domination.

The proto-historical phase of Southeast Asian history can be divided into several stadial stages that corresponded to the periods in which certain varieties of acculturative influence became predominant throughout the region. These periods are presented generally in order of their appearance, but later periods did not completely replace the influence of earlier periods, but only added further complexity on top of the already diverse region.

Furthermore, traces and suggestions of influence from the exogenous sources of later periods are evident during the earlier phases, but remained emergent or sub-critical in their development until their later developmental sequence.

In this way, the historical period of Southeast Asia can be divided into the phases of Brahmanization, Buddhization, Islamization, Confucianization, and Christianization, a fully historic period that can be subdivided into Catholization, Dutch Calvinism, and British Protestantism, and finally, modern secularization.

There is an important and valid reason for dividing and labeling these periods by their religious character—not only does it suggest the primary role that religion has played in the formation of regional Southeast Asian identity, but it also suggests the role religion has had in acculturative expansion and interregional influence of different civilizations.

<u>Southeast Asian Sources</u>

The subsequent phases of Brahmanization (or Hinduization), Buddhization, Islamization, Confucianization and Christianization represented but extensions of a basic historical patterning in the Southeast Asian region that overlaid an indigenous animism and inter-linked local, regional and interregional interests into increasingly complex patterns of interdependency and involvement.

The arrival of Indian Civilization provided the impetus of potent symbolic forms that mandated and sanctioned the augmentation of state power by an elite. Islam penetrated the hinterlands and conferred stability to the peasant resource base of these states.

Chinese influence had long provided critical economic linkages for the articulation of the entire development process. Christianization helped to provide a stable and dependable administrative machinery and a valuation of capitalistic enterprise.

First evidence of Brahmanization is found in the first and second century AD—though the small trickle of sea-faring Indian merchants probably had no real beginning, building trade settlements on foreign shores on top of ancient Neolithic sites.

This trickle gradually flowered into a major stream of culture contact resulting in the founding of "Indian Kingdoms practicing the arts, customs and religions of India, and using Sanskrit as their sacred language." (George Coedes, <u>The Indianized States of Southeast Asia</u> 1968.)

Indian influence is pervasive throughout Southeast Asia, and has become a basic component of Southeast Asian regional identity.

The model of Brahmanization consists of small groups of merchant vessels, either carrying Brahmans or merchants who passed themselves off as priests, mixing with and influencing the local elite, learning the local language, introducing elements of their Hindu civilization, marrying well placed daughters of powerful leaders, who in turn became the best agents for the promotion of Hindu values.

Inheriting land or titles of authority, Indianized chiefs then assembled local peoples into a state organization. A Hindu temple might be built on a near by mountaintop.[67]

Buddhism appears to have swept through Southeast Asia in several waves—in the first and second centuries A.D., later in the 3rd and Fourth, and then again in the 7th and 9th centuries. *Fa Shien* was a Buddhist monk who traveled from India to China via Southeast Asia, who described the ships of the day as carrying 200 persons, (G. R. G. Worcester, The Junks and Sampans of the Yangtze Annapolis, Maryland: Naval Institute Press 1971: pg. 22) left a detailed account of Buddhist Kingdoms he had visited along the way.

Buddhist monks and their temples were the principle purveyors of this faith, and the political and economic ramifications of its influence in Southeast Asia are not clear but may have been considerable. Some Buddhist monasteries appear to have accumulated a great deal of wealth and local control, and Buddhism provided another potent symbolic pantheon for the legitimization of state authority.

Buddhism in many areas appears to have been implicated in the formation of early cities, providing some of the religious

---

[67] "This custom, associated with the original foundation of a kingdom or royal dynasty, is witnessed in all the Indian kingdoms of the Indochinese Peninsula...It reconciled the native cult of the spirits on the heights with the Indian concept of royalty, and gave the population assembled one sovereign, a sort of national god, intimately associated with the monarchy. We have here a typical example of how India, in spreading her civilization to the Indochinese peninsula, knew how to make foreign beliefs and cults her own and assimilate them." (George Coedes, The Indianized States of Southeast Asia, 1968: pgs. 26-7.)

symbolisms of royal authority appropriated by the ruling elites. This kind of influence is evident in much of the early monumental architecture. (Keith Taylor, <u>The Birth of Vietnam</u> 1983.)

Islam spread epidemically from the 7th Century AD onward, and became well rooted among the lowland peasant peoples, especially in Malaysia and the Indonesian Archipelago. Carried by Arab traders, Koranic reading and the *Jawi* script provided the first basis for the spread of literacy. The basic model of Islamization was similar to that of Brahmanization.

It was basically an urban civilization, another factor in the generation of the Southeast Asian city-state complex. The urban model of Islamization had five basic components:

1. A citadel or defensive work.
2. A royal quarter containing the royal residence, administrative offices and royal guards.
3. A central urban complex containing mosques, religious schools and markets, with "special places" assigned for main groups of craftsmen or traders and the homes of the principal merchant and religious bourgeoisie.
4. A core of residential quarters divided among resident foreign ethnic groups and religious minorities that enjoyed a degree of autonomy.

And finally

5. The outer quarters of suburbs, where resided recent immigrants and temporary visitors to the city.[68]

---

[68] A. H. Johns, "Islam in Southeast Asia" in <u>Southeast Asian History and Historiography</u>, edited by C.D. Cowan and O. W. Wolters, 1976: pg. 310.

Confucianization represents the casting of the patriarchal Chinese shadow over the Nanyang, as the basis of tributary-trade relations. Chinese presence in Southeast Asia actually predated the arrival of the grand fleets of Admiral Cheng Ho, and the religion that the earliest Chinese carried with them was undoubtedly the syncretistic Conflation of the "Three Teachings" combined Confucian ethos and ethics with Mahayana and Chan Buddhist symbols and attitudes and Taoist rituals and spiritualism.

There is little doubt that this religious orientation blended quite well with the local religious orientations. Some of its early deities were actually female, like the Goddess Kwan Yin, supporting traits of mercy rather than the patriarchal values of Confucianism and Ancestor worship.

Confucianism itself was not incompatible with indigenous systems—its official "Mandate of Heaven" and its counterpart "Rectification of Names"—and its ethos and ethno-cosmology provided "an inclusive cult that sacralizes the (social) structure and (political) leadership."

These doctrines, where they were encountered in the Southeast Asian setting, undoubtedly lent credibility to the ruling powers, as well as legitimacy to successful revolutionary parties. It also helps to explain the role of the Chinese in Southeast Asia, who could so facilely and successfully submit to the mandate of local authority of whatever shore he found himself washed up upon.

Chinese traditionally practiced humility, subservience, obedience and respect for authority that generalized over to other, non-Sinitic regimes under which they found themselves. Chinese influence in Southeast Asia may have had an effect of opening up the hierarchical regimes of Southeast Asian city-states, not only to greater external influence, but also to greater internal forces of change.

Christianization dates from the arrival of the Portuguese and Spanish, with early Catholic missionary zeal, and followed the later paths of the Dutch, French and English with their Protestant repressions.

Here we find a close alliance between "merchant missionaries" and "missionary merchants," conversion by the Cross accompanied by chastisement by "whips and scorpions," and the introduction of an armaments industry and arms market into the region.

Each European nation had its own interests, its own style of imperial colonization, and its own brand of Christianity to promote "in the name of God and King and Country."

V: The "Plural-Polity Hypothesis"
Primitives, Pioneers, Peasants, Pirates, Princes, Prostitutes, Proletarians, Presidents and Pariahs in Southeast Asian Geography

Inextricably entangled with the problem of such acculturation and the incorporation of diversity, is the problem of "ethnos" as a central organizational principle of Southeast Asian civilization. Ethnicity as the study of ethnic identity and ethno-genesis as the study of ethnic origins, are intrinsic and basic dimensions of Southeast Asian studies in general. "Ethnic diversity is so fundamental in Southeast Asia that it is one of the great laboratories for the study of ethnicity." (D. E. Brown, 1976:99.)

It was in general reference to Southeast Asia, and in specific relation to the pervasiveness of the Overseas Chinese there, that had led J. S. Furnival to formulate his now classic theory of "radical pluralism"—the social integration of people of many cultures in a common market place and under the aegis of a common political structure.

The principle of ethnos lies at the base of Southeast Asian cultural identity. Social organization based upon such a principle of ethnos, is characteristically of a plural and culturally heterogeneous society. Indeed, J. S. Furnival in reference to Southeast Asia coined the ethnic concept of "radical pluralism".

D. E. Brown (Principles of Social Structure, 1976) notes seven conditions necessary for the maintenance of radically plural societies that are typical of Southeast Asian settings:

1. Continuity of stable economic and ecological conditions (ibid.: pg. 82.)

2. Relative isolation of the radically plural society from other similar sized but differently structured societies (ibid.: pg. 85-6.)

3. Demographic ratios between ruling and rule should be maintained or change in favor of the ruling elite (ibid.: p. 86.)

4. Social identities and boundaries are maintained by generalizing differences across all spheres—religious, familial, educational, occupational, economic, etc.—thus restricting inter-group acculturation and mobility (ibid.: pg. 87.)

5. Symbiotic relations offering primary compensations for the subordinate minority and religious or ideological orientations offering deferred compensations are encouraged (ibid.: p. 88.)

6. The corporate exclusiveness, superior organization, solidarity and cohesion of the ruling group should be systematically promoted (ibid.: p. 88.)

7. Authority should be made sacred and legitimated by an inclusive cult offering compensation in another life or advocating withdrawal from worldly affairs. (Ibid.: pg. 90.)

The basic model of corporate social structure based upon the principle of ethnos implied by this formal paradigm is held to characterize the developmental dynamics of typically Southeast Asian civilization, even from its first prehistoric inception perhaps as long ago as several thousands of years until today.

It is a model in which numerous, relatively homogenous, local groups came into increasing contact with one another, and with extra-regional peoples, and resulting in the processes of intercultural contact and transmission, there developed increasing levels of heterogeneity and socio-structural complexity.

This model is critically linked to the development of the economic exploitation of the entire region, and to the emergence of an increasingly complex interregional system based upon commerce and hinterland exploitation, in which local people were to become increasingly integrated and more culturally sophisticated and cosmopolitan.[69]

Civilization is thus also held to be a developmental process of interregional integration, represented by increasing levels of complexity of socio-political organization, increasing economic integration and exploitation, and the increasing influence of religious ideas and orientations upon the structure of social organization.

The political-economic basis of Southeast Asian civilization is discussed in its structural relation to the phenomena of plural-polity role relations between different kinds of people. The political-economy of a region during a particular period cannot be simply understood in formal terms, but has a substantive bases rooted in the culture and the ecological-economic underpinnings of a region.

Identity in Southeast Asia has always been of a shifting focus, dependent upon one's geographical distance from alternative

---

[69] "To examine the role of economic exchange in this region, we must be aware of the ways in which international commerce has penetrated Southeast Asia, and come in contact with local societies and economies. My contention is that the process by which this occurred generally intensified through the centuries, that as time went by more and more parts of the region made contact with foreign trade. While there certainly were fluctuations in this development, we must consider that those societies that at one time had taken part in this trade remained aware of it and interested in it. From this point we may begin to ask about the impact of this commercial involvement on the internal situation...." (J. K. Whitmore, "The Opening of Southeast Asia: Trading Patterns Through the Centuries," in Economic Exchange and Social Interaction in Southeast Asia, edited by Karl L. Hutterer 1977:134)

centers of influence and power. The chameleon quality of Southeast Asia identity is even apparent in the hyphenation of "South-East" which the name implies. The chameleonness of identity is of course rooted in an orientation that emphasized the importance of behaviorally adaptive community context, both social and natural, in the definition of the self.

This posed a fundamental relationship between time and space, and the forms of constraint imposed upon the temporal-spatial organization of experience. Inconsistency becomes a relative measure in the eye of the beholder. The play between the forces of good and evil that are enacted upon the stage of *wayang kulit* are the play of forces that tear at and continually threaten to sunder the self, vis-à-vis different ethnocultural others in a common communal continuum

The hypothesis is held that Southeast Asian identity was spatially ordered in a cyclical, ritual manner that contrasts with the "temporal" organization of western historical recounting of biographical experience and historical events. We are left with the question of the role of cultural constraint and the extent and manner in which context must be taken into our account in our formulas for historical patterning.

Status became a matter of negotiation and manipulation of one's own place, a positioning, in relation to others, for strategic advantage. It also entailed constant competition and conflict, coalitions and crosscutting commitments, as well as centering oneself in positions of greater legitimacy and power. As everywhere, power in Southeast Asia, unevenly distributed, created legitimacy, and legitimacy reinforced relations and positions of power.

The "Plural-Polity Hypothesis"

If we were not the first civilization to actually invent the corporate principles of capitalism, we may also not have been the first peoples to invent the state-market practices of political economy. Power and wealth have always been the unholiest of sanctified unions.

It is the kind of violent force that creates coercive power that states co-opt and also creates the prerequisite and sufficient conditions for the accumulation of wealth that we call today capital and that is more generally referred to as profit. Combining the two in terms of political economy, we can talk about human exploitation of labor and resources for the sake of private gain.

An alternative substantive model of political economy, or political-ecology, is proffered in within a regional context of multiple modes of production within different patchworks of adaptation, which beget different patterns of social relation and stratification at different levels of articulation and transaction.

Each role had its place, and different roles had their different "places" within a larger context in which the payoffs of conflicts always had to be measured against the costs of cooperation.

Southeast Asia has been described as an ethnic mosaic, a cauldron and a laboratory of ethnicity. It has been a region where different groups have coexisted and transacted business, "making a living" time immemorial.

Identity rooted in ethnic distinction and ethno-national diversity demanded that people incorporate themselves into groups in the pursuit and protection of their common interests within a common national forum of a state-marketplace, in competition with some groups, and in complement with others.

The "plural-polity" hypothesis holds that circumscription in terms of social-environmental relations, were systemic mechanisms in the rise and development of regional integration and of early state civilizations.

<u>Southeast Asian Sources</u>

Stratification occurred as asymmetrical interrelations of dominance-dependence were established between different groups of people, and, by extension, between the different niches that they occupied.

State structures and the stratification upon which they are based are expectable outcomes of the critical self-organization and interaction of diverse inter-local areas and peoples. This development has depended upon the incorporation of a broad resource base, and organizational mechanisms that permitted the local-regional articulation of resources.

While most materialist models of state development are built from the ground up, the plural-polity hypothesis turns Marx "inside out" and focuses upon the self-other defining reference behavior of different kinds and groups of people who are tied to and defined in terms of their main ecological modes of adaptation, as these are articulated within an extra-local social-geographical context.

The origin of change of a people, say from a Latifundian slave class into a feudal land-bound serfdom or from a hunter-gatherer or slash and burn primitive to a sedentary-farming peasant, is rooted not so much in the primary modes of production upon which they are held to be based, as they are in the shifting patterns of domestic and extra-domestic social relations and reproduction that arises from asymmetrical relations of dominance/dependence between people.

Dominance and dependency are political relations that control change and the differential access and distribution of resources. They are inherently conflicting and social in nature. These relations are inherently unstable and shifting in character, unless they are firmly rooted to culturally defined patterns of ecological adaptation.

The internal contradictions that are the source of dialectical transformations in social integration are those asymmetries of power that are rooted within systemic social-environmental inconsistencies of ecological adaptation. The development of the birdman cult on Easter Island and the subsequent decline of Polynesia civilization upon the island was rooted in the imbalances and eventual failure of the cultural system to work out a more stable, long-term eco-cultural relation with its island world.

It is in reference to the "plural-polity" relations in Southeast Asian political ecology that we can consider several sets of factors that underlie Southeast Asian regional integration:

1) The patterns of movement and settlement of different kinds of people.

2) The periodic rise and fall of Mandala city-state kingdoms during the proto-historic phase with concentrically diffused spheres of authority and legitimacy, and within which the roles and status-identity of different kinds of people's could be reciprocally defined.

3) The cultural-ecological and economic bases of group-identity and organization of different peoples in Southeast Asia.

We may refer to enduring, long-term structures of continuity that are rooted in the geographical contexts of Southeast Asia, which have preconditioned and underlay the political ecological and economic relations between different peoples of the region, and the resulting patterns of social integration of the region.

Patterns of Migration and Settlement: Primitives, Pioneers
and Peasants

"Wherever they settled, there was Vietnam, because Vietnam, as
a totality and continuity of human existence, was the Vietnamese
Village...(Joseph Buttinger, 1958: pp. 172-3.)

The "Great Divide" may have been as much a culture
geographical relationship between high and low in Southeast
Asia as it has been a culture historical distinction between
"primitive and civilized."

Throughout Southeast Asia the distinction between the dwellers
in the highlands and the lowlands remains one of the most basic
distinctions. This kind of cultural distinction may have been
present even in the remotest of prehistoric times, and may in part
account for the confusing complexity of the ethno-linguistic map
of Southeast Asia.

The highlands have been conservative and isolated. The lowlands
have been a source of contact and convergence of different
civilizations. Highland-lowland distinctions may have maintained
themselves in much earlier times—with isolated pockets of
highland groups that today seem anomalous in cultural
surroundings may have been present before the lowland groups,
and may have witnessed the successive replacement of several
lowland groups.

Different groups were pushed and pulled in different directions.
Two separate routes of movement would also have been open—
highlanders following the mountain valleys and crests,
lowlanders following the flow of rivers and coastlines.

The flow of culture would have tended from one direction to
another along each route, except when unusual historical
circumstances would have dictated a crossing over from one to
the other.

The more widespread traffic would have been lowland. Cultures crossing between mountain chains would be less likely than a common origin of a lowland culture diverging into the highlands and becoming subsequently isolated. We historically privilege more complex social patterns as being more advanced developments, rather than a merely alternative forms of adaptation.

Ways of life in the mountains were separate from, and in many ways complementary to, ways of life in the valleys and lowlands. The ball and chain configuration of the Southeast Asian landscape permitted each group to have its own mountaintop or lowland delta or plain or river or island.

Dense tropical rainforest interiors prohibited the across the grain movements of peoples which may have disrupted the formation of this stable pattern. Pioneers proceeded from the direction of greatest population pressure; Princes proceeded along the lines of least resistance. Within Southeast Asia, power has always flowed along the lines of least resistance.

The patterns of movement that are associated with the lowland rice-cultivating peasant are very different from the patterns that the swidden horticulturalist of the highlands will adopt, although both fit into a "wave of advance model." In this model change is linked to demographic transitions based upon subsistence strategies, while the flow of culture by the transference of an elite, a prince and his court, may be rather dramatic and sudden, as suggested in an "elite-dominance" model in which at least the incoming group must be fairly highly organized.[70]

There is also evidence in Southeast Asian demography suggesting the "system collapse model" in which the demise of a small state organization, either due to internal pressures or

---

[70] Colin Renfrew <u>Archaeology and Language: The Puzzle of Indo-European Origins</u>, 1987: pg. 131-2.

external forces and factors, may lead to a migration and dispersal of once concentrated people.

If we studied the ethno-linguistic map of Southeast Asia, (for instance, see the superbly detailed map accompanying the book <u>Ethnic Groups of Mainland Southeast Asia</u> by Frank LeBar, Gerald Hickey and John Musgrave, New Haven: HRAF Press, 1964) we could probably find evidence of patterning that would fit some variant of all three models. In fact, none of the models are mutually exclusive, and all can be fit within a fourth model of imperialism and possibly a fifth one of colonization (and colonial enslavement.)

Highland population densities are much lower than lowland population densities (130 per square mile compared to densities as high as 500 per square mile). The premium in the highlands that practiced a swidden pattern of slash and burn hoe-cultivation, without draft animals, is for new fertile land.

The premium in the lowlands is for cleared, arable and cultivable land. There is thus a tendency in a shifting cultivation pattern adapted to the highlands towards marginalization or movement towards the periphery, and this marginalizing tendency will be "pushed" from behind by the increasing densities and population pressures of previously used land in which different methods of cultivation must be adopted to maintain satisfactory productive yields.[71]

Evidence suggests that the Miao Mountain people were on the move long before they began cultivating opium. Opium has long

---

[71] Movement in and among the highlands region is governed by the "law of the Mountains"—"land that is not under settlement is everybody's land, and, there being more people behind than in front of him, he is prepared to keep moving onwards." (William Robert Geddes <u>Migrants of the Mountains: The Cultural Ecology of the Blue Miao (Hmong Njua) of Thailand</u>, 1976: p. 28.)

been opportunistic cash crop that fit in well with their cultural incentives that maximized opportunity and freedom of movement.[72]

Movement of both mountain and lowland groups will tend in similar directions—toward the frontier—and in every case the lowland groups will tend to drive out and displace those groups of the lowlands who are practicing a shifting pattern of cultivation.

It is suggested that the wave model in which pioneers are replaced by peasants in the opening and settlement of new frontiers, including peripheral roles in which even primitive hunter-gatherers may become specialized primary foragers such as the *Punan* peoples of Borneo.

Punan is a broad, loosely applied generic label to peoples specialized in a primary foraging adaptation at the peripheries of civilization and who have long been enmeshed in a larger regional or global network, recapitulates to some extent the pattern of state development and regional integration and stratification in Southeast Asia.

The *Punan* are Austronesian speakers who were at one time rice-cultivating farmers who subsequently returned to "commercial hunting-gathering" that is "an adaptation in which the collection

---

[72] "Mountain people are not foot loose. Though they may be 'indomitable pioneers' they are not nomads or 'Driven to travel by an innate compulsion.' Our observation suggests that every Miao, if asked, would say that he prefers to be settled. The people who do follow behind may have a lower range of expectations because they are usually farming land that has already been occupied." (Geddes, pg. 28) "Therefore those in the vanguard tend to stay there because they have the greater incentive. Opportunity, too, is greater at the frontier. Those behind may have to adapt to longer periods of settlement, and modify their farming practices accordingly, because of lack of opportunities to better themselves." (Geddes, pg. 28.)

of natural commodities for trade forms a major, if not primary motivating for hunting and gathering. (Hoffman, 1984: pg. 147.)

Jean Kennedy provides a model for the regional development of Southeast Asia based on growing interdependencies between different specialized groups, leading to a diversification of the spectrum of Southeast Asian society.[73]

There are historical precedents for some of these processes in Southeast Asia. From the period of Chinese domination in North Vietnam from the first century BC, until the 14th Century AD, the expansion of the Vietnamese nation consisted of a slow and steady "march to the south" that was accompanied and punctuated by a series of wars with its southern Champan and Khmer neighbors, a settlement pattern by pioneering peasants and frontier armies that was not too different from the American westward march.

Part of this process was surely a gradual process of fission and dispersal by small peasant villages into outlying hamlets that become strung out along roads and watercourses. This fissioning process has been fairly well described.[74]

They must also be fit within a larger patterning of north to southward migration that was stimulated in Northern China and in part explains the construction of the Great Wall.

----

[73] "Systems of exchange, in maintaining links between old and new forms, not only foster innovation by decreasing the risks of specialization or nonconformity...The increase in diversity and differentiation of productive modes is conducive not only to further economic specialization, but also to the development of intra- and inter-group controls and to the rise of central-place exchange. In such developments, perhaps, lies the origin of the ethnic mosaic of modern Southeast Asia." (Jean Kennedy, <u>Economic Exchange and Social Interaction in Southeast Asia</u> edited by Karl Hutterer, 1977: pg. 35-6)
[74] For instance, see Joseph Buttinger, Keith Taylor, and Gerald Hickey.

A continuous trickle of soldier/peasant/ex-officials/refugees from the Han period, and periodic waves fleeing famine, poverty and persecution made their way South, putting pressure upon and ultimately displacing those who come before them.

The Vietnamese advance southward replicated the Chinese model by the frontier establishment of pioneering farmer/soldier settlements of exiled persons of the state who could earn their own land and freedom while defending and domesticating the frontier against hostile barbarians. These settlements eventually became hamlets and villages that added to the hearth count and the tax revenues of the state.

This process must be seen as multi-layered in its patterns of movement. Undoubtedly the resistance and ultimate demise of the *Champan* state braked, channeled and finally created a vacuum for this process.

The *Chams* themselves were ultimately part of a group of sea-invaders whose numbers could not have been too large, and yet whose cultural presence has left an indelible mark upon the local region. A similar pattern of movement can be detected in the spread of the Thai speaking peoples down into the *Chao Praya* plains, and the intrusion of Sino-Burman speaking peoples in the Northeast region of the Southeast Asian mainland.

All of these movements into the lowland plains and deltas have an historical time frame. Court records document the rise and fall of royal potentates, some of whom fled to safety.

Most of the time, when these movements were not the result of open warfare, conflict and conquest, it can be assumed that a certain modicum of acculturation, assimilation and amalgamation between groups was always occurring. It is certain that the patterns of these movements have played an important part in dictating the resulting distributions of peoples in Southeast Asia today.

Southeast Asian Sources

If we want to look at some of the dynamics of this set of processes, the history of Vietnam provides a good example. First Chinese colonization of Vietnam apparently mostly affected the ruling elite, though evidence suggests intermarriage between Chinese men and local wives from a very early time, and the undoubted influence that indigenous Vietnamese women had upon their husbands and their offspring.

The great stability and conservatism of the peasant in his nucleated, inbound and impenetrable village, is held to have always outlived the vicissitudes of court intrigues and the instability of dynastic succession.

Vietnamese national and cultural sentiment was rooted in the peasant, who survived, from the time of Chinese imperial domination, until even in the most recent era, the violent political forces that have always threatened to destroy them.[75]

Indeed, a lesson hard learned by blundering Americans was that it was the very self-sufficiency of the villages that "gave Vietnam hidden powers of resistance." It has also been ethnographically documented that the average peasant, though conservative, is supremely practical and will accept and adapt any innovation if its usefulness can be proven.[76]

____

[75] "Cultural values and social behavioral patterns are shared because the inhabitants have a common tradition, which in this case is the Vietnamese tradition as it exists in Southern Vietnam. It does not necessarily follow that members of village society have strong social bonds or a sense of social solidarity. These qualities are found within the village but cannot be attributed to the village." (Hickey, 1964: pg. 278.)

[76] "The single form of Vietnamese settlement duplicated the closed circle of the nation. Hidden from sight behind their high hedges of bamboo, the villages stood like nuclei within their surrounding circle of rice fields." (Fitzgerald, 1972: pg. 11.)

Behind the peasant and his village we see the operation of kinship and the political economic role of the family unit—one whose lineage size went from nine ascending generations in the north to five in the central regions to only three in the south. But the family was a corporate productive unit—the minimal community.

And the village was a tight aggregation of families, and the village replaced the clan or lineage organization as the principle unit of organization. In Vietnam, to be exiled from the Village was a fate worse than imprisonment or even death.[77]

Chinese Commanderies were at first interested in the villages only for the purposes of hearth-counts, taxation, Corveé and conscription and pacification. For the most part, they left the local culture of the Village intact.

With independence after the Ninth Century AD, national and court life of the King and subsequent emperors came to intrude more upon the daily lives of the peasant. Yet the Vietnamese Village has always remained a semi-autonomous unit, and the source of much potential conflict—"The laws of the Emperor yield to the custom of the villages."

Annual festivals were held at the village ceremonial center, or *Dinh*, commemorating the official consecration and founding of the village by the Emperor. Before national government, *dinhs* referred to local gods of the earth.[78]

---

[77] "One of the dreads of poverty is that the family may disintegrate as members quit the villages to seek livelihood elsewhere. For the villager, it is extremely important that the family remain together: in addition to the comfort of having kinfolk around, immortality lies in an undying lineage." (Hickey, 1964.)

[78] "In assuming temporal power, the emperors of Vietnam took on the responsibility to perform the rites of the agriculture for all the Vietnamese villages and replaced the local spirits with the spirits of

Southeast Asian Sources

The common factor in the stability of lineages was the possession
of common land, or *huang hoa*, as well as the religious based
symbolic-ceremonial mechanisms that reinforced lineage
solidarity, such as Ancestor Worship, and values built in
patriarchal, patrilineal familism. This links the stability of family
units to the possession of property—the peasant should contribute
not only to the interests of his/her own offspring, but also to the
common welfare of the "main stem" of the family. Similar
processes in hinterland—core relations of modern Southeast
Asian states can be found happening even in modern times.

These institutional mechanisms reinforced the human relationship
to the land at the same time that they reinforced human social
solidarity. Hence, we have a triadic interrelationship between the
individual's own interests, land and property ownership, and the
common, familial-communal interests of the group.

The basis for potential conflict was rooted in the structure of
village society, familial organization and individual peasant-
villagers in possession and usufruct privileges to land, and is
critical to understanding the process of southward expansion
called "Vietnamization."[79]

Perhaps this explains why graft and corruption at higher levels
became so rife—for it meant becoming divorced, physically,

---

national heroes and gene. Under their reign the *dinh* contained the
imperial character that incorporated the village into the empire, making
an elision between the ideas of 'land,' 'emperor' and 'Vietnamese'"
(Fitzgerald, 1972: pg. 14) The *dinh* was "a symbolic bond between the
villages and the emperor." (Hickey, 1964: pg. 6.)
[79] "...Within the villages as within the nation the amount of arable land
was absolutely inelastic. The population of the village remained stable,
and so to accumulate wealth meant to deprive the rest of the
community of land, to fatten while one's neighbor starved..." The earth
took precedence in the definition of society, "for, as the source of life, it
was the basis for the social contract between members of the family
and members of the village..." (Hickey, 1964: pg. 13)

socially and psychologically, from the primary symbolic structure of one's psycho-cultural identity.

But village solidarity was never complete or immune from the competition and intrigue of neighbors. "Land breeds no land," and title and estate property was a legitimate source of wealth, poverty meant the disinheritance of property to someone else. "...But strictly speaking, the distinction is not between richness and poverty, but between privilege and non-privilege." (Stover, 1974: pg. 80-1) States could come and go, but the Vietnamese nation, rooted in the village, would remain.

In this regard, it is worthwhile to consider several other important aspects of the general process. The colonial and dynastic history of Vietnam reveals the struggles of a rising state centralization against the divisive tendencies of a feudal social structure.

Periods of good and honest administration were followed by the corrupt exploitation of degenerate offspring, setting the stage for feudal divisions and rebellion, and subsequent replacement by a new dynasty. The degree of corruption preceding rebellions is documented in the tax records.

Also important is the degree to which the state or alternatively a feudal authority intrudes upon the productive relationship between the peasant and the land.

Promulgation of state laws encouraging partible inheritance, even sexual equality in the matter, constituted an attempt by the state to prevent and break up large land-holdings which represented a source of resistance to state revenue and power.

In a strictly feudal economy, the relationship between the serf or peasant and the central authority of the state is one that is characterized by social distance and regal-ritual symbolism.

Southeast Asian Sources

Otherwise the direct linkages between the royalty and the land are tenuous and easily broken. It is a central economy characterized by the redistribution of levied foods for the maintenance of the court. The move towards a state society entails the bureaucratic and administrative incorporation of the peasant into the orbit of the state.

The emphasis is upon the management of markets and greater administrative efficiency in extenuating the linkages between the state and the productivity of the peasant. The peasant cultivating a basic staple remains the primary source of food and economic basis of the state, whose power to extract and requisition this wealth directly from the peasant is the source of centralized authority and power.

An important motivating factor in territorial expansion of Vietnam was the chronic problem of local over population that the cultural ecology of wet-rice cultivation led to. The harvesting and planting of rice are brief but labor-intensive seasons that are critical to the success of the crop. They require a reserve labor force that is not needed during the rest of the growing season.

Wet rice regions support some of the highest population densities in the world, next to some urban areas, and such densities are in part due to the agricultural involution which wet-rice cultivation supplies—renewable or even increased fertility of the same plot over time, and relatively high yields per unit area of land.

Compounding this problem is the need for essential amino acids and balanced proteins that a dependency upon a staple carbohydrate produces.

An endemic and often pandemic disease of protein-calorie, nitrogen-protein deficiency, referred to as "Boiffoisure d'Annam", characterized the Vietnamese countryside. This disease seems to have been endemic and seems to have resulted in a diet based upon strategies of diversification and opportunistic consumption—a wide-ranging consumption of almost any protein source available, including carrion, worms, rats, and entrails and the characteristic lack of hoarding. A main part of the Vietnamese diet is *nouc mam* or fish sauce that is high in concentrated proteins.

A country confronted with periodic bouts of overpopulation and malnutrition, almost once every generation, has only two means open to it. In the tradition bound feudal economy of Vietnam only the former one of which was seen as a viable alternative.

This is either the opening of new frontiers or imperialistic expansion and colonization of foreign territories, and the seeking out of new economic sectors in a field of "supply and service industries operated by merchants."

Stover talks about these possibilities and it is interesting to compare the more tradition bound Vietnamese peasant, and the later Vietnamese refugee in the United States, with very similar or alternative patterns by Chinese immigrants in the Nanyang or Overseas.[80]

The Le rulers of the fifteenth century instituted a policy of systematic territorial expansion against the *Champan* Empire in the south. A series of wars led to the virtual eradication of the Champs of the lowlands by 1471.

During the following decades "masses of landless peasants" settled during the following decades southward, penetrating the Mekong delta region which was indefensible by the then declining Cambodian empire. "The Vietnamese reached Saigon shortly before 1700 and annexed the rest of the South during the following sixty years." (Buttinger, 1958: pg.47.)

---

[80] Leon Stover, The Cultural Ecology of Chinese Civilization: Peasant and Elites in the Last of the Great Agrarian States, 1974.

<u>Southeast Asian Sources</u>

We may look to yet another factor involved in this process, also characteristic of both the Vietnamese and the Chinese, and that is the "oral" pattern of socialization which distinguishes the indulgences and subsequent corruption of the children of the wealthy and the privations and frequent rising of the children of the poor.

Wealthy parents unconsciously consider their children's leisure and gratification as indicative of their own prestige and prosperity. The mechanism underlying "father-son" identification among the Chinese (and by inference, the Vietnamese) is similar to the mechanism of romantic identification between husband and wife. Children may be raised in very strict, paternalistic and authoritarian regimes, but be "free from restraint with regard to food."[81]

We can compare, as Francis Hsu does, two alternative and clearly contraposed "status personality configurations" that are the result of these factors. Poor children grow up hard working, while the children of the rich grow up "to firmly believe that whatever they desire in life will be forthcoming to them simply for the asking or the taking." (Hsu, 1967: pg. 279.)[82]

---

[81] "The children of the poor must tighten their belts not because of the disciplinary compunctions of their parents, but because of adverse circumstances—they are liable to grow up under food restrictions "regardless of parental intentions." "...Parents do not merely refrain from imposing restrictions on their children's feeding habits. Those who have no cause to worry about food take great pleasure in seeing their young ones eat freely. The same is true regarding the spending of money." (Hsu, 1967: pg. 278.)

[82] The differences between these personalities are that while "the former status group tends to be submissive, careful, rational, frugal, realistic, industrious, and sincere, the personality configuration of the latter group tends to be vain, unsympathetic, licentious, impulsive, unrealistic, extravagant, carefree, insincere and to lack economic and common sense." (ibid: pg. 280.)

Combining these three sets of factors, it is useful to consider this problem in light of Melville Herskovits theory of cultural dynamics that posits that socialization and enculturative conditioning in early childhood and the integration of society and cultural sanctioning, will lead paradoxically both to adaptive reconditioning and relearning and to conservatism in adulthood, and that cultural focus upon certain aspects of culture to the exclusion of others will lead to greater elaboration of those aspects, and subsequently, to 'drift.' (Melville J. Herskovits <u>Cultural Anthropology</u>, 1955).

It seems as if cultural forces are focused upon the dynamic relationships between people, groups, land and resources of the land, in terms of controlling, channeling or facilitating the mobility and mobilization of such resources. Such control is mandatory if a society is to achieve adaptive integration. Such mobilization may take many different patterns. We can refer to upward and downward social mobility, to migration and geographic mobility, and to mass mobilization or social movements.

Pirates and Princes

Piracy, and the attribution of piracy, has always been endemic and widespread in Southeast Asian Historiography as a political ploy and economic strategy. Pirates have continued to operate up until contemporaneous times, afforded haven and hiding among the many small islands and outlets of the seas. Fishermen and traders in one season may become opportunistic pirates in the next.

Piracy has always added flavor and violence to the daily rhythms of Southeast Asia. We must inquire into what piracy has represented to the region, and how it has influenced the character of Southeast Asian Civilization.

Southeast Asian Sources

Southeast Asia has had a long and romantic tradition of piracy. The possibilities for adventure and predation have always been there. The mentality of primitive economics construes smuggling and raiding as merely a para-politically expedient extension of trading—why haggle over prices when one can simply take by force what one wants?

Some economists have argued that the need for finance and protection on the High Seas was one of the main spurs toward government and capitalistic enterprise.

Clearly, the early European trading partners who got together investors to finance long distance trading missions in Further India numbered among the earliest, and perhaps most unscrupulous capitalists western society has produced.

For piracy was more than a human possibility of the variegated Southeast Asian landscape. It was a major off-season pursuit of peripheral fishermen and traders who regularly plied the pliant, warm seas of the region.

Protection from pirates, and from interior raiders and brigands who always lurked just beyond the margins of the concourses of civilization, has been perhaps a major impetus behind early state aggregation and formation.

Early Mandala civilizations surely served, besides a symbolic and possible mercantile function, a police function to protect the trade route sources and interests of the elite, if not the peasants or tribes of peoples who came under the umbrella of their control.

There was a perennial need to secure the lucrative linkages of trade and communication with the outside world. The same forces that could police the hinterlands could also be counted on to enforce tributary relations and to subdue other tribes and peoples.

The arc of control by one potentate over other petty potentates was the symbolic measure of the greatness of a people and a political economic measure of their prosperity and security of their resource base.

In other words, petty pirates were not the only ones to practice piracy in Southeast Asia, and, despite the romanticism, they have been the only ones without the legal charter or moral mandate to reinforce their para-institutional and locally-regionally customary prerogatives.

We must recognize that "piracy" was as much an ascriptive label applied especially by the British as a matter of policy in their pacification and colonization of Malaya and Borneo. Piracy was applied to all groups who showed resistance to British colonial procedures and who sought by brute force to gain profit from victims.

This form of piracy was not too much different from the imperialistic policies of the Europeans themselves, whether we talk about the cutthroat and exploitative policies of merchant-mariners or the policies of British administrators and their military henchmen.[83]

British policy became transformed into a matter of "protectionism" in which "the mark of a protected state or people...is that it cannot maintain political intercourse with

---

[83] Such piracy policy later became transformed into a policy of paramouncy. "...This was the theory that the strongest had a legal duty to keep its weaker neighbors in sufficient order to permit trade. ...The roots really lay in a concept of world order that exalted rights of property, of goods in transit or in warehouses, to be free from interference. Since rival claims to sovereign, law-making authority might interfere with rights of property, the 'paramount' power assumed the right, even the 'duty' to oversea questions of dynamic succession." (Alfred Rubin, Piracy, Paramountcy and Protectorates 1974: p. 54)

foreign powers except through or by permission of the protecting state." (Ibid.: pg. 66)

It is not too difficult to see the implicit "White man's burden" and racial superiority behind this kind of policy.

But the prototypical form of piracy has probably had its place in Southeast Asia long before the Europeans took over. It consisted for the most part of sea-going groups, sometimes numbering in the thousands and in the hundreds of craft, who traveled and marauded ships, coastal settlements, and even raided far inland up rivers.

This was a cultural adaptation, and fishing and trading were undoubtedly a part of the complex. Families lived on boats, headed by a male elder and several sons or in-laws.

Such fleets could hide among the many islets and bays, or escape inland among the many inlets and deltaic tributaries with which they were familiar. Groups that were displaced from their settlements may become "wandering pirates"—sort of sea gypsies.

The principle item of trade of such pirates were slaves, many of whom were inducted into the profession of piracy, and most of whom would be resold in another place on the slave market. They might capture slaves on one shore, and sell them on the opposite shore, or take them in the north and sell them in the south.

Princes kept harems of slaves, and concubines—some of who were recorded to have escaped from a Malay prince to seek safety among the Chinese of Singapore after having been tortured.

Chinese themselves have long been pirates on the Nanyang— capturing slaves from the coasts of Fukien province, attacking a Spanish settlement at Manila in 1570 under the leadership of

Limahon and even plundering ships in Singapore harbor in the 19th century.[84]

Malay pirates were more numerous. They attacked as far as the Gulf of Tonkin in the 8th Century, using poison arrows, throwing darts and slings.

Piracy was no small part of the prosperity of the Indianized states of Southeast Asia, relying as much on control of commerce as upon the exploitation of a sedentary agricultural substratum. We must consider piracy to have been an acceptable form of "primitive economics" in which relations of trading could easily alternate into raiding, competition, conflict and even periodic or perennial warfare.

In considering the Mandala states, we must look at the limitations of power yielded by princes who were as much "big men" of prowess as they were "chiefs" whose authority was legitimated by religion. In this we can see certain characteristic patterns that have been identified by Wolters (1982) as widely represented features of many parts of early Southeast Asia.

Comparative isolation of groups with strong local attachments, cognatic kinship, an indifference towards lineage descent, "and a preoccupation with the present that came from the need to identify in one's own generation those with abnormal spiritual qualities...(Wolters, 1982: pg. 4-9).

These characteristics combined to promote a "big Man" orientation upon "men of prowess" bringing with it the "possibility of mobilizing extended kinship ties within and outside the settlement or network of settlements."

---

[84] Charles Robequain, <u>Malaya, Indonesia, Borneo and the Philippines: A Geographical, Economic and Political description of Malaya, the East Indies and the Philippines</u>. London: Longman, Green and Co., Ltd., 1958.

Southeast Asian Sources

This orientation promoted characteristic regional attitudes towards common expectations for achievement in public life, a common means of gaining prestige.

Leaders regularly bestowed gifts and titles on those of merit. Many Southeast Asian languages came to reflect the differences between the aristocratic and the common people in marked dialectical forms.[85]

These overarching themata of proto-historical Southeast Asian civilization resulted in a map of concentrically radiating, overlapping "Mandalas" or "circles of kings" whose power would wax and wan like so many ripples upon a pond. Power, spiritually sanctioned, radiated in concentric rings of influence and prestige.

The prehistoric map of Southeast Asia evolved from a complicated network of many small settlements into a patchwork of overlapping "spheres of power." Boundaries existed only in the name and influence of the ruler and in the sense of security of the subjects, as "each ruler was acclaimed in his own country as one who had unique claim to "universal" sovereignty.[86]

---

[85] "...Public life would also be the stage for open competition for pre-eminence. Leaders and followers alike needed to validate their status by continuous achievement, and achievement often involved adventures into neighboring settlement areas...Finally, and very important in the extension of communications between networks of settlements, leaders in neighboring areas would recognize the higher spiritual status of a man of outstanding prowess and seek to regularize their relations with him by means of alliances that acknowledged the inequality of the parties. In this way more distant areas would be brought into a closer relationship with one another." (Wolters, 1982: pgs. 4-9)

[86] "...In each of these Mandalas, one king, identified with divine and "universal" authority, claimed personal hegemony over the other rulers in his mandala who were in theory his obedient allies and vassals..." (Wolters, 1982: pgs. 16-17.)

Mandalas were inherently unstable—expanding and contracting in influence in "concertina-like fashion." Chronic warfare or acculturative influence failed to define a stable structural center, while many princes competed for the title of ultimate sovereignty.[87]

Cultural diversity and regional variation led to a consistent pattern of localization or stylization of exogenous acculturative forms in endogenous meanings. Foreign symbols were adapted to local contexts and needs.[88]

The Southeast Asian crossroads created a shared "outward" and open orientation toward a "single ocean."[89]

The single ocean was "a vast zone of neutral water" that all states sought to mutually protect and exploit to maintain the freedom of the seas. It is not surprising then that one of the most important functions of Southeast Asian states was the control of piracy that flourished only upon the peripheries and interstices of Southeast Asian civilization. "The single ocean is a significant fact of Southeast Asian historical geography...." (Wolters, 1982: pg. 40.)

We must consider briefly the political ecology of the symbol as this has become representative of Southeast Asian civilization. The type of proto-historic state characteristic of Southeast Asia

---

[87] "The mandala perimeters continued to replicate court situations at the center. Centers of spiritual authority and political power shifted endlessly." (Wolters, 1982: 17).

[88] "Foreign materials had to be localized in different ways "before they could fit into various local complexes of religious, social and political systems and belong to new cultural "wholes." Only when this had happened would the fragments make sense in their new ambience, the same ambiences which allowed the rulers and their subjects to believe that their centers were unique." (Wolters, 1982: pg. 52).

[89] "The trading connections linked the opposite ends of maritime Asia resemble links in a chain which would join together again even if one link were temporarily broken..." (Wolters, 1982: pg. 39)

can be classified as a regal-ritual city-state in which central power and wealth was relatively limited and the monopoly of power tended to be decentralized across a feudal region of subsidiary areas and regents, kinsmen of the ruler, royal appointees with local power bases, or "autonomous self-made magnates."

Distances become an important function in the amount of autonomy of local rule and power may be reduplicated in kind or form at many levels throughout the state. The rural/urban dichotomy is not a qualitative difference but more quantitative in terms of "simply more wealthy, prestigious and powerful."

The political-religious roles of the urban residents provided a model of emulation for the countryside, and were the only means of solidarity in an otherwise weakly cohesive society. Leaders may come and go, but there must always be a contender. Corporate ideological links survive ties of actual power to be redefined in contexts of new people but the same tradition.

The chief inhabitants of the city are the members or associates, artisans, bureaucrats, retainer so the prince and his court. The court consists of family and kin, officials, advisors, servants, concubines and "others whose presence is solely a reflection of the ruler and his court." (Fox, 1977)

Such centers are parasitic consumers—economically dependent upon exploitation and taxation of the surrounding areas. A sumptuous court life provides a model, a style of life, embodied by a ceremonial complex reinforcing the status hierarchy. "The life-style is defined by the Calendric round of state rituals, kingly ceremonies, coronations, funerals, preparations for war, royal feasts, and divine sacrifices, rather than by individualism and secularism..."(Fox, 1977: pg. 54)

Symbolically, the function of the center is that of paramouncy over the surrounding area. Centralization depends heavily upon a shared ideology and emulation of the ruler's prestige. There exists ideological continuity between center and periphery and definition of symbolic forms and elements in the center will "influence the nature of settlement throughout the society" and will be approximated more-or-less throughout.

Design motifs, patterns of behavior, speech and symbols will be duplicated and become the basis of status determination at every level of the society. "Emulation of the attributes of the capital cities can continue down to the simplest village and homestead. In ancient Siam, for example, the village headman was lord of the village in a manner similar to the King who was lord of the state."

It follows that the most important function of the regal-ritual center and the court is to preserve, protect and reinforce its symbolic and ideological legitimacy. These states are referred to as "theater states" or "segmentary states" rather than merely feudal or tribal.

Segmentary states widely disperse power throughout various sub-units of organization. They rely heavily upon lineage or kin-based or even pseudo-familial paternalism for assuring solidarity.

They are theatre states because they highlight the symbolic function of legitimization by the ruler and his household, a function replicated through the levels of society, in lieu of real political cohesiveness.[90]

---

[90] "...Even if, in South-East Asia, the old dynasty is deposed, the new ruler who sits in the regal-ritual capital quickly becomes a hitherto unknown reincarnation of the divine. The symbolic aspects of rule thus continue even though the actual leadership of the state society changes. In state societies where centralized power is limited, the ideology of kinship or the divine nature of rule stabilizes the framework of political organization even if its personnel undergoes frequent changes through revolt and usurpation..." (Fox, 1977: pg. 21-22.)

Prostitutes, Pariahs, Presidents and Proletariats

It is in this context that we can infer an historical phase in the development of the "administrative mercantile" city-state in Southeast Asia, one that largely accompanied the extension of trading empires and the need for the protection and regulation of such commercial activity.

In this we can consider the affect of the intrusion of a global market oriented political economy which tended to everywhere upset the earlier, domestic based division of labor upon which society was founded. The tendency was to emphasize the basic difference between the countryside and the urban center.

In the third world, at least, it has resulted in the growth of "primate cities" characterized by huge slums of displaced proletarians.

It is in regard to these subsequent phases of the regional integration of Southeast Asian civilization that we can make reference to the rise into preeminence of four categories of people whose status-role identity were defined by the new relations established. These four types of people are prostitutes, pariahs, proletariats and presidents.

Prostitution. The status of women in Southeast Asia has everywhere been noted to be relatively high and equal to that of men, at least in traditional definitions. They are active agents and traders in many local markets, virtually monopolizing some sectors of commerce.

One common consequence of political-economic intrusion has been the de-emphasis and denigration of the domestic mode of production and hence the relegation of the role of women and their participation in the market economy to a second-class position. This is perhaps best represented in Southeast Asia by the rise of the widespread profession of "GI/tourist prostitution" that has accompanied the poverty of underdevelopment. This form of prostitution was greatest in Thailand, Vietnam and the Philippines.

Though prostitution has had a long history, and though all of these categories have had some precedence time immemorial in Southeast Asia, we must consider the economic place that this particular "profession" has had in a modern setting as a kind of marginal "service" economy and a form of "sexploitation" that has accompanied the lack of sexual repression and alienation upon which developmental organization and socialization has in part depended, and political economic asymmetries that result in such forms of exploitation.

Pariahs. Secondly, the role of pariahs in Southeast Asia is also been, in the colonial and post-colonial eras, a vital one in the political economic organization and mobilization of the entire region.

In this, Chinese merchant-middlemen, the "Asian Jewry," have figured prominently. They are necessary and efficient intermediaries in the long-distance networks that have established the regional integration. Their position as resident aliens is inherently ambiguous and ambivalent in society—often charged with exclusive, usurious and exploitative practices resulting from their superior social organization and money-handling skills, they have also been some of the main agents in the innovation, pioneering and development of Southeast Asia.

The British not only used them as a coolie labor force and a merchant-middleman sector, but also as bureaucratic officials who interceded from them in the daily business of colonial administration.

Pariah groups thus frequently serve the function in complex societies as one of intermediary between potentially hostile and asymmetric social groups, and thus as the convenient "scapegoats" for conflict and targeted aggression by both the elite and the masses.

Brian Foster writes of such an important intermediary role, in which the breakdown of "minority trading mechanisms provide large-scale, inter-group conflict which, in extreme cases, can take the form of genocide. Persecution of minorities who are active in commerce has been known for centuries."

Such pariah groups are in an inherently, structurally insecure position. They are symbolic targets for both the machinations of the elite who wish to focus blame upon some convenient out-group, and for the hatred, feelings of failure and insecurity of the masses that is born in the frustration of their own poverty, failings, false promises and exploitation. They come to embody, culturally and structurally, the contradictions and conflicts inherent in the integration of the region.

Political economic asymmetries can become the source of "exchange-generated conflict" characterized by a mode of "negative solidarity" and by the focal point of strategic relations/transactions negotiated in the market place.

In complex societies, trading specialists emerge who, along with political authorities and property owners, become major foci of conflicting relations, by which compensating effects of other cross-cutting conflicts may be diffused and their relative forces diffused. (B. L. Foster, 1978:pg.10)

There occurs special distancing mechanisms to regulate such conflict—jural mechanisms or ritual proscription regulating and limiting the range of interaction, displacement of conflict upon a third pariah party, and by spatial/social distancing between the parties of the negotiation who come together only in the marketplace.

Conflicting relations become focused on these trading out-groups, diminishing other possible conflict and further insulating different communal groups from maintaining potentially conflicting relations between one another. It also "helps relieve the trader from the expectations of fair dealing and generosity that the peasants have among themselves.

This change of expectations, as does the market place, constitutes a mechanism for displacement of the exchange-generated conflict by focusing some of the tension on inter-ethnic group relations rather than on the parties to an individual transaction. Such displacement helps explain the remarkable hostility often encountered by minority trading groups.

It also helps explain why traders who are the object of such hostility are not readily replaced by traders from the majority group: the latter are destroyed by the conflict inherent in their commercial activities or by the uneconomic behavior required of them if they are to avoid conflict." (Foster, 1978:pp. 14)

Proletarians. Proletarians can best and most simply be described as landless peasants who are destined to become the slum-dwelling poor of Southeast Asia's primate cities. They are, most important, a readily exploitable and cheap source of labor, and resources.

Witness the market in some countries for the selling of donor organs. They have high rates of crime, substance abuse, birth, infant mortality, malnutrition, and debt, and low rates of longevity, employment, literacy, education and opportunity.

They can be a volatile source of instability and fodder for cannons and machine guns. They are the most despised people on earth, and no one wants to be a part of them—they are the untouchable symbols of the failings of our system.

Southeast Asian Sources

Their youth becomes primary targets for recruitment to criminal organizations and for ideological thought-control in resocialization for Neo-Marxist revolutionary movements.

Presidents are, I maintain, another distinctive feature of the modern political economic order. They too are important national and cultural symbols—they too are inherently ambivalent and insecure. They are rational symbols of the rational, administrative order of the secular state too concerned with balancing budgets and taxes to be concerned with moral-religious precepts.

They are thus supremely middle class, suburban symbols whose only religion is the false consciousness of a new Nationalism. They stand for democracy, republicanism, equality, as well as for corruption, violence and stratification.

Their administrations come and go faster than the nations they control. They say a lot and accomplish little. Independent or puppets, they are all enmeshed inescapably in a web of political economic entanglements.

Pontianak and the Political Ecology of Human Possibility

Pontianak is a Malay story about a beautiful woman who comes out at night at lonely places. Usually she will say she is in trouble so men, and sometimes women will help her. Once she has them in her clutches she changes suddenly into an ugly monstrous woman and kills her victims by sucking their blood, if they do not die by fright. But if one manages to hammer a nail into the nape of her neck, then she will forever remain a beautiful woman, and never become a Pontianak any more.

One time, a young man managed to put a nail into the back of her neck, and they married and had a beautiful daughter. Many years passed and the daughter grew up. One day the daughter was combing her mother's hair, and said "Mother, there is something in the back of your neck."

Her mother told her to pull it out, and as soon as she pulled it out, that night following she transformed back into a Pontianak. She did not hurt her husband or her daughter, but ran off into the forest and was never seen again.

The political economy of a people cannot be merely described in terms of "modes of production" and social relations of production. The style of life a people pursue, and the values and interests with which they pursue it, and is critically rooted in and constrained by a wider social context in which the values, interests and styles of life of others must be taken into account in formulas and strategies for success.

In other words, the political economy by which a broad group or nation of peoples achieve social integration is accomplished by cultural means. The adaptability of Chinese immigrant society in Southeast Asia owes its success as much to the organizational ethos and practical strategies open to a group because of its shared cultural values and orientations, as it does to any notions of "innate" Chinese cunning or business acumen.

As sojourning merchant middlemen with extraordinary skills in merciless money handling and in business organization, the Chinese have been able to out compete practically any group they have come into relation, with the exception perhaps in many contexts of highly specialized and niched Indian minority groups.

In a similar vein we can speak of the cultural political economy of the Miao speaking peoples who have a considerable interest in the production of poppies in the highlands of Northern Southeast Asia. The world, it seems, must always be short of opium, and the Hmong must understand this very well.

Identity in the world becomes established as a function of our role-relations and place occupied within the world. Within each identity there is possibility for alternation and symbolic subjectification of meaning that relates the biography of personal experience to the larger streams of social and political history.

There is an inherent political-ecological relativity about such identity and of human possibility. We are what we are in relation to others who are what they are in relationship to ourselves.

This relationship is dynamic and is always defined in a context that has a sense of space and time, of a geographical history about it. We are actors cast upon a stage not of our own choosing, and however long or short our entrances or exits, we may have many parts to play.

VI: The "Circular Center Hypothesis"
Symbolic Ecology in Southeast Asian Civilization

Some symbolisms have such an enduring character that they transcend the vicissitudes of time and cultural change. Southeast Asian culture and civilization has always remained closely tied to its natural setting and environment, and this close, often dangerous and unpredictable relationship, is deeply embedded in the cultural symbolizations and symbolic themes recurrent throughout the region.

The conventional functionalist, materialist and ecological models of cultural-environmental adaptations are contraposed to a symbolic model that claims that cultures will draw directly from the symbolism in its environment and utilize these in social institutions, practices and relations.

The symbolic structure of its socio-cultural organization will thus be highly congruent with its local and trans-local settings. This congruence will extend to the regional character of its civilization in certain basic forms. An animistic Southeast Asian spirit complex that is rooted in a basic relationship to nature is held to be a common defining feature of Southeast Asian civilization.

A culture has a more direct relationship with nature than most cultural materialists and ecologists would want to admit. People draw readily and directly from nature's cornucopia the symbolisms that they employ in the organization and mobilization of their cultural resources. Totemic relationships did not end or become merely submerged beneath the rise of states.

We do not need to speculate upon the protein requirements of a tropical forest or the ecology of rice to understand the impact that the introduction of the cultivation of rice had upon Southeast

Southeast Asian Sources

Asian civilization—rice became a principle means, as well as metaphor, for health and success.

We do not need to observe evidence of ancient irrigation works to understand that the harnessing of rivers that brought life and death to peoples was a major source of symbolisms about death, fertility and the renewal of life.

This symbolisms and their function did not necessarily take effect only after the "techno-environmental foundations of irrigation" had already been laid—humans had thought about, realized and experienced the potentialities of the rivers long before they figured out how to go about building dikes and irrigation canals.

If anything, such symbolisms probably formed the necessary mental connections that paved the way for such invention. The invention of an artificial civilization, if anything, tended to sever the direct human symbolic connection with its natural world. In devising technologies to overcome the forces and harness the power of nature, we began creating mythologies in which this natural connection became reversed and subdued by a human embodied supernatural force.

Early Southeast Asian statecraft may have always relied upon the promotion of the sacred legitimacy of certain nature symbols as totems of state authority and power. The dragon, the phoenix, the Naga, and the crocodile, all were all recurrent totemic symbols of Southeast Asian peoples.

A functionalist perspective maintaining such symbols would serve a secondary legitimating institutions which serve to provide universal omnipotence and legitimacy, and which serve to annihilate "marginal" episodes or alternative sources which threaten the legitimacy of the center. A materialist orientation would maintain that these mechanisms are largely epiphenomenal and exist only as secondary feedback mechanisms rather than as "primary determinants" of social change.

A socio-structural perspective rooted in Durkheim holds such symbols as the sacred embodiment of the social order. While all of these functions of symbolism are undoubtedly important, the more direct socio-ecological function of symbolisms in mediating the relationship of people to their natural environment must be entertained.

Briefly, it can be said that symbolisms directly mediate the boundary between people and the social group, and their relationship with the natural world. Symbolisms serve to locate, mobilize and transform people within natural landscapes.

Symbols will also locate nature and the social body or state within the body. Symbols serve to express and to map the relations between the body and the primarily social, humanized world of nature, and then between the world and the cosmos.

In Southeast Asia, these symbols are primarily spatial and a-temporal in orientation. It is this same boundary-mediating mechanism which defines the ecological relationship, the relative equilibrium or imbalance of people within their world, that also defines human social relationship and identity with one another, and which thus serves to bridge the important gap between natural and historical patterns of adaptation and change.

Symbols are both religious and aesthetic, and have been a vital agency in the mobilization and organization of human actions and in providing direction for the development of human civilization.

Ethnographic evidence supports the belief that for the most part primitive man was both more environmentally aware as well as aesthetically sensitive to its natural environment than modern humankind, and that they had long ago worked out complex cycles and strategies that were rooted in the natural rhythms of their environmental settings.

<u>Southeast Asian Sources</u>

They knew which plants to eat, and which to avoid, which plants could cure and which could kill. They knew when to burn off the forest underbrush, and where to clear the forest for their new settlements.

They knew where they were in the forest, and which direction they wanted to go in. They had a time for peace and a time for war, and even instituted complex ritual and symbolic cycles to help signal and regulate the management of the environment.

It is in regard to the symbolic ecology of human adaptation in its natural world that various aspects of Southeast Asian civilization will be considered:

- The role of basic nature symbolism in Southeast Asian cultures and in Southeast Asian statecraft.
- The transformational and frequently destructive effect of Western acculturation in the symbolic alienation and redefinition of the basic social-environmental relationship that had been long worked out in Southeast Asian civilization.
- The rise of revitalization movements in response to Western contact.
- The symbolic ecological contradictions inherent to predominant nation-building policies of development in the modernization of Southeast Asia.

Finally, basic linkages between symbols and the environment is hypothesized, rooted in human nature that entails that similar symbolic forms and functions will be independently adopted by historically unrelated peoples, and that historical relationship will tend toward the convergence of such shared symbolism.

Furthermore, basic differences that are symbolically defined and ecologically rooted will tend to be positioned between peoples in a predictable and cross-culturally consistent fashion, and will lead to a predictable pattern of status-role identification and boundary-maintenance between peoples.

Thanatophidia and Symbolic Ecology

Humankind everywhere has had a fascination with snakes. Primates are claimed to have an instinctive fear of snakes, and some have specific calls for snakes.

Human fear and horror towards snakes is certainly widespread, if not universal, although many mythological traditions exist that claim great snakes as benefactors, as creators of the land, and as symbols of good and fertility.

The myth of the Serpent in the Garden of Eden is certainly very ancient and probably has its origin in the Gilgamesh era during early Mesopotamian and Sea of Sunrise civilization. Snake skeletons were found buried in pottery jars with pearls, and sometimes other precious stones, in *Dilmun*.[91]

It is perhaps fitting in this regard that the beautiful queen Cleopatra should end her life by being bitten in the breast by an adder. The latter Christian mythology that associates the snake with wisdom, death, and the devil and evil, is clearly an elaboration rooted in the earlier Gilgamesh epic, which in turn was probably based upon every earlier myth.

---

[91] Bibby, in his <u>Looking For Dilmun</u> (1970), describes the discovery of pots at the level contemporaneous with the temple circa 2000 BC, in which they had found, "coiled up at the bottom, the skeletons of snakes." "...In over half the bowls there was found in addition, loose among the coiled snake-bones, a single bead, in most cases a tiny turquoise...Beyond a doubt we have here clear proof that the legend of Gilgamesh was still a living and integral part of the religion of Bahrain at the time when the palace was built and inhabited. We have since found many more of these snake-burials, beneath the floors of other rooms, and their total must be well up into the forties." (Bibby, 1970: pg. 164-5.)

<u>Southeast Asian Sources</u>

We can find mythology, folklore, superstition, magic and religious ritual associated with the snake in practically every major region on earth. In Europe there were Cretan and Danish snake goddesses, Medusa of Greek mythology, the Caduceus, the medieval Danish tradition of burying an adder beneath the threshold to keep out evil spirits.

The European-style Dragon is clearly a snake-like creature that hoards treasure and steals young maidens. In Indigenous North America the Indians of the Pueblos had a rattlesnake cult-ritual in which costumed men danced and carried the rattlesnake that was captured, and latter returned, to the wild. Similar snake rituals have been reported in Meso-America and in South America.

In contemporary North America there is a snake-handling cult of Southern White Anabaptists who believe that the handling of venomous, feral snakes is a gift from God, and who also practice trance, eating of fire, and drinking of strychnine.

In the American Southwest there are annual rattlesnake roundups where rattlesnake dens are raided, the snakes killed and dressed and sold for meat, and the skins, heads and tails are also sold as tourist trinkets. From the crowd that these roundups draw, one must wonder about the symbolic character of the great interest and energy people put into this activity.

In India, the snake has a different mythological tradition. A Great python is held to have created the land, and is held as a great benefactor. The snake is therefore more positively associated with fertility and annual renewal than in the more Occidental tradition.

The lingum itself an eti-phallic symbol, is associated with the raised head of the hooded cobra. It is no wonder that a resident cobra is considered a sign of good luck for an Indian villager, that snake charmers abound and form their own caste in India. In Sri

Lanka the albino cobra is considered a sacred creature and is the object of many pilgrimages.

In East Asia, among other things, the snake is considered as an aphrodisiac and thus as a source of renewable fertility.

In Okinawa, once rife with the "Habu" snake (tree viper) until the introduction of the mongoose, it is still possible to buy Saki fermented with snakes as an aphrodisiac and as a rejuvenator of life.

It is in Southeast Asia that we might expect, and find, well developed mythology and cultural practices associated with the snake, for snake fauna in this region is perhaps some of the most diverse, representing most of the major genera and all of the forms of venomous snakes, and in which human contact and consociation with the snake is the closest.

It is the region with by far the highest number of annual snakebite deaths in the world. And this close association between humans and snakes can be taken as a direct measure of the extent to which nature intrudes upon and surrounds human life and cultural adaptation in the region.

Thus the overseas Chinese and Thai people of Bangkok regularly eat snake flesh and drink snake blood, sometimes sucking it directly from the snake, as a source of strength and sexual potency. This market has been so thriving that locally it is serving to upset the ecological balance of the snake fauna—leading to an increase in rats, the main prey package of snakes, and to the lose of grain.

In Burma, tribal women capture a king cobra and train it as a dancing partner. During their dance they will kiss the raised snout of the cobra, before releasing it back into the wild. King Cobras, natural culture fleers will during courtship in the wild do a kind of mating dance.

<u>Southeast Asian Sources</u>

The snake-temple in Penang, Malaysia, is world renowned for its lithe green tree adders that are very venomous. The snakes were said to have come of their own to the temple after it was constructed, and this was considered to be a propitious sign.

The number of snakes has dwindled there over the years, and now the temple is not as popular a tourist attraction as it once was. Presumably, the snakes have stopped coming on their own to the temple, and the local care-taker/photographer must go out and find fresh snakes.

The "Thanatophidia hypothesis" holds that the symbolic and ecological relationship between humankind and snakes, as well as other natural forms, are interconnected.

It is this common relationship which lies at the core of so many common themes of mythology, religion and folklore, and which can be counted as thematic convergences about a central symbolic complex that does not have to be explained in historical terms of diffusion or common origin.

We might refer the "Thanatophidia hypothesis" as a concept of the symbolic unity of human experience and culture that is rooted in common thematic relationships with the natural environment.

While certain specific thematic motifs, such as the story of Gilgamesh, are likely candidates for diffusion and elaboration, symbolic complexes as a whole that are thematically recurrent do not need to be explained in terms of a common historical connection, but can be used instead as a basis for cross-cultural comparison.

Snakes and serpents as symbols are clearly common, even panhuman motifs. As such, the symbolic associations are inherently ambivalent and ambiguous—they may simultaneously be symbols of death, fear, and evil as well as of fertility, rebirth, strength, and benevolence.

A part of the "Thanatophidia hypothesis" is that such symbolisms and their thematic complexes are what might be called marginal symbols that have the common thematic characteristics of dealing with marginal experiences.

Death, alienation, asymmetry and separation, of being universalistic and cosmological in orientation in providing a sense of unity of experience and in serving to orient or locate such experience in space and time, they are organic in being based upon natural forms, and of being dialectically synthetic and syncretic.

We may only speculate upon the connections of such symbolism in the depths of the human psyche. They are basic and prototypical and thus might be counted as collective archetypes of the panhuman symbolization of experience.

As marginal symbols, they serve a totemic function reinforcing the normal boundaries of cognitive and normative experience that are rooted in human social relations and human relations with the environment.

They serve to annihilate and to reincorporate the marginal experience, and shape and modify our expectations of such experiences. Because of their inherent ambivalence, they serve to embody and represent the very existential contradictions of the historicity of our constructions of reality, and thus by their reification serve to cover over the facticity and objectivity of our constructions.

As marginal symbols, they can be thought of also as boundary symbols which define and demarcate the normal bounds of experience from the marginal, and which help to shape and give substance to our expectations of marginal experiences (desymbolization, deculturation, and marginalization), events (death, violence, disaster) and episodes (war, Acts of God, etc.).

<u>Southeast Asian Sources</u>

It is small wonder that they come to express basic divisions such as male and female, life and death, good and evil, and that they often serve as emblematic representations of group identity.

Their functional capacity and versatility is derived from several aspects of their design:

- Their basicness and rootedness to natural motifs and themes.
- Their capacity for the "incorporation of contradiction" and the resolution of opposites by embodying as a single, substantively real referent those dialectical differences which otherwise threaten or undermine the identity and unity of experience.
- Their symbolic structure in which open-ended symbolic chains and complexes are built up on the basis of loose associations.
- Their transferability and flexibility in being adapted to a range of alternative experiences and reinterpreted to fit changing circumstances.

   And

- Their capacity for accreting new symbolic forms and associations, or for accreting to other symbolisms.

The question to be answered is the conservatism of such symbolisms, their potential for being carried and diffused across space in some basic form, and how we might readily identify an old from a new form, or a primitive versus a derived form or an original versus borrowed form.

Certainly, the connection of the snake with the Gilgamesh epic underlying western mythology and religious cosmology is a very old one, but one which probably would not have been guessed had not the tablets been discovered in which the epics had been inscribed. There seems to be no straightforward way of showing a common thematic origin to stories which have a similar thematic structure or that employ similar forms of symbolisms.

Finally, it must be emphasized that thematic aspects of design can be borrowed as ideas as readily as the actual symbolic elements themselves as the forms in which the ideas take shape.

Thematic design expresses recurrent patterns of ordered relation between elements that has some form of intentional, symbolic significance that is beyond the significances of the individual components. It is possible that themes may remain pretty much the same, while the elements that compose the design have been replaced.

Vietnamese Nature Mythoi

In Vietnamese Mythology, the snake, the crocodile, and the dragon are all closely associated symbolisms that seem to have an inherently ambivalent nature.

They are both creatures of the land and the sea, and are thus both symbolic of death and life, male and female, yin and yang. While the dragon is clearly a patriarchal symbol of Kingship and authority, in Vietnamese mythology, Kings and men regularly transformed into snakes that dove into the sea.

In *Feng Shui*, of geomancy, the Mountains are the backs of dragons and the streams the concourses of their movement. Supernatural power is held to originate in the highlands of Tibet and flow through dragon's veins along the mountain ranges, branching out and carrying spiritual energy to all corners of the earth. This energy of the earth collects in certain propitious, and inherently dangerous, locations.

In Vietnamese folklore, "*Long do*" or "Dragon's belly" is the geographical and spiritual center of the Vietnamese realm, and it represented the political center of gravity and stability—in the

197

location of Hanoi—and the Emperors in a special spirit cult elaborated this powerful geographic position.

"Coiled Dragon" was the god of the earth that the Vietnamese Kings who sought to maintain control over the heartland worshiped, and that subsequently became the national symbol of the Vietnamese.

It must be understood that the Dragon-Man-Snake motif is clearly associated with the water, a female element. Snakes in Vietnamese mythology are the Water King's children "and announce floods and deluges to come" and are associated with magical amulets and talismans.

Lac Long Quan, the dragon king and original father of the Vietnamese, made his home in the sea. The renewed fertility of the sea is unsurprisingly associated with female fertility—and with the power of both giving and taking life.

Thus water symbolism associated with snakes is, in this tradition, symbolisms of darkness and death as well as rebirth. The water kingdom is an important netherworld in Vietnamese mythology associated with fertility, death and the female-principle of *am*, or darkness. In popular folklore, it is often confused with Hell.

The way to the underworld and to hell is often through the Water Kingdom—the great womb of Vietnamese mythology from which many of its culture heroes issue with their mandate to rule. In Vietnamese mythology, the tortoise and the lotus are two symbols that are clearly associated with the female, fertility and the water element.

The tortoise is a symbol of longevity and perfection that is "usually found with a coral branch in its mouth and a crane on its back."

The crane usually has a lotus in its mouth—a Buddhist symbolism of the female principle—the "most popular flower in Vietnam" standing for femininity, sexuality and grace.

The lotus was associated with the florescence of Buddhism in Vietnam that was linked to the art of rainmaking, and Buddha spirit cults of "clouds, rain, thunder and lightening" as well as the worship of trees and aquatic powers.

Buddhism became a widespread religion among the common Vietnamese as "a new method of controlling the vagaries of nature in the interests of agriculture"

The moon is another female symbol associated with beauty and fertility, and that is understandably implicated in the calendric rites associated with the lunar calendar that is so important in the timing of seasons, tides and fishing. (Taylor, 1983:p. 83) Many village temples were dedicated to Buddhist spirits of agricultural fertility.

Water is also associated with death. For Vietnamese, drowning is a particular horrible form of death, associated with errant and wandering ghosts. There are a host of water spirits possessing ambivalent forms of power—"some are inherently wicked, and some occasionally wicked, and others capricious or benevolent."

The Water Goddess, or *Ba Thuy* is associated with "*Noi*" or "an irresistible urge to plunge one's face into water." "It is not surprising that many legendary culture heroes and fallen kings killed themselves by drowning. The *T'rung* Sisters, or Rain maidens, drown themselves in the *Hat-Giang* River after their defeat. Lady *Trieu* rode her elephant into the sea."

The *Thuch* family overthrew the last king of the old dynasty who threw himself into a well, and *Thuc Phan* himself, subsequently defeated by the Chinese, 'walked into the ocean' while his son also jumped into a well. The last of the Tran rulers, *Buy Khoach*,

jumped into the sea from a boat that took him to China etc."
(Buttinger, 1959: pg.113.)

Many Vietnamese culture heroes and heroines alike returned to
the watery realm in apotheosis, from which their mandate
originally derived.

The "Man-Dragon-Mountain-Water" thematic motif provides
evidence of "symbol chains" that are found on the early *Dong
S'ong* bronze drums.

Apparently these drums were power and status symbols of
aboriginal chiefs among the *Yueh* tribes throughout Southern
China—their distribution covered an area embracing many of the
sub-cultures of the region, and their symbolic function was
closely associated with government, rain-making, fertility rituals,
decision-making, justice and war.

Frog motifs and a "water-chain" are associated with water
animals, the dragon, frogs and fish, and bronze boats. Another
motif is that of the ship of the dead, associated with drowning,
drowning sacrifices and female shamans.

Finally, it is worthwhile to consider the extent to which nature
symbolisms are found in the poetry and the Vietnamese language.
Early erotic poetry contains a great many references to nature.

The character of the Vietnamese is closely connected to an
almost romantic love of nature. The Vietnamese language lends
itself, in its tonality and homophonous resonances, to double
punning and word play, as well as to a musical quality of speech
that can frequently, when the mood is right, erupt into melodious
singing.

Balinese Character and Culture

Bateson (1972) described the Balinese as being in a "steady state" in which equilibrium and the balance of the middle ground is valued over extremes. It is said that the Balinese desire a continuing "plateau" of intensity in interactions than the attainment of climactic junctures.

This lack of climax is notable in its music, in its art, in trance, in quarrels. Competition and direct conflict are thus avoided, and, under these circumstances, hierarchy is rigid.

Bateson notes several points regarding Balinese ethos: they are a culture of plenty:

- They are penny-wise but pound-foolish.
- They are very dependent upon spatial orientation.
- They value activity for itself, aesthetically, than as goal-oriented or purposive.
- There is evident enjoyment of doing things in large crowds.
- Many Balinese actions are accounted for sociologically rather than psychologically in terms of individual goals or values.
- Culturally correct actions are acceptable and aesthetically valued, permissible actions are regarded with neutrality, and inappropriate actions are deprecated.
- Postural balance and coordination are highly valued for their correctness of form, such that there is fear of loss of support, there is preoccupation with elevation as a means of asymmetrical support, there is a preoccupation with problems of balance.

Southeast Asian Sources

In comparing Balinese culture with Von Neumann games, he considers it the primary problem of the Balinese to maintain a complex steady state of the cumulative factors of the system.[92]

Bateson searches for the self-correcting mechanism that underlies this "non-schismogenic system" and finds it in the balance of opposite poles of turbulence and serenity as is evident in the style of Balinese artwork.[93]

Clifford Geertz has written about the cultural preoccupation and pervasiveness of cockfighting in Bali, and refers to the "migration of the Balinese status hierarchy into the body of the cockfight."[94]

"Along with everything else that the Balinese see in fighting cocks—themselves, their social order, abstract hatred, masculinity, demonic power—they also see the archetype of status virtue, the arrogant, resolute, honor-mad player with real fire, the ksatria prince." (Geertz, 1973: pg. 442)

The cockfights help to render everyday experience more comprehensible in its presentation in forms that are not "really real" but in which forms the basic themes of such experience have been raised to a level where they can be more powerfully

---

[92] "In sum it seems that the Balinese extend to human relationships attitudes based upon bodily balance, and that they generalize the idea that motion is essential to balance." (Bateson, 1972: pg. 125)

[93] "...The unity and integration of this picture assert that neither of these contrasting poles can be chosen to the exclusion of the other, because the poles are mutually dependent. This profound and general truth is simultaneously asserted for the fields of sex, social organization and death."(Bateson, 1972: pg. 152)

[94] Clifford Geertz "Deep Play: Notes on a Balinese Cockfight" in The Interpretation of Cultures: pg. 436. He refers to cockfight as the symbolic reenactment of the "status bloodbath" of the participants' social matrix. It is fundamentally "a dramatization of status concerns." (Geertz, 1973: pg. 437)

articulated. It is a construction, a medium of expression of these basic themes.

The aggression of the fight is a reversal of the normal experience of the reticent Balinese—while it shares as a focused microcosm a characteristic of ordinary Balinese life, the "lack of temporal directionality.""...Their life, as they arrange and perceive it, is less a flow, a directional movement out of the past, through the present, toward the future than an on-off pulsation of meaning and vacuity...(Geertz; 1973: pg. 446).

For Geertz, the Balinese cockfight does not reinforce the status quo of the Balinese system, so much as it is a cultural text, a meta-social dialogue in which fighting cocks are connected to status—and it effects a transfer of emotions, perception and value from the former onto the latter. Culture is an ensemble of such texts.

In another important text by Geertz which describes Balinese worldview, he lays out a theory of culture and its integration as "significant symbols, clusters of significant symbols, and clusters of clusters of significant symbols—the material vehicles of perception, emotion, and understanding—and the statement of the underlying regularities of human experience implicit in their formation."

He refers to this symbol system as "more variable, less tightly coherent, but nonetheless ordered 'octopoid' systems of them, confluences of partial integrations, partial incongruences and partial independencies." (Geertz, 1973: pg. 66)

He sees Balinese culture as rooted in a tightly integrated system of person perception and identity, conduct and propriety, and conceptions of time. He refers to the ceremonial formalization of interpersonal relations—the contemporizing of relations and identities in shared time but not shared space, to the "stage fright" that accompanies shame, and to the "absence of climax" found in social life and action, as the three main characteristics of Balinese culture.[95]

Other analysis of Balinese culture and character have yield similar interesting aspects which point to the symbolic spatialization of the culture—the geographical orientation of the Balinese about the central mountain *Gunung Agung* and the sense of confusion that results from disorientation in relation to the mountain. The Balinese, for instance, are a rather extreme example of a people whose orientation is spatial.[96]

The phenomenological aspects of Balinese experience, especially in ceremonialism, trance and the religious symbolism, describe a cultural orientation that is well adapted and integrated to its island homeland.

J. Stephen Lansing describes the Water Temple system of Bali that had been used traditionally to regulate the irrigation system of the island according to the agricultural calendar. This system had eluded Dutch interests, who had established their own separate system of regulation, and its elucidation has figured importantly in the debate between Geertz's argument for the

---

[95] "What binds Balinese symbolic structures for defining persons (names, kin terms, teknonyms, titles, etc.) to their symbolic structures for characterizing time (permutational calendars, etc.), and both of these to their symbolic structures for ordering interpersonal behavior (art, ritual, politesse, etc.), is the interaction of the effects each of these structures has upon the perceptions of those who use them, the way in which their experiential impacts play into and reinforce one another." Clifford Geertz <u>Person, Time, and Conduct in Bali: An Essay in Cultural Analysis</u>, Cultural Report Series No. 14: Southeast Asian Studies, Yale University, 1966: pg. 65-66.

[96] . Errington, Shelly <u>Meaning and Power in a Southeast Asian Realm</u>, Princeton, New Jersey: Princeton University Press 1989: p. 65.)

peasant regulation of the irrigation, or for the Wittfogelian hydraulic theory of a despotic centralization.[97]

The temple system is enmeshed in a wider temple system, and, like these is hierarchically stratified such that the chief Temple of the Crater Lake devoted to the water goddess that spiritually regulates with holy water the water that flows through the irrigation network. "The entire mandala of the lake forms the center of a much larger mandala, consisting of the island of Bali and the seas that surround it."[98]

In this regard, he considers Marxian theory, retaining its relationships between nature, society and history while transposing its levels of analysis to the symbolic system and its constitutive role, of the humanizing of nature as the mapping onto the physical geography and cosmos of the social order, as civilization transforms the landscape it occupies with each succeeding generation and the new generation come to regard the transformed, manmade, reified landscape, as if the embodiment of society.

The images of society that the Balinese see in their terraced landscape do not reflect the progressive linear order that Marx and Hegel understood as "history." Instead, for the Balinese nonlinear patterns of temporal order emerge from the regular progression of natural cycles, the seasons of growth and change.

When Balinese society sees its self as reflected in a humanized nature, a natural world transformed by the efforts of previous

---

[97] Karl Wittfogel, Oriental Despotism: Comparative Studies in Total Power, Yale University Press, 1957.
[98] "The 'flow' of holy water from temple to temple establishes hierarchical relations between temples. Thus water temples define the institutional structure—the hierarchy of productive units—that manages the rice terraces as a productive system." (Lansing, 1991: pg. 128)

generations, it sees a pattern of interlocking cycles that mimic these cycles of nature. Whereas Marx looked at nature and saw evolutionary progress, a Balinese farmer may look at nature and see the intricate patterns of the *tika* calendar or hear the interlocking cyclical melodies of a gamelan orchestra. (Lansing: pg. 133.)

It is evident from these illustrations of Balinese culture and character that in many aspects it can be considered prototypical of the degree of symbolic-ecological integration and adaptation of Southeast Asian civilization to its local and regional environments.

Symbol systems have a direct part played in the constructive articulation of the social forces of history, in the dynamics that have brought about historical and social change. Such systems can be both conservative and adaptive at the same time.

Animism and Syncretism

It is worthwhile to consider in this regard a more basic cultural substratum that is widely held to be characteristic of Southeast Asian civilization. This is the common and pervasive spiritual animism and animistic ethos that underlies even Islam, Christianity and Buddhism.

It can be called the Dionysian id of the Southeast Asian, over which is laid the Apollonian superego of one or another of the Great Religions traditions. Because animistic beliefs are held to represent the projection of impure beliefs, while beliefs of the later religions are associated with pure ideals, the later are much more powerful in commanding social veneration, such that the dialectic between the Great Tradition and local spirit cult is always asymmetrical, with the local animistic beliefs always yielding ground before the Grand traditions.

There are several basic traits that can be expected with this animistic complex:

1. The belief in a supernatural spirit world which interpenetrates the natural order such that a pantheon spirit beings, ghosts, local deities and spirit-familiars may inhabit local sites.

2. The use of a shaman who may go into trance or spirit possession.

3. The use of magic amulets, potions, poisons to affect human beings in certain ways.

4. A belief in the supernatural power that suffuses the natural world and which may come to reside differentially in powerful human beings.

5. The use of ritual ceremonies in affecting cures, purification, fortune telling.

It can be argued that this kind of animistic complex is to be found wherever a traditional non-hierarchical style of society is found. This is true, but the particular combination and style of this complex is uniquely Southeast Asian.

Take for example the widespread practice of the ritual bath in Southeast Asian animism. Water is held to be the boundary weakener that allows passage between states of being.[99]

---

[99] "Power exists, independent of its possible users...In Javanese traditional thinking there is no sharp division between organic and inorganic matter, for everything is sustained by the same invisible power. This conception of the entire cosmos being suffused by a formless, constantly creative energy provides the basic link between the 'animism' of the Javanese villages and the high metaphysical pantheism

<u>Southeast Asian Sources</u>

It is the manner in which this animistic complex has intermeshed itself into the mythos, ethos and pathos of Southeast Asian civilization, and how it has come into a dialectical tension with the organized religions in the areas with which it is associated.

Even modern secularism has not gone unaltered by its contact with this spirit animism. The key quality of this complex seems to be in its encompassing and syncretic character, in its capacity to absorb new symbolisms and to coexist with contradiction, and to adapt itself to a wide range of situations and alternative interpretation.

Melford Spiro, in his ethnographic analysis of Burmese supernaturalism, emphasizes the expressive, affective, instrumental and mechanical aspects of animistic beliefs, which he contrasts with the repressive and meditative aspects of Buddhism.[100]

When viewed as ideal types, Spiro contrasted Buddhism and animism in terms of the moral, ascetic, rational, serene personality and otherworldly social orientation of the former, against the amoral, libertarian, non-rational, turbulent personality and worldly social orientation of the later. (Ibid.: pg. 258.)

---

of the urban centers." (Benedict Anderson "The Idea of Power in Javanese Culture." In <u>Culture and Politics in Indonesia</u> edited by Clare Holt Benedict Anderson, and James Siegel 1972: pgs. 1-69; p. 7)
[100] The two systems are complementary—"Using Buddhist means, they pursue *nat* like, non-Buddhist ends; cathecting Buddhist goals, they attempt to achieve them by nat like, non-Buddhist means. In short, between the polar extremes of animism and Buddhism, we see a continuum of beliefs and practices which show attributes of both systems." (Melford Spiro <u>Burmese Supernaturalism: A Study in the Explanation and Reduction of Suffering</u>, Englewood Cliffs, N.J.: Prentice-Hall, Inc. 1967: pg. 270-1.)

Whereas Buddhists seek wisdom and enlightenment, animists seek the possession of power. This basic conflict is the source of an inner ambivalence of Burmese towards animism.

The animism that is common to Southeast Asia may be accountable for the remarkable religious and symbolic syncretism that has characterized many religious revitalization movements in Southeast Asia. Cao Daoism and the *Hoa Hao* movement in Vietnam were well known examples of such syncretism

Hue-Tam Ho Tai's study of the "*Buu Son Ky Huong*" (Strange Fragrance from the Precious Mountain) sect which flourished in South Vietnam since its pre-colonial founding on the very frontiers of Vietnam along its border with Cambodia, is a fitting example of such syncretism combining animism with elements from several religions, that was almost unknown outside of South Vietnam.

The prophet named *Doan Minh Huyen*, or "Buddha Master of Western Peace," began his movement during a great cholera epidemic in 1849 which claimed half a million lives. He practiced shamanistic curing in which he was said to be particularly effective against madness, and legend holds that he soon attracted a large number of pilgrims seeking cure, such that his credibility as a Buddha master grew.

He preached salvation and apocalypse, and provided a powerful spiritual motivation for the early pioneers. This religious tradition, characteristic of South Vietnam, was rooted in the Sino-Vietnamese folk religion.

The contrast between the temple priest in the articulation and mediation of the authority of the state and the interest of the populace, and the shamanistic prophet in being the divine voice, or the direct incarnation of the divine, and the healer and revitalizer of the populace, is a basic, recurrent theme throughout the world

<u>Southeast Asian Sources</u>

According to the study by Susan Ackerman and Raymond Lee of religious movements in modern Malaysia, animism was the only truly indigenous religion of Southeast Asia. (Susan E. Ackerman and Raymond L. M. Lee <u>Heaven in Transition: Non-Muslim Religious Innovation and Ethnic Identity in Malaysia.</u> Honolulu, Hawaii: University of Hawaii Press, 1988)

Subsequent introduction of different religions created a competition among a number of alternatives. Secularization meant a detachment of political involvement in religion, a greater degree of choice in the selection of religion, and an individual atomization of religion as a personal affair.

Such secularization, particularly prominent in urban areas, has brought with it greater experimentation. The presence of a number of alternative religions sets up a relational field between them that define, at various levels of mutual compatibility and incompatibility, define the ways and degrees to which such religions can coexist or become integrated.

The "Circular-Center Hypothesis"

Symbols, and the systems they construct, have played an important part in Southeast Asian Civilization and its scholarship. Symbols mediate the boundaries of identity between person, place, experience, the social world, and the supernatural cosmos.

In Southeast Asia, such symbolizations are commonly "spatial" in organization, and time is conceived as circular. Power which symbols contain, which pass through symbols, becomes centered in local places, and levels of power are concentric rings from the center.

Such centers exist in the thoughts, in the being and body of the individual, in the home, in the public realm, in the state and the nation, and in the world and universe.

In regard to this Southeast Asian spatialization of symbols, several points can be made:

1. Symbols come to express and contain a spiritual energy invests the universe and can come to reside in certain places, persons or things which are centers of power.

2. Symbols as spatial metaphors of place mediate the boundary between the body and person hood and the state and social body, such that the state becomes embodied in the person, and state becomes the embodiment of the person.

3. Symbols as spatial metaphors of centers mediate the boundary between the state and the cosmos, such that the humanized natural world becomes the mapping of the supernatural world and the supernatural world becomes the projection of the state.

4. Symbols also spatially mediate the boundary between the individual, his/her body and person hood, and the cosmos, such that they orient and locate the individual spiritually in the cosmos and spiritually map the cosmos in the individual.

5. Symbols form multiple overlapping "network hierarchies" of relations that serve to locate power differentially and dynamically in people, places, social relations and the cosmos.

6. Symbols serve an anti-structural mediating function which allows for the manipulation of power relationships which are otherwise uncontrollable and can be expected to be emphasized or exaggerated when power relationships are inherently, structurally ambiguous.

7. Symbols come to coalesce into chains and complexes, which define topographically uneven regions of a shared, social "symbol scape" that form the multiple network-

hierarchies. In these complexes we can recognize core and dominant symbols, distinguished from peripheral and antithetical symbols. We can distinguish as well between "basic" symbols and "elaborated" symbols.

8. Symbolic complexes provide for mediation of many marginalizing experiences and protects unconsciously from the ever-present possibility and uncertainty of such marginalization, both for individual psychology and for group social psychology.

Magic and Animistic religious beliefs were originally held by Western observers to be chaotic. Subsequently scholars have taken notice of an underlying order of such symbol systems, the parallelism between "micro-cosmos" and "macro-cosmos."[101]

This parallelism between the state and the Cosmos also occurs between the macrocosm of the universe and microcosm of the person, as well as between the macro-cosmos of the state and the microcosm of the person.

Symbolism mediates the relationships between spirit and matter, and their ritual manipulation as "receptacles of spirit" is a means of manipulating and regulating these boundaries. The manipulation and management of symbols through religious ritual and magic, is a form of power, or a "playing with power" that is supernatural.

---

[101] "...According to this belief humanity is constantly under the influence of forces emanating from the directions of the compass and from stars and planets... Harmony between the empire and the universe is achieved by organizing the former as an image of the latter, as a universe on a smaller scale." (Robert Heine-Geldern; Conceptions of State and Kingship in Southeast Asia Southeast Asia Program, Ithaca, New York 1958: pg. 1.)

Clive Kessler notes a similar parallelism between "the body personal and the body politic" that is evident in the ritual performances of the Malay bomoh.[102]

According to Kesseler, this parallelism is not simply a dualism, but a parallelism between the body, the state and the cosmos, and in this matter the state is the political embodiment and mediator of the power.[103]

And if the social body constrains how we define the human body, as Mary Douglas would have it, it might also happen that the human body may become the metaphor for the state. The political idioms shared by a variety of symbolic complexes become the fundamental organizing idea or design of a culture.

To what extent do symbolic complexes, as partially integrated networks in the patterning of culture, overlap or are congruent with the ecological patterns of adaptation, as well as the historical patterns of borrowing and alteration.

For instance, if we compare two cultures known to be historically related, that nonetheless diverged in different environments, would we be able on the basis of their comparison to select those aspects of symbolic complexes that remain basically unchanged.

---

[102] —"...The body is a realm, at once unitary and multiplex. Its various components are ideally coordinated and integrated, subordinated to a governing center, the palace of personality, and the head. Since this conception of the body as a realm is not merely abstract and static, it permits illness or disorder within the person to be presented in political terms." (Clive Kesseler "Conflict and Sovereignty in Kelantanese Malay Spirit Séances" in Case Studies in Spirit Possession, edited by Vincent Crapanzano and Vivian: pg. 319)

[103] "Hence, mediating between person and cosmos, the state, in its concretized conceptual form as the _balai_, provides the appropriately potent instrument or receptacle...for ritually manipulating and transferring powerful, and therefore potentially dangerous, spiritual essences." (ibid., 1958; pg. 321.)

Southeast Asian Sources

Alternatively, if we compare cultures that are known not to be related but which seem to share similar kinds of environments, or cultures which are distantly related and which share similar kinds of environments, though they presumably have never been in contact, would we find convergent symbolic systems. [104]

There are different analytical levels of complexes of meaning—the more primary the complex in which concrete individual phenomena are given a place, the more available it is to our senses and our understandings and the less equivocal in interpretation.

But the more the complexity of meaning is removed in terms of its inferable connotations, the more it will depend upon its appropriate placement within a systemic framework, such that lower order complexes become subsumed within higher order complexes.

Symbols also have ecology about them, about their use and their meaning, one that was well described, if in somewhat overly functionalistic terms, by Roy Rappaport. (Pigs For the Ancestors, Yale University Press, 1968)

The connection between symbols and the human world does not need to depend upon a functionalist, materialist or ecologist account. Symbols are "direct metaphors" of experience which allow both perceptive disembodiment of the experience through the symbols incorporation and representation of that experience.

---

[104] As J. S. van Leur quotes in full the working method of Werner Sombart in culture history as it applies to economic history (J. C. van Leur, Indonesian Trade and Society: Essays in Asian Social and Economic History, The Hague, Bandung: W. van Hoeve, Ltd. 1955: pp. 42-3), there is no reason that such a method could not be applied as well to other topical aspects of cultural symbolism.

It is therefore no great surprise that symbols should be widely employed by human beings to for the expression of relationships and significances which are either not directly available to experience, or for one reason for another, must be repressed from experience. Among all other things, symbols can stand for other symbols as well as for themselves—because they may mean so many different things, they may mean no one thing at all.[105]

Thus agricultural ritual becomes an integral component of the technology of farming, which in turn becomes an intrinsically "social" as well as technical productive process.[106]

A common theme shared by symbolism in Southeast Asian civilization is the belief that all beings are hierarchically ranked according to relative proximity to the sacred. The higher one's rank, the more sacred power one possessed in one's being and one's place.

Status was legitimized by one's sacred power and rank. Because of this rank, higher status people were regarded as more efficacious channels in tapping spiritual and supernatural powers, which could be distributed to the followers. This belief therefore

---

[105] Georges Condominas has built upon the notion of the symbolic significance of production, or work, in social life, and the use of symbol systems in the regulation and expressive reiteration of the value of such production. (George Condominas, We Have Eaten the Forest: The Story of a Montagnard Village in the Central Highlands of Vietnam. New York: Hill and Wang, Inc., 1977.)

[106] "...It is a meaningful series of interactions between social groups and the natural world. The field rituals that accompany each stage of agricultural labor form a kind of commentary on the productive process...Moreover, the rituals of work in the fields may be 'performative,' in that they call forth particular social groups to engage in activities such as planting and harvesting." (J. Stephen Lansing Priests and Programmers: Technologies of Power in the Engineered Landscape of Bali Princeton, New Jersey: Princeton University Press, 1991; pg. 6.)

defined leadership and the expectations that surrounded it in traditional Southeast Asia.

Linked to this belief is a "circular conception of space in which potently charged centers were thought to radiate power outward and downward toward less-charged peripheries. Not surprisingly, higher-status people were found in centers—were, in fact, conceived to _be_ centers—and were surrounded by people declining in proximity to power and hence in status as one moved outward."[107]

This preoccupation with a certain style of leadership that animated Southeast Asian politics, statecraft and hierarchy, can be thought of as the distinctive pattern of stylization and genius of traditional Southeast Asian civilization.

---

[107] Lorraine Gesick, editor. <u>Centers, Symbols and Hierarchies: Essays on the Classical States of Southeast Asia</u> Monograph Series No. 26: Yale University Southeast Asia Studies, 1983; pg. 1-2.

VII: The "Dialectical Dynamics Hypothesis"
Synthesis and Synergism of Southeast Asian Civilization

A culture historical approach is revived to explain a central principle of Southeast Asian civilization that is at the unchanging center of so much change, that is at the hub of a wheel composed of many different spokes.

A multi-disciplinary approach is demanded for such synthetic perspectives, because the kind of integrative synthesis underlying the historical synergy of Southeast Asian civilization cannot be approach analytically from any single standpoint or methodological strategy alone.

We can refer to the basic dialectical dynamics underlying the rise of human civilization and development of regional integration in Southeast Asia, as the central axis of contrast about which the patterns of history have unfolded from the remotest of times.

This dynamic provides a regional continuity of character, as an "historical structure of the long run" which has witnessed unchanged the coming and going of many peasants and the rise and fall of many states.

These factors remain in the background as pervasive constraints and limits to the possibilities of human action and development, and have set the stage for the enactment of many Southeast Asian dramas.

Sources and Conclusions

It is from this analytical schema that we can identify different levels of integration, and that we can summarize with certain basic conclusions drawn from the themes explored within these essays.

Broadly speaking, because we are dealing with models tied to the reconstruction of past events in Southeast Asia, we are dealing with a form of history in its most general sense. Such a perspective forces us to adopt a notion of "Southeast Asia" and "Southeast Asian Civilization" as if these were preexisting, coherent and possible to define entities that actually existed out in the world.

Many scholars would reject the notion that there is such a thing amongst all the diversities present in the region, while others have argued for a larger unity, either underlying the region as a substratum or as a Sukarno-type theme of "unity in diversity."[108]

Without a doubt, the subject matter of Southeast Asia lends itself to certain broad thematic outlines, outlines that have been a source of dilemma and of dialectic.[109]

There are several summary points in regard to the study of Southeast Asia which deserve to be pointed out:

1. Though the areal studies of Southeast Asia are multi-thematic and dialectical, a survey of the literature would

---

[108] For instance, see J. C. van Leur's Indonesian Trade and Society: Essays in Asian Social and Economic History (1955) for an early thesis of broader regional continuities and unity; George Coedes, Indianized States of Southeast Asia (1968) for the substratum hypothesis; and Lea Williams Southeast Asia: Its History (1976) for the development of the theme of "unity in diversity." On the other hand, see Nicolas Tarling's A Concise History of Southeast Asia (1966) and John Cady's The History of Post-War Southeast Asia (1974) for an emphasis upon the intrinsic diversity of the region.

[109] For instance, Neil L. Jamieson "Toward a Paradigm for Paradox: Observations on the Study of Social Organization in Southeast Asia." Journal of Southeast Asian Studies. 1984

reveal that certain themes and thesis of the dialectic have been emphasized more than others. Donald Emerson, in a review of the History of the region, notes several basic dialectical themes that he organizes into a rectangular cube—historicism versus modernism, continuity versus change, diversity versus unity, originality of Southeast Asian civilization versus dependence on exogenous influence, and macro-system versus micro-system.

2. While some combinations of these themes are recurrent throughout the literature, there has been an overall emphasis upon the historicism and modernism, change, diversity and unity, and dependence, and much less emphasis upon continuity, originality, macro-system and micro-system approaches to understanding Southeast Asian History.[110] In general, we may say that a perspective that deals with the originality of Southeast Asian civilization, with a systemic perspective at both a broader global and local analysis, and with the problems of change and continuity in the region, have been under-emphasized.

3. Southeast Asian Scholarship, written in a western idiom, largely reflects the implicit Western values and worldviews of its scholars.[111]

4. The point of view of the exogenous/endogenous dynamics of Southeast Asian social history in terms of social

---

[110] Donald Emerson "Issues in Southeast Asian History: Room for Interpretation: A Review Article," Journal of Asian Studies Vol. XL, No. 1, November, 1980: pg. 43-68.

[111] For instance, Joseph Fischer, Foreign Values and Southeast Asian Scholarship Research Monograph No. 11, Center for South & Southeast Asian Studies. University of Calif., Berkeley, 1973. Thus such regional studies and histories often failed to critique or move beyond the role which Western colonialism has played in the modern historical development of the region. Hugh Tinker "The Search for the History of Southeast Asia" in The Journal of Southeast Asian Studies Sept. 1980.

stratification and class-ethnic struggle remains to be fully synthesized.

From these points, it is fitting that I should briefly offer a thematic outline of some of the broader perspectives. First, Southeast Asia as a coherent region can only be approached from a cross-disciplinary perspective that combines in balanced proportion history, folklore, geography, ecology, sociology, archaeology, linguistics, anthropology and the understandings derived from a miscellany of other fields of study.

Not wanting to leave out of the picture a statement about the modern era and the role which Western imperialism, colonialism, and subsequent modernization has played in Southeast Asia, it is worthwhile to briefly highlight some of the more salient milestones—a review I will undertake in reverse of chronological ordering of history.

Contemporary Southeast Asia suffers the blights of underdevelopment shared by all third world nations. Except for the tiny little City-State of Singapore and perhaps the small nation-state principality of Brunei, certain broad common features can characterize almost all the rest of Southeast Asia—

- Radical pluralism.
- Ethnic competition.
- Strife and conflict.
- Political corruption.
- Diminishing democratic institutions.
- A large and rapidly growing poor population.
- A thoroughly self-interested elite.
- Continuing neo-colonial dependency and domination by Western interests.
- The growing role of the Japanese, of other foreign diaspora communities, and of "New" mainland Chinese, and the shrinking role of the Overseas Chinese.

Many of the distortions and imbalances that remain to be worked out were a direct or indirect consequence of colonialism.

If we take one step back, we can see the period of late colonialism in the U.S. involvement in Vietnam, a thoroughly destructive and tragic historical accident which brought out the worst racist values of Americans and which lead to the systematic genocide, ecocide and ethnocide of the Vietnamese—and the Vietnamese eventually won their struggle for independence from foreign domination.

One step further back, we can see the chain of retreat from the colonial political domination; of Southeast Asian countries and the struggles which took place—the Americans in Vietnam and the Philippines, the French in Indo-China, the British in Burma, Malaysia, and Sarawak, and the Dutch in Indonesia and Kalimantan.

Though this period is too recent to characterize in terms of its net outcomes, it is safe to claim that the communist insurrections that were commonplace during this period can be seen historically as the rationalist, ideologically secular or religiously fundamentalist political counter movements to capitalistic colonial domination.

One step further back, there is the period of colonialism proper in which racially biased European powers conquered and political-economically encapsulated and exploited Southeast Asia as a zone of primary resource acquisition, cheap labor, and as dumping grounds for cheap industrial commodities produced in the West.

Before this era, we can talk about the early phases of colonialism before the process of Western imperialist expansion became industrially driven. This period deserves broader treatment, like that by Eric Wolf.[112]

But Southeast Asian history also deserves a more detailed survey of the local events, encounters and patterns of response that occurred as the result of contact, trade and the unscrupulous efforts of Western agents of imperialism to establish political and economic control of the region.

Before this era, we reach the phase of the late proto-history and early history of the region, and the more creative influences of Indian, Chinese and Arabian acculturation upon Southeast Asian civilization.

To summarize this very brief history in reverse of Southeast Asia, I wish to stress an important dialectical dynamism of the development of Southeast Asian civilization as a continuous historical process of emerging critical complexity in its intra/inter-regional integration.

With each subsequent phase of contact in which exogenous forces came into interplay with endogenous factors, there arose a broader and more complex level of integration.

Such interplay between internal and external forces was more creative in the earlier phases, and became more destructive in the later phases, until we get the final horror of the Vietnam War. With increasing integration there has been the opportunity for both increased constructive and destructive patterns to have an effect upon the region.

In summary, if we wish to seek a common style pattern and "genius" that we can characterize as inherent and distinctive to Southeast Asian civilization, we can claim that its genius has

---

[112] Eric Wolf, <u>Europe and the People's Without History</u>, 1982: pgs. 231-262.

been in its syncretistic and creative capacity to respond adaptively and deal with complexity and the entropic consequences of external contact.

The style pattern of its civilization is evident in its mosaic and in its organization of diversity which has more often than not precluded conflict and violence and has promoted an outward looking attitude of openness and a live and let live tolerance of human difference.[113]

Furthermore, this style pattern is evident in the way that the symbolic cosmography of Southeast Asian consciousness is symmetrical and reflective of its geography, and in how the metaphor of the body and the metaphor of the social state interpenetrate and resonate with one another, such that the boundaries between these realms are everywhere fluid, dynamic, fuzzy and shifting in focus.

Hypothetical Reconstruction

Several broad hypotheses have been presented in this work. Briefly, they may be summarized:

1. The "Waterways" hypothesis focuses upon the systemic, circumscriptive, consequences of a maritime-riverine-coastal orientation that is predominant in Southeast Asia as a "single ocean" in the developmental integration and adaptation of Southeast Asian civilization.

2. The "Crossroads" hypothesis considers the role of intercultural contact and transmission in reconstruction of the

---

[113] It can be seen in the consistent capacity to maintain a core sense of "Southeast Asianess" that is both an animistic and nature-oriented substratum and a social-symbolic and syncretic synthesis of this dynamic interplay and complexity. (Alfred Kroeber An Anthropologist Looks at History, 1963 and Style and Civilization, 1957.)

process of the historical evolution of a region and its people, from the standpoint of a sui-generis "*Austric*" origin in the Northern Highlands of Vietnam for the Austro-Asiatic, Austro-Thai and Austronesian speaking peoples of Southeast Asia and the Pacific.

3. The "Autochthony Hypothesis" reconsiders the evidence for the autochthonous origins of Southeast Asian civilization in the Northern Highlands of Vietnam, South China, Northern Thailand and Laos.

4. The "Market-place Hypothesis" considers the role of trade and traffic in the regional integration and rise of "central places" throughout the proto-historical period, focusing upon the long-term structures and network patterns that may have been in place time-immemorial, especially in Borneo.

5. The "Plural-Polity" hypothesis focuses upon the characteristic Southeast Asian "organization of diversity" in which the sense of "person-hood" is defined political-ecologically in relation to a Southeast Asian landscape, as this landscape is integrated into the current political-economy of the region.

Such local-regional-global integration has long relied upon the appropriation of symbols of identity and "equivalence structures" by which such potentially disruptive and conflicting diversities could be rendered mutualism in interrelation.

This was accomplished by shared religion that defined the relation between the individual and the group, and between groups, and by status-role identities which defined the appropriate and expected behaviors of a variety of peoples, and which were defined spatially and temporally in terms of the political economic/ecological positionalism or "place" the individual occupied, both geographically and cosmologically.

6. The "Thanatophidia Hypothesis" and the "Circular-Center Hypothesis look at the congruence of certain basic symbolisms and the structure of symbolism in Southeast Asia, as this served to coordinate and orient the individual in relation to both the world and to the social group. These symbolically mediated relationships have been more direct and more consequential in the historical style patterning and genius of Southeast Asian civilization than materialists and functionalists would presuppose.

7. The "Dialectical Dynamism Hypothesis" looks at the poly-thematic representation of Southeast Asian civilization as a complex dialect around certain central axis of diversity and unity, continuity and change, micro-dynamism and macro-systematics, endogenous origination and exogenous dependency and acculturation.

At certain periods and places, these processes combined to create very constructive and very destructive patterns.

The inherent complexity of these polythetic dialectical dynamics makes necessary a systematic and organized cross-disciplinary approach that attempts to comprehend all the available information and understanding relating to Southeast Asia.

This perspective is rooted in the problem of reconstruction that attempts to combine ethnocultural with ethno-historical methods at several levels of analysis—local, regional and global—and in a way such that these levels are mutually coordinate and informative.

This broad-based and yet regionally focused approach in ethnocultural studies thus requires a critical and open attitude toward all forms of evidence and varieties of experience. Least this seem like a resurrection of the archaic Culture Historical methodology, it is, with the proviso that this methodology is divorced from ideological spiritism and is anchored empirically and historically in the scientific approaches to analysis and in the data discovered from such systematic and controlled analysis.

Synthesis rests upon and gives rise to analysis. Finally this approach demands a self-critical, reflexive and self-corrective approach to reconstruction. We must always take into account in our reconstructive formulas the relativities of our own limited knowledge.

There have been several critiques of methodological orientations implicit in this work. These have been to argue for an expanded role of counter-factuality in hypothesis construction, a critique of the taxonomic tendency that uncovers a central root underlying homologically related patterns and elements.

It provides as well a suggestion of an alternative network which does not implicitly deny the inherent complexities of the remoter past and that allows for the possibility of re-convergence and reversibility of cultural process of development, a network pattern that is rooted in a hypothesized "correspondence and covariance structures" between polythetic sets of characteristics.

These themes rooted in basic, prototypical cores, and alternative systematic methodology for inference formulation, testing and decision-making regarding the confidence of diverse sources of different kinds of data, the problem of "inter-translation" and credibility and the use of dynamic "equivalence structures" in explaining the organization of diversity in processes of constructive integration, and the problem of congruence and correspondence of the mechanisms and structure of symbolic mediation which are rooted in basic thematic contrasts.

Finally, in closing, it is worth reconsidering the productive, textual de-petrification that is possible with the deliberate attempt to develop in essay form a transcendent dialectic which achieves a metalogue between the text and its theme.

Each one of the themes presented in this manuscript could be easily developed into a manuscript of its own. The point of the work has been in part to bring to the fore and to investigate certain basic and recurrent themes in Southeast Asian studies that usually remain only in the background, for their implications both for such regional studies and for how we go about reconstructing the past.

The value of the synoptic perspective provided here is to seek the deeper sense of order and meaning behind the complexities of the problem. It is tempting to carry this synthesis one step further and to offer a basic model of Southeast Asian civilization, locating in the process the primary factors or ultimate causes that define its coherence and basic contiguities. Such a model will be left to another time and place, to another person (perhaps, an indigenous Southeast Asian) to develop.

A Comprehensive BIBLIOGRAPHY

A.

Ackerman, Susan E

    1981   *"Communication and Cognitive Pluralism in a Spirit Possession Event in Malaysia"* <u>American Ethnologist</u>

    1988   <u>Heaven in Transition: Non-Muslim Religious Identity and Ethnic Identity in Malaysia</u> Honolulu: Univ. of Hawaii Press.

Ackerman, S. E and Raymond M. Lee
    1981   Communication and Cognitive Pluralism in a Spirit Possession Event in Malaysia. American Ethnologist 8(4): 789-799.

Anderson, Benedict
    1972   The Idea of Power in Javanese Culture. Culture and Politics in Indonesia. Claire Holt, Benedict Anderson & James Siegel, eds.; Ithaca: Cornell University Press.

B.

Bakhtin, Mikail
    1981 <u>The Dialogic Imagination</u>. Austin: University of Texas Press.

Balibain, John
    1932 <u>Hail, Penang!</u>

Bastin, John and Harry J. Benda
    1968   A History of Modern Southeast Asia: Colonialism,
    Nationalism and Decolonization Englewood
    Cliffs, New Jersey: Prentice-Hall, Inc.

Bastin, John and R. Roolvink, eds.
    1964   Malayan and Indonesian Studies: Essays
    Presented to Sir Richard Winstedt on his Eighty-
    Fifth Birthday. Oxford: Clarendon Press.

Bateson, Gregory
    1972   Steps to an Ecology of Mind. San Francisco,
    California: Chandler.

    1979   Mind and Nature: A Necessary Unity. New York:
    Bantam Books.

Beliak, Leopold
    1971   The Thematic Apperception Test and The
    Children's Apperception Test in Clinical Use,
    Second Edition. New York: Grune & Stratton.

    1975   The Thematic Apperception Test, The Children's
    Apperception Test and The Senior Apperception
    Technique in Clinical Use, Third Edition. New
    York: Grune & Stratton.

Bellwood, Peter
    1975   *The Prehistory of Oceania.* Current Anthropology
    16 (1): 9-28.

    1978   The Polynesians: Prehistory of an Island People,
    Revised Edition. London: Thames and Hudson.

    1980   *The Peopling of the Pacific.* Scientific American,
    Vol. 243(5): 174-185.

Southeast Asian Sources

    1985   <u>Prehistory of the Indo-Malaysian Archipelago</u>.
             Orlando: Academic Press.

    1991   *The Austronesian Dispersal and the Origin of
             Languages*, <u>Scientific American</u>, Vol. 265(1): 88-
             94.

Benda, Harry J. and John Larkin
    1967   <u>The World of Southeast Asia</u>. New York: Harper
             & Row.

Benedict, Paul K.
    1975   <u>Austro-Thai Language and Culture: With a
             Glossary of Roots</u> HRAF Press, Inc.

Berger, P. L.
    1988   An East Asian Development Model? In Search of
             an East Asian Development Model, P. L. Berger
             and H. H. M. Hsiao, eds. Oxford: Transaction
             Books.

Berger, Peter L, and Thomas Luckmann
    1967   The Social Construction of Reality: A Treatise in
             the Sociology of Knowledge. New York: Anchor
             Books.

Bibby, Geoffrey
    1970   <u>Looking For Dilmun.</u> New York: Alfred A Knopf,
             Inc.

Blumberg, Paul, ed.
    1972   <u>The Impact of Social Class: A Book of Readings</u>.
             New York: Thomas Y. Crowell Company.

Blust, Robert
    1976   *Austronesian Culture History: Some Linguistic
             Inferences and Their Relations to the*

Archaeological Record. World Archaeology, 8(1):
19-43.

Bonacich, Edna
      1980   *Middleman Minorities and Advanced Capitalism.*
             Ethnic Groups, Vol. 2:211-219.

Bronson, B.
      1977   *Exchange at the Upstream and Downstream Ends:
             Notes Towards a Functional Model of the Coastal
             State in Southeast Asia.* Economic Exchange and
             Social Interaction in Southeast Asia: Perspectives
             from Prehistory, History and Ethnography. K.
             Hutterer, ed. Center for South and Southeast Asian
             Studies, Michigan Papers on South and Southeast
             Asia, No.13: University of Michigan Press.

Brown, D. E
      1964   Southeast Asia: Its Historical Development New
             York, N.Y: McGraw Hill 1976 Principles of
             Social Structure: Southeast Asia. Westview Press.

      1976   Principles of Social Structure: Southeast Asia
             Westview Press, Inc.

Buchanan, Keith
      1967   The Southeast Asian World: An Introductory
             Essay. London: G. Bell and Sons, Ltd.

Buell, Hal
      1968   Vietnam: Land of Many Dragons New York:
             Dodd, Mead and Co.

Burling, Robbins
      1967 (1965, 1966)

Southeast Asian Sources

Hill Farms and Paddi Fields: Life in Mainland
Southeast Asia Englewood Cliffs, New Jersey:
Prentice-Hall, Inc.

Buttinger, Joseph
1958   The Smaller Dragon: A Political History of
Vietnam New York: Frederick A. Praeger.

1972   A Dragon Defiant: A Short History of Vietnam
New York: Frederick A. Praeger.

Butwell, Richard and Amy Vandenbosch
1966   The Changing Face of Southeast Aaia Lexington,
Kentucky, University of Kentucky Press.

C.

Cady, John F.
1954   The Roots of French Imperialism in Eastern Asia
Ithaca, New York: Cornell University Press.

1964   Southeast Asia: Its Historical Development.
McGraw Hill Book Co.

1964   The Development of Southeast Asian Civilization

1974   The History of Post-War Southeast Asia Athens:
Athens: Ohio University Press.

Cavalli-Sforza, Luigi L.
1986   "*Diffusion of Cultures and Genes*" in On
Evolutionary Anthropology: Essays in Honor of
Harry Hoijer, 1983. Edited by B. J. Williams
Malibu, Ca.: Undena Publications.

Cavalli-Sforza, Luigi L. and Feldman, M. W.
    1981   Cultural Transmission and Evolution: A
            Quantitative Approach. Princeton: Princeton
            University Press.

Cavalli-Sforza, Luigi Luca, Piazza, Alberto Piazza, Paolo
            Menozzi, and Mountain, Joanna
    1988   "Reconstruction of Human Evolution: Bringing
            together Genetic, Archaeological and Linguistic
            Data" in Proceedings of the National Academy of
            Sciences, USA. Vol. 85: pp. 6006-4 August.

Chaliand, Ge'rard
    1968   The Peasants of North Vietnam Baltimore,
            Maryland: Penguin Books, Ltd.

Chan Kwok Bun and Claire Chiang
    1994   Stepping Out: The Making of Chinese
            Entrepreneurs. New York: Prentice Hall.

Chang Kwang-chih, Grace, George W., and Solheim, Wilhelm
            G., II
    1964   "Movement of the Malayo-Polynesians: 1500 B.
            C. to A. D. 500. Current Anthropology Vol. 5, # 5,
            December: 359-406.

Cheng Te-Kun
    1969   Archaeology in Sarawak. Cambridge: W. Hetter
            and Sons.

Chew, Daniel
    1990   Chinese Pioneers on the Sarawak Frontier 1841-
            1941. Singapore: Oxford Univ. Press.

Chew, Ernest C. T. and Edwin Lee
    1991   A History of Singapore. Singapore: Oxford Univ.
            Press.

Southeast Asian Sources

Chia, Felix
    1994   The Babas Revisited. Singapore: Heinemann Asia.

Chin, John M.
    1981   The Sarawak Chinese. London: Oxford Univ.
            Press.

Clammer, John
    1979   *The Ambiguity of Identity: Ethnicity Maintenance
            and Change Among the Straits Chinese
            Community of Malaysia and Singapore.* Institute
            of Southeast Asian Studies Occasional Paper, #54
            Singapore: University of Singapore Press.

    1980   Straits Chinese Society. Singapore: Singapore
            Univ. Press.

    1983   "Studies in Chinese Folk Religion in Singapore
            and Malaysia" Contributions to Southeast Asian
            Ethnography, Editor, No. 2; August. Singapore:
            National University of Singapore.

Coedes, George
    1968   The Indianized States of Southeast Asia Honolulu,
            Hawaii: East-West Center Press.

Condominas, Georges
    1977   We have Eaten the Forest: The Story of a
            Montagnard Village in the Central Highlands of
            Vietnam New York: Hill and Wang, Inc.

Coppel, Charles A.
    1983   Indonesian Chinese in Crisis. Oxford: Oxford
            Univ. Press.

Coughlin, Richard J.
  1960   Double Identity: The Chinese in Modem Thailand.
          Hong Kong: Hong Kong Univ. Press.

Coughlin, Richard J., Donn V. Hart, and Phya Anuman Rajadhon
  1965   Southeast Asian Birth Customs: Three Studies in
          Human Reproduction New Haven, Connecticut:
          Human Relations Area Files Press, Inc.

Cowan, C. D. and O. W. Wolters, eds.
  1976   Southeast Asian History and Historiography:
          Essays Presented to D.G.E. Hall Cornell, New
          York: Cornell Univ. Press.

Crawford, Ann
  1966   Customs and Culture of Vietnam Rutland,
          Vermont: Charles E. Tuttle Company, Inc.

Crissman, Lawrence W.
  1967   The Segmentary Structure of Urban Overseas
          Chinese Communities. Man: Vol. 2 (New Series):
          185-204.

D.

Dawson, T R P
  1969   Tan Siew San: The Man from Malacca
          Singapore: Donald Moore Press, Ltd.

de Moubray, G A de C
  1931   Matriarchy in the Malay Peninsula and
          Neighbouring Countries London: Rutledge &
          Sons, Ltd.

<u>Southeast Asian Sources</u>

Ding Choo Ming
    1978   *An Introduction to the Indonesian Peranakan Literature in the Library of the Universiti Kebangsaan Malaysia*
            <u>Journal of the Malayan Branch of the Royal Asiatic Society</u> Vol. 51

E.

Edmonds, Juliet
    1968   *Religion, Intermarriage and Assimilation: The Chinese in Malaya.* <u>Race</u>, X (1): 57-67.

Elliott, Allan J. A.
    1955   <u>Chinese Spirit-Medium Cults in Singapore</u> Monographs on Social Anthropology, No. 14, London: The London School of Economic and Political Science.

Emmerson, Donald K.
    1980   *The Case for a Maritime Perspective on Southeast Asia* <u>The Journal of Southeast Asian Studies</u>, XI (1): 139-145.

    1980   *Issues in Southeast Asian History: Room for Interpretation-A Review Article.* <u>Journal of Asian Studies</u>, XL (1): 43-68.

    1986   *'Southeast Asia': What's in a Name?*, <u>Journal of Southeast Asian Studies</u> Vol.19: 1-21.

Endicott, Kirk Michael
    1970   <u>An Analysis of Malay Magic</u>. Oxford: Clarendon Press.

Errington, Shelly
    1989   Meaning and Power in a Southeast Asian Realm.
             Princeton: Princeton University Press.

Evans, Ivor H. N.
    1970   Studies in Religion, Folk-Lore & Custom in
             British North Borneo and the Malay Peninsula.
             London: Frank Cass & Co.

F.

Fabian, Johannes
    1983   Time and the Other: How Anthropology Makes its
             Object. New York: Columbia University Press.

Fairservice, Walter
    1959   The Origins of Oriental Civilization. New York:
             Russell and Russell.

Fauconnier, Giles
    1985   Mental Spaces: Aspects of Meaning Construction
             in Natural Language. Cambridge, Mass.: M.I.T.
             Press.

Felix, Alfonso Jr., editor
    1969   The Chinese in the Philippines, 1570-1770, Vol. I,
             Manila: Solidaridad Publishing House.

    1969   The Chinese in the Philippines, 1770-1898, Vol. 2,
             Manila: Solidaridad Publishing House.

Finney, Ben R.
    1976   Pacific Navigation and Voyaging Wellington,
             New Zealand: The Polynesian Society
             Incorporated.

Southeast Asian Sources

Fischer, Joseph
    1973 Foreign Values and Southeast Asian Scholarship: Research Monograph No. 1. Center for South & Southeast Asia Studies, Univ. Calif. Berkeley.

Fitzgerald, C P
    1965 The Third China Univ. of British Columbia

Fitzgerald, Francis
    1972, 1973
        Fire in the Lake: The Vietnamese and the Americans in Vietnam. New York: Random House, Inc.

Flannery, Kent
    1971 "Archaeological Systems Theory and Early Mesoamerica" in Anthropological Archaeology in the Americas; Washington D. C.: The Anthropological Society of Washington, D. C., pg. 67-87.

    1972 "The Cultural Evolution of Civilizations" in Annual Review of Ecology and Systematics" 3, pp. 399-426

Fortes, Meyer
    1953 *The Structure of Unilineal Descent Groups.* American Anthropologist 55(1): 17-41.

Fortier, David H.
    1957 "The Chinese in North Borneo" in Colloquium on Overseas Chinese, edited by Morton H. Fried, New York, N.Y.: International Secretariat, Institute of Pacific Relations.

Foster, Brian
  1974   *Ethnicity and Commerce.* American Ethnologist l
          (3): 437-448.

  1977   *Trade, Social Conflict and Social Integration:*
          Rethinking Some Old Ideas on Exchange.
          Economic Exchange and Social Interaction in
          Southeast Asia, edited by Karl Hutterer, Univ. of
          Michigan Press.

Fox, Richard G.
  1977   Urban Anthropology: Cities in their Cultural
          Settings. Englewood Cliffs, New Jersey: Prentice-
          Hall, Inc.

Freedman, Maurice
  1958   Lineage Organization in Southeastern China.
          Monograph on Social Anthropology, No. 18.
          London: London School of Economics. The
          Athlone Press.

  1959   *The Handling of Money: a Note on the*
          Background to the Economic Sophistication of
          Overseas Chinese. Man, LIX(87-107): 64-65.

  1962   *Chinese Kinship and Marriage in Early*
          Singapore, Journal of Southeast Asian History,
          3(2): 65-73.

  1966   Chinese Lineage and Society: Fukien and
          Kwangtung. Monograph on Social Anthropology,
          No. 33. London: London School of Economics.
          The Athlone Press.

Southeast Asian Sources

Freedman, Maurice and Marjorie Topley
    1961 *Religion and Social Realignment among the
          Chinese in Singapore.* Journal of Asian Studies,
          Vol. 21: 3-23.

Freedman, Maurice and William E. Willmott
    1961 *South-East Asia: With Special Reference to the
          Chinese.* International Social Science Journal, 13:
          245-270.

Fried, Morton H., ed.
    1958 Colloquium on Overseas Chinese. New York:
          International Secretariat, Institute of Pacific
          Relations.

Fryer, Donald W.
    1979 Emerging Southeast Asia: A study in Growth and
          Stagnation, 2nd Edition. New York: Wiley.

Fung, Yu-Lan
    1948 A Short History of Chinese Philosophy. New
          York: The Free Press. Geertz, Clifford
    1966 Person, Time, and Conduct in Bali: An Essay in
          Cultural Analysis. Cultural Report Series No. 14.
          Yale University: Southeast Asian Studies.

G.

Geddes, William Robert
    1976 Migrants of the Mountains: The Cultural Ecology
          of the Blue Miao (Hmong Njua) of Thailand
          Oxford University Press.

Geertz, Clifford
    1963 Agricultural Involution Berkeley, Calif. University
          of California Press.

1966   Person, Time, and Conduct in Bali: An Essay in
Cultural Analysis. Cultural Report Series No. 14:
Southeast Asian Studies, Yale University.

1973   "Deep Play: Notes on a Balinese Cockfight" in
The Interpretation of Cultures

Gesick, Lorraine
   1983   Centers, Symbols and Hierarchies: Essays on the
          Classical States of Southeast Asia. Monograph
          Series No. 26: Yale University Southeast Asia
          Studies.

Giddens, Anthony
   1979   Central Problems in Social Theory: Action,
         Structure and Contradiction in Social Analysis.
         London: MacMillan. 1984 The Constitution of
         Society: Outline of the Theory of Structuration.
         Cambridge: Polity Press.

Gosling, L.A.P.
   1964   *Migration and Assimilation of Rural Chinese.*
         Malayan and Indonesian Studies. John Bastin and
         R. Roolvink, eds. Oxford: Clarendon Press.

   1983   *Changing Chinese Identities in Southeast Asia: An
         Introductory Review.* The Chinese in Southeast
         Asia: Identity, Culture & Politics, Vol. 2. L. A.
         Peter Gosling & Linda Y. C. Lim, eds. Singapore:
         Maruzen Asia.

Gosling, L. A. P. and Linda Y. C. Lim, eds.
   1983   The Chinese in Southeast Asia: Ethnicity and
         Economic Activity, Vol. I. Singapore: Maruzen
         Press. 1983 The Chinese in Southeast Asia:
         Identity, Culture and Politics, Vol. H. Singapore:
         Maruzen Press.

1983   The Chinese in Southeast Asia: Identity, Culture and Politics Vol. II, Singapore: Maruzen Press, Ptc. Ltd.

Gould, Richard A. and Watson, Patty Jo
1982   *A dialogue on the meaning and use of analogy in ethnoarchaeological reasoning* in Journal of Anthropological Archaeology I: 355-381

Graff, Edward and Harold Hammond
1967   Southeast Asia: History, Culture, People New York: Cambridge Book Co., Inc.

H.

Hall, Kenneth R.
1985   Maritime Trade and State Development in Early Southeast Asia. Honolulu: University of Hawaii Press.

Hall, Kenneth R. and John K Whitmore, eds.
1976   Explorations in Early Southeast Asian History: The Origins of Asian State-craft. Michigan Papers on South and Southeast Asia, No. 11. Michigan: University of Michigan Press.

Hamilton, Gary
1978   *Pariah Capitalism: A Paradox of Power and Dependence.* Ethnic Groups, Vol. 2:1-15.

Hamill, James F.
1990   Ethno-Logic. Urbana, Illinois: University of Illinois Press.

Hanks, Lucien
>	1972	Rice and Man: Agricultural Ecology in Southeast Asia, Arlington Heights: AHM Publishing.

Harrison, Brian
>	1967	South-East Asia, New York: St. Martin's Press.

Harrison, Tom
>	1967	*Niah Caves: Progress Report to 1967.* The Sarawak Museum Journal, XV: 95-6.

Harrison, Tom & Stanley J. O'Connor
>	1970	Gold and Megalithic Activity in Prehistoric and Recent West Borneo Data Paper # 77 Southeast Asia Program, Department of Asian Studies Cornell University, Ithaca, New York.

Hawkes, Jacquetta
>	1971	Nothing But or Something More. The John Danz Lecture Series.

Heine-Geldern, Robert
>	1958	Conceptions of State and Kingship in Southeast Asia. Data Paper # 18 Southeast Asia Program, Department of Asian Studies. Ithaca, New York: Cornell University.

Hendry, James B.
>	1964	The Small World of Khanh Hau. Chicago, Ill.: Aldine Pub. Co.

Herskovits, Melville J.
>	1947	Man and His Works New York: Alfred A. Knopf.

>	1955	Cultural Anthropology New York: Alfred A. Knopf

<u>Southeast Asian Sources</u>

1958 <u>Acculturation: The Study of Culture Contact</u>
Massachusetts: Peter Smith.

Hickey, Gerald
1964 <u>Village in Vietnam</u> England: Yale University
Press.

1982 <u>Sons of the Mountains: Ethnohistory of the
Vietnamese Central Highlands to 1954</u>. New
Haven, Connecticut: Yale University Press

Higham, Charles
1984 *Prehistoric Rice Cultivation in Southeast Asia.*
<u>Scientific American</u> 250(4): 138-146.

1988 <u>The Archaeology of Mainland Southeast Asia:
From 10,000 B. C. to the Fall of Angkor.</u>
Cambridge: Cambridge University Press.

Higham, C. F. W. and R. Bannanurag
1991 <u>The Excavation of Khok Phanom Di: A
Prehistoric Site in Central Thailand: Volume I:
The Excavation, Chronology and Human Burials.</u>
London: The Society of Antiquaries.

1991 <u>The Excavation of Khok Phanom Di: A
Prehistoric Site in Central Thailand: Volume II:
The Biological Remains (Part I)</u>. London: The
Society of Antiquaries.

Hobart, Mark and Robert H. Taylor, eds.
1986 <u>Context, Meaning and Power in Southeast Asia.</u>
Ithaca: Cornell Southeast Asia Program.

Hodgen, Margaret T.
    1964   Early Anthropology in the Sixteenth and Seventeenth Centuries. Philadelphia: University of Pennsylvania Press.

Hoffman, Carl L.
    1984   *Punan Foragers in the Trading Networks of Southeast Asia.* Past and Present in Hunter Gatherer Studies. Carmel Schrire, ed.: 123-149. New York: Academic Press.

Holloman, Regina & Serghei A. Arutiunov, editors
    1978   Perspectives on Ethnicity Mouton Publishers.

Holmgren, Jennifer
    1980   Chinese Colonization in Northern Vietnam Australia: Australian National University.

Hsu, Francis
    1967   Under the Ancestor's Shadow. Stanford: Stanford University Press.

Hue-Tam Ho Tai
    1983   Millenarianism and Peasant Politics in Vietnam Cambridge, Massachusetts: Harvard University Press.

Hunter, Guy
    1966   South-East Asia: Race, Culture and Nation London, England: Oxford University Press.

Hutterer, Karl L., ed.
    1977   Economic Exchange and Social Interaction in Southeast Asia; Perspectives from Prehistory, History and Ethnography Center for South and Southeast Asian Studies, Michigan Papers on

Southeast Asian Sources

South and Southeast Asia, No.13. Michigan:
University of Michigan Press.

Hy Van Vuong
    1977   'Brother' and 'Uncle'": An Analysis of Rules,
          Structural Contradictions and Meanings in
          Vietnamese Kinship, American Anthropologist
          Vol. 19(2)

J.

Jamann, Wolfgang
    1994   Chinese Trading Firms in Transition. The Moral
          Economy of Trade: Ethnicity and Developing
          Markets. Hans-Dieter Evers and Heiko Schrader,
          eds. 126-147. London: Routledge.

Jamieson, Neil L.
    1984   "Toward a Paradigm for Paradox: Observations on
          the Study of Social Organization in Southeast
          Asia." Journal of Southeast Asian Studies

Jiang, Joseph P. L.
    1966   "The Chinese in Thailand" Journal of Southeast
          Asian History Vol. 7, no. 1, March.

Johns, A. H.
    1976   "Islam in Southeast Asia: Problems of Perspective"
          in Southeast Asian History and Historiography:
          Essays Presented to D. G. E. Hall, edited by C. D.
          Cowan and O. W. Wolters Ithaca, N. Y.: Cornell
          Univ. Press.

K.

Kebschull, Dietrich
  1986   Transmigration in Indonesia: An Empirical
          Analysis of Motivation, Expectations and
          Experiences Hamburg Institute of Economic
          Research.

Keeler, Ward
  1987   Javanese Shadow Plays, Javanese Selves
          Princeton Univ. Press.

Karim, Wazir Jahan
  1990   Emotions of Culture: A Malay Perspective.
          Singapore: Oxford Univ. Press.

Kennedy, Jean
  1977   *From Stage to Development in Prehistoric
          Thailand: An Exploration of the Origins of
          Growth, Exchange and Variability in Southeast
          Asia.* Economic Exchange and Social Interaction
          in Southeast Asia. Karl Hutterer, ed. Michigan:
          Univ. Michigan Press.

Kern, Hendrik
  1889   "Linguistic Theories about the Austronesian
          Homeland" Brill, the Netherlands

Kesseler, Clive S.
  1977   *Conflict and Sovereignty in Kelantanese Malay
          Spirit Seances.* In Case Studies in Spirit
          Possession. Vincent Crapanzano and Vivian
          Garrison, eds.: 295-332. New York: Wiley.

Khoo Kay Kim
  1991   Malay Society: Transformation &
          Democratization. Selangor Darul Ehsan, Malaysia:
          Pelanduk Paperbacks.

Southeast Asian Sources

Khoo Su Nin, editor & writer
    1989-1991 Pulau Pinang: A Guide to the Local Way of
        Life & Culture of Penang.

    1991   *Clan Complex*. Pulau Pinang 2(1): 26-28.

    1991   *Thai menora: The Initiation Ceremony*. Pulau
        Pinang 2(3): 20-24.

Koller, John M.
    1970   Oriental Philosophies. New York: Charles
        Scribner's Sons.

Kroeber, A. L.
    1957   Style and Civilization. New York: Cornell Univ.
        Press.

    1963   An Anthropologist Looks at History. Berkeley:
        University of Calif. Press.

Kuchler, Johannes
    1965   Penang Chinese Population: A Preliminary
        Account of its Origin and Social Geographic
        Pattern. Asian Studies, Vol. 3, no. 3

L.

Lai Ah Eng
    1986   *Peasants, Proletarians and Prostitutes: A
        Preliminary Investigation into the Work of
        Chinese Women in Colonial Malaya*. Research
        Notes and Discussions Paper No. 59.Singapore:
        Institute of Southeast Asian Studies.

Lansing, J. Stephen
    1991   Priests and Programmers: Technologies of Power
            in the Engineered Landscape of Bali. Princeton,
            New Jersey: Princeton University Press, 1991.

Leach, Edmund
    1954   Political Systems of Highland Burma. London:
            London School of Economics.

Leaf, Murray J.
    1972   Information and Behavior in a Sikh Village:
            Social Organization Reconsidered. Berkeley, Ca.:
            University of California Press.

Lebar, Frank M., Hickey, Gerald C. and Musgrave, John K.
    1964   Ethnic Groups of Southeast Asia, Vols I &
            II.(New Haven: Human Relations Area Files

Lee, Poh Sing
    1978   Chinese Society in 19th Century Singapore.
            Melbourne: Oxford Univ. Press.

Lent, John A., ed.
    1977   *Cultural Pluralism in Malaysia: Polity, Military,
            Mass Media, Education, Religion and Social
            Class*. Special Report No. 14. Northern Illinois
            Univ.: The Center for Southeast Asian Studies.

Leonard, Jane Kate
    1984   Wei Yuan and China's Rediscovery of the
            Maritime World. Harvard East Asian Monographs
            DI, Council of East Asian Studies, Harvard Univ.

Levi-Strauss, Claude
    1963   Structural Anthropology. New York: Basic Books.

Southeast Asian Sources

Lewis, David
    1974   *Wind, Wave, Star and Bird*. National Geographic
               146(6): 747-8.

Lind, Andrew W.
    1974   Nanyang Perspective: Chinese Students in Multi-
               Racial Singapore: University Press of Hawaii.

M.

Mackie, J. A. C., ed.
    1976   The Chinese in Indonesia. Singapore: Heineman.

Manguin, Pierre-Yves
    1980   *The Southeast Asian Ship: An Historical
               Approach*. Journal of Southeast Asian Studies XI
               (2):266-276.

McCloud, Donald G.
    1986   System and Process in Southeast Asia: The
               Evolution of a Region. Westview Press.

McVey, Ruth, ed.
    1963   Indonesia. Southeast Asian Studies: Yale Univ.
               Press.

Milner, G. B., editor
    1978   Natural Symbols in South East Asia. London:
               School of Oriental and African Studies.

Minchin, G
    1870   Notes and Queries on China and Japan,
               n.s. 4, no. 6 Hong Kong

Mitchell, Robert E.
    1973   Levels of Emotional Strain in Southeast Asian
               Cities: A Study of Individual Responses to the

Stress of Urbanization and Industrialization Vols. 1-11.

Moench, Richard
1961   A Preliminary Report on Chinese Social and Economic Organization in the Society Islands Paper presented at the Tenth Science Congress of the Pacific Science Association: University of Hawaii

Mohammed, Mahathir bin
1970   The Malay Dilemma. Kuala Lumpur. Times Books International.

Mohammed Taib, ed.
1885   Malaysian World-View. Singapore: Institute of Southeast Asian Studies.

Mortensen, Karen Vibeke
1991   Form and Content in Children's Human Figure Drawings. New York: New York Univ. Press.

Murdock, George P.
1964 "Genetic Classification of the Austronesian Languages: A Key to Oceanic Culture History" in Ethnology 3.2, pp. 117-26.

N.

Nagata, Judith
1974   *"What is a Malay?" Situational Selection of Ethnic Identity in a Plural Society.* American Ethnologist 1 (2): 331-350

Southeast Asian Sources

    1979   Malaysian Mosaic: Perspectives from a Poly-
ethnic Society. Vancouver Univ. of British
Columbia Press.

Nelson, S. M.
    1990   "Diversity of the Upper Paleolithic 'Venus'
Figurines and Archaeological Mythology." In
Archaeological Papers of the American
Anthropology Association, 1990: pg. 11-22)

Newell, William H.
    1962   Treacherous River. Kuala Lumpur Univ. of
Malaya Press.

Ng, Cecilia Siew Hua
    1983   *The Sam Foh Neo Neo Keramat: A Study of a
Baba Chinese Temple*. Contributions to Southeast
Asian Ethnography John R. Clammer, ed.
Singapore: National University of Singapore.

Noyes, James L.
    1993   Artificial Intelligence with Common LISP:
Fundamentals of Symbolic and Numeric
Processing

O.

Oliver, Victor L.
    1976   Caodai Spiritism: A Study of Religion in
Vietnamese Society Leiden: E. J. Brill.

Omar, Roziah
    1994   The Malay Woman in the Body: Between Biology
and Culture. Kuala Lumpur Penerbit Fajar Bakti,
Sdn. Berhad.

Omohundro, John T.

    1977   *Trading Patterns of Philippine Chinese: Strategies of Sojourning Middlemen.* <u>Economic Exchange and Social Interaction in Southeast Asia.</u> Karl Hutterer, ed., The Univ. of Michigan Press.

    1981   <u>Chinese Merchant Families in Iloilo: Commerce and Kin in a Central Philippine City</u>. Athens, Ohio: The Ohio Univ. Press.

Ong, Aihwa

    1986   Spirits of Resistance and Capitalist Discipline: Factory Women in Malaysia. Albany: State University of New York Press, 1987.

P.

Pakir, Anne Geok-In Sim

    1987   <u>A Linguistic Investigation of Baba Malay</u> PhD. Dissertation, Ann Arbor, Mi.: Dissertation Abstracts International, A: The Humanities and Social Sciences, 12(1), June.

    1988   *The Baba Malay Lexicon: Hokkien Loanwords in Baba Malay* <u>Applied Linguistics Association of Australia: Occasional Papers</u>, 10: 3-30.

    1989   "Linguistic Alternants and Code Selection in Baba Malay" <u>World Englishes</u>, Vol. 8, no. 3, Winter: pages 379-388.

    1991   "The Range and Depth of English-knowing Bilinguals in Singapore" <u>World Englishes</u> Vol. 10, no. 2: 167-179.

    1991   The Range and Depth of English-knowing Bilinguals in Singapore. World Englishes, 10(2): 167-179.

Southeast Asian Sources

Pan, Lyn
    1991   Sons of the Yellow Emperor: The Story of the Overseas Chinese. Singapore: Mandarin.

Pandian, Jacob
    1982   The Other in Us: An Essay Concerning the Function of Anthropology in the Western Intellectual Tradition [unpublished manuscript]

Png Poh-Seng
    1969   *The Straits Chinese in Singapore: A Case of Local Identity and Socio-Cultural Accommodation* Journal of Southeast Asian History, Vol. 10, no. 1

Purcell, Victor
    1947   *Chinese Settlement in Malacca.* Journal of the Malayan Branch of the Royal Asiatic Society, XX (1): 115-25.

    1948   The Chinese in Malaya. London: Oxford Univ. Press.

    1956   The Chinese in Modem Malaya. Singapore: Donald More.

    1965   The Chinese in Southeast Asia, 2nd Edition. London: Oxford Univ. Press. 1965 South And East Asia Since 1800. Cambridge: At the University Press.

    1965   South And East Asia Since 1800. Cambridge: At the University Press.

Pryzluski, Jean and Emile Senart
    1925   "La Princesse a l'odeur de poisson et la Nagi dans les traditins de l'Asie oriental" Etudes Asiatique,

Publications, E'cole Francaise d'Extreme-Orient, vols. 19-20: 2: 265-285. Paris.

Q & R

Rabushka, Alvin
   1973   Race and Politics in Urban Malaya. Stanford University: Hoover Institution Press.

Rashid, Rehman
   1993   A Malaysian Journey. Malaysia Selangor Darul Ehsan.

Rappaport, Roy
   1968   Pigs for the Ancestors. Yale University Press.

Ratcliffe, Peter, ed.
   1994   "Race" Ethnicity and Nation: International Perspectives on Social Conflict London: University College London Press.

Raybeck, Douglas
   1980   *Ethnicity and Accommodation: Malay-Chinese Relations in Kelantan, Malaysia.* Ethnic Groups, Vol. 2:241-268.

   1983   *Chinese Patterns of Adaptation in Southeast Asia.* The Chinese in Southeast Asia: Identity, Culture & Politics Vol 2. L. A. Peter Gosling & Linda Y. C. Lim, eds. Singapore: Maruzen Asia, Pte. Ltd. Reid, Anthony and Lance Castles, eds.

   1975   Pre-Colonial State Systems in Southeast Asia: The Malay Peninsula Sumatra, Bali-Lombok, South Celebes. Kuala Lumpur. Council of the Malaysian Branch of the Royal Asiatic Society.

Southeast Asian Sources

Reid, Anthony and Castles, Lance, editors.
  1975   Pre-Colonial State Systems in Southeast Asia: The
         Malay Peninsula Sumatra, Bali-Lombok, South
         Celebes. Kuala Lumpur, Malaysia: Council of the
         Malaysian Branch of the Royal Asiatic Society.

Renfrew, Colin
  1987   Archaeology and Language: The Puzzle of Indo-
         European Origins. London: Jonathan Cape.

Robequain, Charles, translated by Laborde, E. D.
  1958   Malaya, Indonesia, Borneo, and the Philippines: A
         Geographical, Economic and Political description
         of Malaya, the East Indies, and the Philippines.
         London: Longmans, Green and Co., Ltd.

Roff, William R., ed.
  1974   Kelantan: Religion, Society and Politics in a
         Malay State. Kuala Lumpur: Oxford University
         Press.

Rogers, Marvin L.
  1993   Local Politics in Rural Malaysia. Kuala Lumpur:
         S. Abdul Majeed.

Ross, Philip E.
  1991   "Hard Words" Scientific American April, pp. 139-
         147.

Rubin, Alfred P.
  1974   Piracy, Paramouncy and Protectorates. Kuala
         Lumpur, Malaysia: Penerbit Universiti Malaysia

Ruhlen, Merrit
  1976   A Guide to the Languages of the World. (Stanford
         University: Language Universals Project.

Runciman, Stephen
    1960   The White Rajahs: A History of Sarawak From 1841 to 1946. Cambridge: At the University Press.

S.

Salaff, Janet W.
    1981   Working Daughters of Hong Kong: Filial Piety or Power in the Family? Cambridge: Cambridge Univ. Press.

Salmon, Claudine
    1981   *The Contribution of the Chinese to the Development of Southeast Asia: A New Appraisal.* Journal of Southeast Asian Studies, XII (1): 260-275.

Sauer, Carl O.
    1952   Agricultural Origins and Dispersals: The Domestication of Animals and Foodstuffs. Cambridge: M.I.T. Press.

    1969   Seeds, Spades, Hearths & Herds: The Domestication of Animals and Foodstuffs. Cambridge: M.I.T. Press.

Schaie, K. W. and R. Heiss
    1964   Colour and Personality. Bern: Huber.

Scharfstein, Ben-Ami
    1978   Philosophy East/Philosophy West Basil Blackwell. Oxford.

Sebeok, Thomas A.
    1971   Current Trends in Linguistics, Vol. 8: Linguistics in Oceania. The Hague, Paris: Mouton & Company, Printers.

Southeast Asian Sources

Shorto, Harry L., Paul Sidwell, Doug Cooper and Christian
        Bauer, Eds.
    2008   *A Mon–Khmer Comparative Dictionary.*
        Canberra: Australian National University. Pacific
        Linguistics.

Shutler, Richard, Jr. and Shutler, Mary Elizabeth
    1975   Oceanic Prehistory Menlo Park, Calif.: Cummings
        Publishing Company.

Siaw, Lawrence
    1981   *The Legacy of Malaysian Chinese Social
        Structure.* Journal of Southeast Asian Studies, XU
        (2): 395-402.

    1983   Chinese Society in Rural Malaysia: A Local
        History of the Chinese in Titi Jelubu. Singapore:
        Oxford Univ. Press

Simoniya, N. A.
    1961   Overseas Chinese in Southeast Asia—A Russian
        Study. Data Paper No. 45. Ithaca: Cornell
        University.

Siow, Moli
    1983   *The Problems of Ethnic Cohesion among the
        Chinese in Peninsular Malaysia: Intraethnic
        Divisions and Interethnic Accommodation.* The
        Chinese in Southeast Asia: Identity, Culture &
        Politics, Vol. 2. L. A. Peter Gosling & Linda Y. C.
        Lim, Eds. Singapore: Maruzen Asia, Pte. Ltd.

Skeat, Walter William
    1984   Malay Magic: Being An Introduction to the
        Folklore and Popular Religion of the Malay
        Peninsula. Singapore: Oxford Univ. Press.

Skinner, G. William
    1957   *The Chinese of Java*. Colloquium on Overseas
            Chinese. Morton H. Fried, ed. New York:
            International Secretariat, Institute of Pacific
            Relations.

    1963   *The Chinese Minority*. Indonesia. Ruth McVey,
            ed. New Haven: HRAF Press.

Smith, R. and W. Watson
    1979   Early South-East Asia: Essays in Archaeology,
            History and Historical Geography. New York:
            Oxford University Press.

Solheim, II, Wilhelm
    1972   "*An Earlier Agricultural Revolution*" Scientific
            American: April.

Somers-Heidhues, Mary F.
    1974   Southeast Asia's Chinese Minorities. Hawthorn,
            Vic.: Longman Press.

Somers, Mary F
    1965   Peranakan Chinese Politics in Indonesia
            Ph. D. Dissertation, Ithaca, N.Y.: Cornell
            University Indonesia Project.

Song Ong Siang
    1967   One Hundred Years' History of the Chinese in
            Singapore. Singapore: University of Malaya Press.

Sophie Mohd. Noordin
    1973   *The Penang Secession Movement, 1948-51*
            Journal of Southeast Asian Studies, Vol. 4

Southeast Asian Sources

Spencer, J. E.
> 1966   Shifting Cultivation in Southeast Asia. Berkeley: University of California Press.

Spiro, Melford
> 1967   Burmese Supernaturalism: A Study in the Explanation and Reduction of Suffering. Englewood Cliffs: Prentice-Hall, Inc.

Steadman, John
> 1969   The Myth of Asia. New York: Simon and Schuster.

Steinberg, David Joel
> 1987   In Search of Southeast Asia. Honolulu: Univ. of Hawaii Press.

Stover, Leon
> 1974   The Cultural Ecology of Chinese Civilization: Peasants and Elites in the Last of the Agrarian States. New York: The New American Library.

Strauch, Judith
> 1980   The Chinese Exodus from Vietnam: Implications for the Southeast Asian Chinese. Boston, Harvard Univ. Press.

> 1981   *Multiple Ethnicities in Malaysia: The Shifting Relevance of Alternative Chinese Categories.* Modem Asian Studies, 15(2): 235-60.

> 1981   Chinese Village Politics in the Malaysian State. Mass.: Harvard Univ. Press.

Suryadinata, Leo
>1981   Peranakan Chinese Politics in Java, 1917-1942
>Singapore: Singapore Univ. Press

Swaminathan, M. S.
>1984   *Rice* Scientific American: Jan. 1984.

T.

Tan Chee-Beng
>1979   *Baba Chinese, Non-Baba Chinese and Malays: A Note on Ethnic Interaction in Malacca.* Southeast Asian Journal of Social Science, 7(1-2): 19-28.

>1980   "*Baba Malay Dialect*" Journal of the Malayan Branch of the Royal Asiatic Society Vol. 53, Part 1:150-166.

>1982   "*Peranakan Chinese in Northeast Kelantan*" Journal of the Malayan Branch of the Royal Asiatic Society Vol. 55, part 1.

>1983   *Acculturation and the Chinese in Melaka: The Expression of Baba Identity.* The Chinese in Southeast Asia: Identity, Culture & Politics, Vol. 2.; L. A. Peter Gosling & Linda Y. C. Lim, eds. Singapore: Maruzen Asia Pte. Ltd.

>1993   Chinese Peranakan Heritage in Malaysia and Singapore. Kuala Lumpur Penerbit Fajar Bakti Sdn. Berhad.

Tan Giok-Lan
>1963   The Chinese of Sukabumi: A Study in Social and Cultural Accommodation Ithaca, New York: Cornell Univ. Modem Indonesia Project, Southeast Asia Program, Department of Asia Studies.

Southeast Asian Sources

Tan, Rosie Kim Neo
    1958   The Straits Chinese in Singapore. Unpublished
              Diploma Social Studies Dissertation, University of
              Singapore.

Tan Sooi Beng
    1990   *Thai Menora.* Pulau Pinang, 2(3): 16-19

Tan, Thomas T.W., ed.
    1990   Chinese Dialect Groups: Traits and Trades.
              Singapore: Opinion Books.

Tarling, Nicholas
    1966   A Concise History of Southeast Asia. New York:
              Frederick A. Praeger.

Taylor, Keith Weller
    1976   "Madagascar in the Ancient Malayo-Polynesian
              Myths" in Explorations in the Early Southeast
              Asian History: The Origins of Southeast Asian
              Statecraft, edited by Kenneth R. Hall and John K
              Whitmore: pg.27)

    1983   The Birth of Vietnam. Berkeley, Ca.: University
              of California Press.

Tham Seong Chee
    1977   Malays and Modernization. Singapore: Singapore
              University Press.

Tinker, Hugh
    1980   *"The Search for the History of Southeast Asia"* in
              The Journal of Southeast Asian Studies; Sept.

Turnbull, C. M.
    1972   The Straits Settlements: 1826-1867: Indian
            Presidency to Crown Colony. University of
            London: Athlone Press.

Turney, A. H.
    1955   Differentiation of the Phenomenal Field.
            Lawrence, Kansas: University of Kansas
            Publications.

Tweddel, Colin and Kimball, Linda
    1985   Introduction to the Peoples and Cultures of Asia
            (New Jersey: Prentice-Hall, Inc.)

U. & V.

Valeri, Valerio
    1991   "Afterword" in Priests and Programmers:
            Technologies of Power in the Engineered
            Landscape of Bali, 1991: pg. 137)

van Leur, J. C.
    1955   Indonesian Trade and Society: Essays in Asian
            Social and Economic History. The Hague,
            Bandung: W. van Hoeve, Ltd.

Vaughn, J. D.
    1854   "Notes on the Chinese of Penang"
            Journal of the Indian Archipelago

    1879   Manners and Customs of the Chinese of the Straits
            Settlements, 1971 reprint. London: Oxford Univ.
            Press.

Southeast Asian Sources

Voegelin, C. F. and Voegelin, F. M.
     1977   Classification and Index of the World's
             Languages. New York: Elsevier North-Holland,
             Inc.

                        W.

Wallerstein, Immanuel
     1979   The Capitalist World Economy. Cambridge:
             Cambridge University Press.

Wallace, Anthony F. C.
     1970   Culture and Personality. New York: Random
             House.

Wang, Tai Peng
     1994   The Origins of the Chinese Kongsi. Selangor
             Darul Ehsan, Malaysia Pelanduk Publications Sdn
             Bhd.

Weber, Max
     1946   Class, Status, Party in Max Weber: Essays in
             Sociology. Hans H. Gerth & C. Wright Mills, eds.
             & translators. New York: Oxford University Press.

Wheatley, Paul
     1966   The Golden Khersonese: Studies in the Historical
             Geography of the Malay Peninsula Before A.D.
             1500: Kuala Lumpur: University of Malaya Press.

Whitfield, Danny
     1976   Historical and Cultural Dictionary of Vietnam.
             Carbondale Illinois.

Whitmore, J. K.
    1977   *The Opening of Southeast Asia: Trading Patterns Through the Centuries*. Economic Exchange and Social Interaction in Southeast Asia. Karl Hutterer, ed., Michigan: The Univ. Michigan Press. Pg. 134

Wickberg, Edgar
    1964   *The Chinese Mestizo in Philippine History* Journal of Southeast Asian History Vol. 5, no. 1, March.

    1965   The Chinese in Philippine Life: 1850-1898 Yale Univ. Press.

Willetts, William
    1964   *"The Maritime Adventures of Grand Eunoch Ho"* Journal of Southeast Asian History Vol. 5, no. 2, Sept.

Williams, Lea E.
    1964   *"Chinese Leadership in Early British Singapore"* Asian Studies, Vol. 2, no. 2

    1966   The Future of the Overseas Chinese in Southeast Asia New York: McGraw Hill.

    1976   Southeast Asia: Its History Oxford University Press.

Willmott, W. E.
    1960   The Chinese of Semarang: A Changing Minority Community in Indonesia Ithaca: Cornell Univ. Press.

    1966   *The Chinese of Cambodia*. Journal of Southeast Asian History, Vol. 7, no. 1, March.

Southeast Asian Sources

Willmott, W. E., ed.
  1972 <u>Economic Organization in Chinese Society.</u>
     Stanford: Stanford Univ. Press.

Win, Shein
  ? *The Chinese Community of Burma: Problems in*
     Relations between Different Ethnic Groups?

Winstedt, Richard
  1961 <u>The Malay Magician: Being Shaman, Saiva and</u>
     <u>Sufi</u> London: Routledge & Paul Kegan.

Winzler, Robert L.
  1970 <u>Malay Religion, Society and Politics in Kelantan.</u>
     PhD. Dissertation, Chicago, Illinois

  1983 *The Ethnic Status of the Rural Chinese of the*
     Kelantan. <u>The Chinese in Southeast Asia: Identity,</u>
     <u>Culture & Politics, Vol. 2.</u> L. A. Peter Gosling &
     Linda Y. C. Lim, eds. Singapore: Maruzen Asia,
     Pte. Ltd.

  1985 <u>Ethnic Relations in Kelantan: A Study of the</u>
     <u>Chinese and Thai as Minorities.</u> Singapore:
     Oxford Univ. Press.

Wittfogel, Karl
  1957 <u>Oriental Despotism: Comparative Studies in Total</u>
     <u>Power,</u> Yale University Press, 1957.

Wolf, Eric
  1966 <u>Peasants.</u> New Jersey: Prentice-Hall, Inc.

  1982 <u>Europe and the Peoples Without History.</u>
     Berkeley: University of California Press.

Wolf, Margery
    1972   Women and die Family in Rural Taiwan. Stanford,
            California: Stanford University Press.

Wolters, O. W.
    1982   History, Culture and Religion in Southeast Asian
            Perspectives. Singapore: Institute of Southeast
            Asian Studies.

Wood, William, ed.
    1977   Cultural-Ecological Perspectives on Southeast
            Asia. Papers in International Studies, Southeast
            Asia Series No. 41. Athens, Ohio: Ohio University
            Press.

Woodside, Alexander
    1971   Vietnam and the Chinese Model. Harvard Univ.
            Press, Cambridge, Mass.

Worsley, P.M.
    1956   The Kinship System of the Tallensi: a
            Reevaluation. Journal of the Royal
            Anthropological Institute, 1956: 37-75.

Worcester, G. R. G.,
    1971   The Junks and Sampans of the Yangtze
            Annapolis, Maryland: Naval Institute.

Wu Yuan-li & Wu Chun-hsi
    1980   Economic Development in Southeast Asia: The
            Chinese Dimension Hoover Institution Press.

Wylie, Alison
    1985   "The Reaction against Analogy" in Advances in
            Archaeology: Method and Theory, Vol 8, pp. 63-
            111.

<u>Southeast Asian Sources</u>

Y. & Z.

Yang, Martin
  1945 <u>A Chinese Village: Taitou, Shantung Province</u>.
     New York: Columbia University Press.

Yeap Joo Kim
  1993 <u>The Patriarch</u>
     Singapore: Lee Teng Lay Pte. Ltd.

Yeh Hua Fen
  1936 <u>Historical Guide to Malacca</u>. Singapore.

Yen Ching-Hwang
  1976 <u>The Overseas Chinese and the 1911 Revolution:
     With Special Reference to Singapore and Malaya</u>.
     <u>Kuala Lumpur</u>: Oxford Univ. Press,

  1981 *Ch'ing Changing Images of the Overseas Chinese*
     (1644-1912). <u>Modem Asian Studies</u>, 15(2): 261-
     285.

  1986 <u>A Social History of the Chinese in Singapore and
     Malaya: 1800-1911</u>. London: Oxford Univ. Press.

Yong, Paul
  1994 <u>A Dream of Freedom: The Early Sarawak
     Chinese</u>. Selangor Darul Ehsan, Malaysia:
     Pelanduk Publications.

Yousof, Ghulam-Sarwar
  1982 *Nora Chatri in Kedah: A Preliminary Report*
     <u>Journal of the Malayan Branch of the Royal
     Asiatic Society</u>, 55(1)52-61.

FINI

Indie Anthropology

<u>Auto-Anthropology</u>
Auto-Anthropology (1992-1998)
A Room In China (2000)
It Makes a Difference (1990)

<u>Anthropological Essays</u>
Anthropological Aesthetics, Rationality,
Ideology & Humanity (1982-1992)
Essays in Anthropological Knowledge (1995)
An Anthropologist in the Larger World (2017)

<u>The Anthropology of Knowledge</u>
Anthropologos & Anthropologia (1992)
Cultural Cybernetics (1996)
Cultural Cognition & Cybernetics (1996)

<u>Archaeological Anthropology</u>
Digging the Past (2002)
Relativity & Relativism (1992)
Southeast Asian Sources (1993)

<u>Ethno-Cultural Studies</u>
Ethnoculture (2005)
Boat People (1986)
The Jetty Chinese (1995)
Malaysian Hokkien Chinese Ethnoculture (1996)
The Overseas Chinese (2005)
Peranakan (1991)
Modern Americana (2003)

<u>Symbolic-Linguistic Studies</u>
English & Education (2000)
Language and Culture 1
Language and Culture 2
Language and Culture 3

Lewis Micropublishing Series

1. General System Notebooks

2. Indie Anthropology

3. Robidoux Stories

4. Hugh's Versography

5. Earthbound Primers

6. West Indie Tales

7. Mil-Anth Studies

8. Global Edge Studies

9. Indo-Pacific Studies

10. Poor Hugh's E-Press

11. Lewis Micropublishing